KT-463-210

HOUSE OF LORDS

House of

phone

House of Lords Library

001008

Drug Policy Harmonization and the European Union

Drug Policy Harmonization and the European Union

Caroline Chatwin
University of Kent, UK

© Caroline Chatwin 2011

All rights reserved. No reproduction, copy or transmission of this publication may be made without written permission.

No portion of this publication may be reproduced, copied or transmitted save with written permission or in accordance with the provisions of the Copyright, Designs and Patents Act 1988, or under the terms of any licence permitting limited copying issued by the Copyright Licensing Agency, Saffron House, 6-10 Kirby Street, London EC1N 8TS.

Any person who does any unauthorized act in relation to this publication may be liable to criminal prosecution and civil claims for damages.

The author has asserted her right to be identified as the author of this work in accordance with the Copyright, Designs and Patents Act 1988.

First published 2011 by
PALGRAVE MACMILLAN

Palgrave Macmillan in the UK is an imprint of Macmillan Publishers Limited, registered in England, company number 785998, of Houndmills, Basingstoke, Hampshire RG21 6XS.

Palgrave Macmillan in the US is a division of St Martin's Press LLC, 175 Fifth Avenue, New York, NY 10010.

Palgrave Macmillan is the global academic imprint of the above companies and has companies and representatives throughout the world.

Palgrave® and Macmillan® are registered trademarks in the United States, the United Kingdom, Europe and other countries.

ISBN 978–0–230–27186–9 hardback

This book is printed on paper suitable for recycling and made from fully managed and sustained forest sources. Logging, pulping and manufacturing processes are expected to conform to the environmental regulations of the country of origin.

A catalogue record for this book is available from the British Library.

Library of Congress Cataloging-in-Publication Data
Chatwin, Caroline, 1978–
    Drug policy harmonization and the European Union / Caroline Chatwin.
        p.   cm.
    Includes index.
    ISBN 978–0–230–27186–9 (hardback)
    1. Drug abuse—Government policy—European Union Countries—
    Evaluation.   2. Drug control—European Union Countries—
    Evaluation.   I. Title.
    HV5840.E8C43 2011
    362.29′1561094—dc22   2011004889

10   9   8   7   6   5   4   3   2   1
20 19 18 17 16 15 14 13 12 11

Printed and bound in Great Britain by
CPI Antony Rowe, Chippenham and Eastbourne

Contents

List of Tables   vi

Introduction   vii

Part I   Harmonization, Drug Policy and the European Union

1   Policy Making at a European Level   3

2   Drug Policy in the European Union   28

3   Statistical Information on the Drug Problem in the
   European Union   47

Part II   Drug Policy in Individual Member States

4   Sweden   89

5   The Netherlands   105

6   Denmark   121

7   Portugal   130

Part III   Multi-level Governance and the Way Forward for European Drug Policy

8   Multi-level Governance and the Way Forward for European
   Drug Policy   149

References   165

Index   178

List of Tables

3.1   Lifetime prevalence all adults: last survey available for
each member state (from 2000 onwards)   50

3.2   Lifetime prevalence young adults: last survey available
for each member state (2000 onwards)   52

3.3   Last 12 months prevalence all adults: last survey
available for each member state (2000 onwards)   54

3.4   Last 12 months prevalence younger adults: last survey
available for each member state (2000 onwards)   56

3.5   Estimates of prevalence of problem drug use at national
level, summary 2003–08, rate per 1000, age 15–64   60

3.6   Prevalence of HIV infection among injecting drug users
in the EU, 2008 or most recent year available   65

3.7   Summary of characteristics of the deceased in
drug-induced deaths according to national definitions   68

3.8   Drug law offences 1995–2008, part (i) number of reports
of offences   71

3.9   Drug law offences 1995–2008, part (ii) methodological
notes   73

3.10   Quantities (kg) of heroin seized, 1995–2008   76

3.11   Quantities (kg) of cocaine seized, 1995–2008   78

3.12   Quantities (kg) of amphetamine seized, 1995–2008   80

Introduction

The issue of illicit drugs is, undeniably, an international one. Drugs that originate in one country will often be trafficked through other countries before being consumed elsewhere. Nor is it just these geographical facts that make drugs an international issue. Every country has people within it that use drugs as well as people that have become problematic in their use, making the issue international in the sense that it is universal – one that is experienced by all societies and one to which those in authority must seek solutions. There is some sense of this international facet to the issue of illicit drugs in that many countries are signatories to international conventions committing them to a broadly similar style of drug policy centred around the notion of prohibition. International bodies, such as the United Nations (UN) through its office on drugs and crime, or the European Union (EU) through its monitoring centre for drugs and drug addiction, also seek to take ownership of the problem and to develop strategies that will be employed across the globe.

Largely, however, individual countries have developed their drug policies in isolation, resulting in a wide variety of policies being in operation today. This individualization of national drug policy has most obviously occurred since the well-documented explosion of drug use in the 1960s when the link between drugs and popular culture was forged. Different countries reacted in various ways to this initial rise in use and, since then, have developed policy along, in some cases, radically different lines. While all countries can agree that drug trafficking should be prioritized and drug traffickers should be met with the full weight of the law, it is in their attitudes towards drug use and drug users that most of the policy differences are to be seen. Some governments have conceptualized drug users as either diseased and in need of help or young and in an experimental phase of their lives, and, as such, have afforded them a certain degree of leniency and tried to protect them from unnecessary contact with the criminal justice system. Others have pursued drug users as aggressively as drug dealers and traffickers as they believe that if drugs are to be eradicated from society then demand reduction must be as much of a priority as supply reduction.

Since its inception, in 1951, the EU has grown in both the strength and breadth of its power, until it has become, arguably, the most powerful supranational institution in the world today. While its beginnings were very much concerned with uniting the economies of the powerhouses of Europe, it has become involved, although less successfully, with political and social policy. As time has passed, efforts to harmonize and coordinate ever-increasing aspects of national policy in these three areas have grown and European powers have expressed the desire to draw "ever closer". Drug policy, then, should have been an early contender for the development of a harmonized European agenda. The international nature of the problem, as well as its universality, should have ensured its suitability for concerted integrative efforts. Yet it is an area that has remained remarkably resistant to attempts to harmonize. Individual countries have remained wedded to their separate, and often idiosyncratic, national policies and, ultimately, the decision has been made to declare drug policy an area in which national governments should retain control of policy making.

This book attempts to understand why this has been the case and what the future possibilities are for harmonization in this area. It explores the desirability for harmonized drug policy within the EU, from the perspectives of both the institutions of the EU itself and the heads of the individual member states. It also considers the viability of a harmonized European drug policy under traditional top-down methods of control through the formulation of policy at both the European and the national level. Finally, it attempts to apply the increasingly popular theory of multi-level governance to the issue of the control of illicit drugs and suggests that, if the aim of a harmonized policy in this area is a serious one, then multi-level governance presents the only realistic way forward to achieve this aim.

A guide to this book

In order to systematically and comprehensively examine the possibilities for harmonization of drug policy at the European level, this book has been divided into three distinct parts. The first deals with harmonization of policy, including drug policy, in the EU, the second with historical case studies of the development of drug policy in individual member states and the third with a summary of both the desirability and the viability of a harmonized European drug policy and the application of the European integration theory multi-level governance to policy development in this area.

Chapter 1 outlines key concepts and theories relevant to the harmonization debate in Europe and gives a historical presentation of the development of economic, political and social policy at a European level. Chapter 2 charts the course of the development of drug policy at a European level and documents the fundamental inability of European powers to decide whether a broadly liberal or broadly repressive strategy is more appropriate in seeking to control this issue. Statistics collected by the European Monitoring Centre for Drugs and Drug Addiction are presented and critiqued in Chapter 3. Ultimately they are judged to be too beset by comparative problems and too inconclusive to provide evidence of the superiority of either a liberal or a repressive drug policy approach.

In the second part of the book, the variety of national drug policy currently in operation within the EU is explored in more detail. The introduction to this part provides a brief round-up of current policy practices in Europe and emphasizes the differences between them. The drug policies of Sweden, the Netherlands, Denmark and Portugal are then examined in more detail in the following four chapters using a historical framework for analysis. The policies of Sweden and the Netherlands have been chosen for further exploration due to their respective positions at opposite ends of the liberal–repressive drug policy continuum. Sweden, with its aim of a drug-free society and its strategy of targeting users as much as dealers, represents a relatively restrictive drug policy and the Netherlands, with its strategies of normalization of drug use and separation of the markets, represents one that is relatively liberal. Together, the case studies provided for these two countries demonstrate the depth of difference in national style of drug policy in operation in Europe.

While Sweden and the Netherlands are revealed as being strongly attached to their national drug policies, other countries within Europe have shown more willingness to change policy direction in recent years. The case studies of Denmark and Portugal have been chosen to reflect this tendency. Denmark has long been a country with a national drug policy that falls directly in between Sweden and the Netherlands: law enforcement strategies have been consistent and sometimes forcefully applied, yet cannabis users have been treated relatively leniently. Since 2001, however, Denmark has abandoned this strategy of leniency towards cannabis users and has introduced a raft of new measures directed against them. Portugal, meanwhile, introduced a radical new law in 2001 based firmly on the principle of harm reduction and decriminalizing the possession of all drugs for personal use. Case studies of these two countries therefore evidence movement towards both more liberal and more repressive approaches to drug policy within Euorpe.

Finally, the third part of the book draws together the arguments and evidence presented thus far and provides an overall assessment of first the desirability of increased harmonization in this area and then the viability of the implementation of such a policy at the European level. In the final chapter, the theory of multi-level governance, outlined in Chapter 1, is returned to and applied to the development of drug policy at the European level. The suggestion is made that should increased harmonization of European drug policy occur, it would be most likely to prosper under a system of multi-level governance.

Part I

Harmonization, Drug Policy and the European Union

The course of integration between member states of the EU has not been smooth. Historically, desire to increase levels of harmonization and to cede powers to a higher European authority has been greatest where clear benefits in doing so can be determined by national governments. For example, as a single economic entity, Europe, theoretically at least, presents a much more powerful player than any individual member state can hope to be. For this reason, European economic policy represents the most fully developed facet of European integration. In some cases, for example the sphere of political or foreign policy, the benefits of increased cooperation are clear. Once again, Europe as a whole presents a much more powerful opponent or lobbying force than any individual member state can hope to be. However, in the case of political policy, allegiances to national values and ideals run high, making compromise and cooperation a difficult and decidedly complex process. In other areas, for example European social policy, few discernable benefits are obvious to individual member states and, in consequence, development has been slow in these areas and has often been inspired only to facilitate other areas (usually economic) of integration. In sum, there is a general desire, certainly within the power structures of the EU itself and to some extent endorsed by the member states, to steadily increase levels and areas of harmonization. In practice, however, this increase is dependent on the recognizable benefits of harmonization to member states themselves, the levels of complexity of the policies in question and the strength of national allegiances in the relevant area.

With these fundamentals in mind, the case of potential harmonization of European drug policy is an interesting one. In many respects, the benefits of increasing levels of harmonization in this area are obvious.

In particular, drug trafficking is, by its very nature, an international crime, making the illegal drug issue an international one. Criminals involved in the illegal drug trade must operate on an international basis and it therefore follows that those involved in detecting them should also do so. Additionally, illegal drug use is an issue affecting all countries of the EU, without exception, further suggesting the appropriateness of an international response. In practice, however, both the complexities of national policies, particularly where they relate to the social sphere (for example, the treatment of dependent drug users), and the level of allegiance to national policies are extremely high, making it difficult to fully integrate in this area. Given that the EU itself has openly expressed a desire for greater levels of harmonization in this area, a state of relative stalemate has been reached.

While the case for desirability of a European response to the illegal drugs problem is a strong one, the viability of such a policy is much less clear. A closer examination of the development of illegal drug policy at a European level reveals a deep divide between liberalism and repression in relation to the use of illegal drugs and to illegal drug users. This has further contributed to the state of stalemate that exists in this field and has severely hindered progress in this area. Before going on to examine the range of individual national policies in operation against the illegal drugs problem, this part of the book contextualizes the development of illegal drug policy at a European level within general models of European integration and examines the case for both the desirability and viability of a fully integrated European drug policy.

1
Policy Making at a European Level

Despite its relatively humble beginnings, the EU is, today, a complicated and highly sophisticated set of interrelating institutions governing wide-ranging aspects of policy at a European level. The foundations of European integration were fundamentally born out of a desire to avoid the destructiveness and dangerous nationalistic feelings associated with individual European governments. The devastation of the Second World War had provoked the realization, by some countries at least, that there was a need for national governments to work together so that their economic affairs and national interests were, to some extent, entwined. From this tentative desire for increased cooperation, the EU has burgeoned into the most powerful supranational institution in the world. Originally motivated out of a desire to link governments economically, both to avoid war and to increase European prosperity, integration now exists not only in the economic, but also in the social and political spheres.

In a speech made at Zurich University in September 1946, Winston Churchill, the former British Prime Minister, called for the need to build a "kind of United States of Europe" (Churchill, 1998, p. 8). Although the construction of such a project was not immediately forthcoming, some would argue that the EU does now look more like a "United States of Europe". Progress towards this goal, however, has not been rapid or taken the form of simple progression. Integration has been more achievable in certain areas and the desire for national sovereignty has remained strong in others. Important theories have been developed to explain these phenomena and shape future integration processes. This chapter will examine the development of integration in the EU with specific relation to the economic, political and social spheres. It will also explore some of the major integration theories and concepts relating to the balance of national and supranational power, with a view to later relating these theories and concepts to the field of drugs.

The Beginnings of a United Europe

After the Second World War, the main proponents of the desire to prevent over powerful nationalistic feelings from redeveloping in Europe were France and Germany. The integration of policy between these two countries would provide the key to stabilizing Europe and to preventing the outbreak of any further war. Robert Schuman, the French foreign minister, enshrined the beginnings of action towards this goal in his famous declaration of 1950, in which he advanced the idea that the pooling of coal and steel industries, the basis of German economic success, would provide the foundations for common economic development. He hypothesized that "the solidarity in production thus established will make it plain that any war between France and Germany becomes not merely unthinkable but materially impossible" (Schuman, 1998, p. 14). If France and Germany irrevocably linked their national production policies in these areas, then the prospect of further war and destruction in Europe would be, to all intents and purposes, removed.

In 1951, Schuman's proposal was realized in the Treaty of Paris, committing countries to the establishment of a supranational power structure dealing with coal and steel. The European Coal and Steel Community (ECSC), launched in 1952, joined the industries of France and Germany with Italy and the Benelux countries (Belgium, the Netherlands and Luxembourg). McCormick (2008, p. 52) describes how this common policy granted powers that had previously been national to a higher authority, for example, the ability "to reduce tariff barriers, abolish subsidies, fix prices and raise money by imposing levies on steel and coal production".

Although never very successful in creating a truly common coal and steel market, the ECSC, and Schuman himself, were influential in extending economic integration of coal and steel production and trade to all other goods. In 1957, the Treaty of Rome committed the six countries towards extending the ECSC common market to all other goods and created the European Economic Community (EEC). The creation of the EEC fully committed these countries to launching a common economic market and harmonizing their economic policies. It also recognized that economic integration of this nature would not be possible without some integration in the areas of political and social policy. The EEC thus often became known more simply as the European

Community (EC). In his ideas of European integration, firstly in the areas of coal and steel and later in all areas, Schuman was aided and advised by a French civil servant and diplomat – Jean Monnet.

Monnet has been the most enduring figure in the creation of European unity. He described Schuman's proposals as "a modest beginning" (Monnet, 1998, p. 22) and vocally envisaged a scheme of European integration that would go much further than the merging of national economic policy. He described the process of integration as "a ferment where one change induces another" (Monnet, 1998, p. 23). For Monnet, the creation of the ECSC, and later the EC, were just the beginnings in a process that would inspire integration, not only in economic areas, but also in political and social ones. He predicted that this process would entail a series of small steps towards a Europe that was comprehensively unified in all areas of policy making. This venture would eventually encompass not just the original six countries, but the whole of Europe and beyond.

Theories of European Integration

Since the creation of the ECSC and the beginnings of harmonized policy within Europe, many theories about the precise nature and form of the integration process have been expounded. As more countries have joined the venture, and integration between them has deepened, these theories have been developed and more vigorously debated. They are concerned with both the allocation of power within the EU and the path which European integration should follow.

Integration of European affairs in economics and beyond brings with it both benefits and drawbacks for national governments. Integration and harmony of European policy induces peace and stability as Europeans are encouraged to recognize their similarities and to work together to achieve goals. It also has strong economic benefits. The creation of a Single European Market, for example, put Europe on a level with the USA and Japan in terms of trading power as well as global influence (Smith, 1986). Integration is also beneficial to Europeans in that it encourages countries to meet minimum standards, develops a system of aiding poorer parts of Europe under its European regional development policy and generally stresses the importance of the individual.

However, these benefits must be measured against potential drawbacks for participating member states. Primarily, these drawbacks can be related to a loss of national sovereignty. To a greater or lesser extent, member states have not embraced policies that infringe on powers normally allocated to national governments. As ideals of freedom of movement within Europe have been advanced, concerns have also grown about the increased ease of drug trafficking and international organized crime. In addition, many countries have baulked at the imposition of uniform laws and controversial policy moves. Not all participators in European integration have agreed on the balancing of these pros of European integration against the cons.

Perhaps the most disputed area of European integration is whether it should be of a supranational or intergovernmental nature. Proponents of a supranational system of government advocate the development of integration towards the creation of an independent European authority that has autonomy and superiority over national systems of government. Intergovernmentalists, on the other hand, decree that national governments should work in partnership but should, ultimately, remain in control of their individual policies rather than passing control to a higher authority. These fundamentally opposed visions of a united Europe have led to the development of two main theories of integration: realist and neo-functionalist.

Realists are firmly intergovernmentalist in nature and believe that the EU exists only because it is in the best interests of member states (Hoffman, 1966; Moravcsik, 1994). Integration is implemented to meet the needs of individual national governments and should not exceed this need. Realist theories of European integration have been widely expounded throughout the history of the development of European integration, but the powers now ascribed to the EU are generally believed to go beyond those compatible with realist theory. European integration has progressed to a stage in which powers have been allocated to a European governance that cannot be recalled. For better or worse an enduring European authority has been created.

Neo-functionalism has enjoyed more prosperity and perseverance among European integration theorists, although there have been periods where its popularity has declined or disappeared altogether. Neo-functionalism builds on the work of functionalists such as Mitrany (1998), who advocated integration of separate sectors, but introduces the concept of spillover. Neo-functionalist theory of European integration relies heavily on the idea of "spillover" as propounded by American social scientists Ernst Haas and Leon Lindberg, whose ideas have thus become associated with the term "neo-functionalism" (Haas, 1998; Lindberg, 1963).

"Spillover" refers to the idea that integration or joint action in one area of European policy will create "a situation in which the original goal can be assured only by taking further actions, which in turn create a further condition and a need for more action" (Lindberg, 1963, p. 10). Haas and other neo-functionalists therefore believe that European integration is a step-by-step process, whereby the beginnings of European integration will inevitably lead, eventually, to a fully united Europe. McCormick (2008) further divides the idea of "spillover" into three distinct areas: functional spillover, which relates to the idea that if states integrate in one area of economics this will lead to the integration of other sectors and the eventual decline of national governments; technical spillover from disparities in national standards, which could mean that individual countries will be forced to rise or sink to the highest or lowest standards operating in Europe; and political spillover, which refers to the fact that, once policy sectors have become integrated, functional sectors and lobbying groups will focus their attention at the international rather than national level. Springer (1992) describes neo-functionalist theory of European integration as a process rather than an objective. As attachment between European citizens and a European integrative authority grows, so will the areas in which integration is perceived as desirable and therefore possible.

From the theories of realism and neo-functionalism two concrete objectives of European harmonization have been advanced: confederalism and federalism. Confederal, in this instance, refers to a system whereby countries retain their own separate national identities but certain specialized powers are given to a higher authority for reasons such as convenience, security or increased efficiency. A higher, central authority is developed but it is relatively weak and exists at the discretion of the countries that implemented it. This objective is closely associated with the intergovernmentalist/realist position.

The EU, as it exists today, can be described as confederalist in that member states are still distinct units, rights in areas such as foreign affairs, security and defence remain limited and allegiance by most European citizens is primarily to their own nation rather than to Europe (McCormick, 2008; Nugent, 2003). However, a sticking point is that it is only marginally still possible for EU member states to maintain that the EU exists only at their discretion. Over the years, increased powers meted out to the EU, as well as increased governmental structure within the EU, have eroded the argument that member states remain fully in control of EU legislation. Researchers who have noted this tendency now advocate the possible development of the EU into a fully federalist structure, especially since the long-awaited ratification of the Lisbon Treaty in 2009.

A federal power structure, in this instance, refers to a system whereby countries have both shared and independent powers, neither of which has supreme authority over the other. There must also be an elected government which enjoys sole power over foreign and security policy. This objective is closely associated with supranationalism/neo-functionalism. Although a fully fledged federal structure is still just a pipe dream for the EU, there is evidence that achieving a federal system is an EU aim as well as signs of progress towards this aim. Some characteristics of a federal system, such as those operated in Germany or America, are nowhere in sight for the EU; for example, the development of a common defence policy or the establishment of a comprehensive and universal foreign policy.

In other areas, however, progress towards a federal system has been made. A single currency has been established in most EU member states, a European Court of Justice (ECJ), albeit with as yet very limited powers, has been founded and attempts to draft a European constitution have long been underway, admittedly without comprehensive success so far. In terms of government, the EU has its own budget, a supranational commission which has the sole power to initiate European legislation and a European Parliament elected by European citizens rather than national governments. In addition, certain policy structures within the EU are already based on a federal organization. For example, European monetary policy is organized federally through a system of European central banks, including a European Central Bank. It is therefore possible to say that, since the engineering of the ECSC in the 1950s leading to the establishment of the EC, harmonization within Europe has spread to numerous policy areas and is moving, although not inevitably, towards a European system of federal government. European integration currently lies somewhere between the "motors of integration that supranationalists have contended... [and the] impotent actors of intergovernmentalist theorizing" (Beach, 2005, p. 254).

Development of European Unity and Integration Theory

After the development of the ECSC into the more pervasive EC, functionalist ideas of European integration associated with both Monnet and Mitrany enjoyed popularity. For several years the prospects for continued and deepening European harmonization developed without check. Confidence was high that the EEC would eventually develop into a supranational power operating at all levels of European policy. However, in 1965, a crisis, in the form of Charles de Gaulle, the first President of France's fifth republic, befell the EC and its burgeoning powers.

At this time, the EC was involved in creating a customs union which would involve an increase in the budgetary powers of the European Parliament (EP). Britain, which had thus far abstained from participation in affairs related to European integration, had expressed a desire to become part of the economic union. French President Charles de Gaulle wanted France to stay in the EC for economic reasons, but believed that he spoke on behalf of the French people in opposing the further development of supranational powers (George, 1996). His vision of European unity is encapsulated in the "belief that a united Europe could not today, any more than in previous times, be a fusion of its peoples, but that it could and should result from a system of rapprochement... [his policy] therefore aimed at the setting up of a concert of European states which in developing all sorts of ties between them would increase their interdependence and solidarity" (de Gaulle, 1998, p. 34). For this reason, he blocked British membership of the EC and recommended that the package regarding increased powers for the EP be sent back for further revision.

Although de Gaulle did not succeed in blocking the package (the customs union was successfully completed in 1968), he did block Britain's accession to EC membership at this time. His subsequent actions also had further, far-reaching consequences for European unity. When his proposal to send back the customs union package was denied, de Gaulle withdrew France from all participation in EC business. This period is referred to by many as the "empty chair crisis". Such a situation was a disastrous setback to European harmonization. In order to placate France and allow European integration to further develop serious concessions had to be made.

One of the proposals contained in the customs union package that had particularly provoked de Gaulle's attack was the move from unanimous voting to a system of Qualified Majority Voting (QMV). De Gaulle felt that "although it is perfectly natural for the states of Europe to have specialist bodies available to prepare and whenever necessary to follow up their decisions, those decisions must be their own" (de Gaulle, 1998, p. 44). Under the QMV proposal, rather than having to secure the support of every member of the EC for new European developments, a clear majority would be satisfactory. After six months of living with an "empty chair" the EC reversed adoption of this practice in what is termed the "Luxembourg compromise", and returned to the veto system. This meant a definite loss of power for the Commission and a serious check on neo-functionalist and supranational theories of European union.

De Gaulle's influence, and the economic recession which then hit Europe in general, ensured that further functionalist or supranationalist developments did not take place throughout the rest of the 1960s and most of the 1970s. Economic recession stemmed progression towards European integration because a lot of national willingness to cooperate with other governments was based on desire for greater economic power. As national governments had to increasingly concentrate on their own economies, international development in this area suffered. Neo-functionalist theories seemed disproved and intergovernmentalism gained credibility, however, a gradual return to these ideals was engendered. In 1973, the EC expanded to include Britain, Denmark and Ireland, and, in 1981, Greece, followed by Spain and Portugal in 1986. As well as this expansion in members, the late 1970s saw a tentative increase in depth of EC supranational powers under the Commission presidency of Roy Jenkins, beginning in 1976. These developments in the depth of decision-making included the foundation of a European Council in 1975 and the launch of the European Monetary System (EMS) in 1979.

This launch of an EMS, combined with the election of Jacques Delors to Commission president in 1985, reinvigorated neo-functionalist theories of European integration, and was influential in leading to the adoption of the Single European Act (SEA) in 1986. Delors was a staunch proponent of federalism and firmly believed in the allocation of further powers to the EC in a bid to ensure it developed into a strong world power, and in almost direct opposition to the earlier ideology practised by Charles de Gaulle. "Neither the European Community – nor the peoples and nations that form it – will truly exist unless it is in a position to defend its values, to act on them for the benefit of all, to be generous" (Delors, 1998, p. 57). Together with the French President of the time, Mitterand, Delors refocused lapsed European functionalist integration theory on the drive for harmonization of economic policy and the extension of integration to other areas.

The SEA was necessary as the doubling of membership of the EC had complicated the Community's decision-making processes and altered the economic balance of the EC (McCormick, 2008). It returned to the possibility of QMV that had been blocked by de Gaulle and had resulted in the "Luxembourg compromise". In addition, the SEA furthered economic powers by creating the biggest market and trading unit in the world and expanding the objective of economic and monetary union within the community. The SEA also incorporated areas outside of the less controversial economic policy sector, expanding EU powers in a manner predicted by neo-functionalists (Sandholtz and Zysman, 1992). The most important of these increased powers was to give legal status to European Political Cooperation (EPC). Other areas of increased power included environmental policy, social policy and research and development policy.

This gradual road to increased harmonization between greater numbers of European countries has continued since the 1986 SEA. In 1992, the name European Union (EU) was officially given for the first time to the supranational power that had begun as the ECSC. In the same year, the Treaty on European Union (TEU), or Treaty of Maastricht as it is also known, forged a massive expansion in areas of supranational concern and interest as well as restructuring existing powers under a new "pillar" system. This treaty paved the road to a European economic and monetary union (first pillar), a common foreign and security policy (second pillar) as well as intergovernmental cooperation on Justice and Home Affairs (JHA) (third pillar). It also inspired a further expansion in territory in 1995 which absorbed Austria, Finland and Sweden.

The Treaty of Amsterdam (1997), intended to prepare the existing EU for the incorporation of ten new central and Eastern European member states, extended interest and cooperation in JHA, setting an objective to achieve an area of freedom, security and justice by the accession date in 2004. It also incorporated the "Schengen Agreement" relating to the free movement of people between EU member states and thus increased the sense of a European citizenship. Finally, a common European currency, the legacy of a long desire for greater economic and monetary harmony within Europe, was launched in 1999. On 1 February 2003, the Treaty of Nice continued the development of European integration in two main areas. Firstly, the treaty was concerned with continuing preparations for the enlargement date in 2004, namely by making changes regarding numbers of members to its institutions. Secondly, the treaty made further steps towards shifting decision-making in the council from unanimity to qualified majority voting (QMV). In addition, the need for a reform of the Union's judicial system was recognized and procedures regarding the breach of fundamental rights of a member state were updated and improved.

Since the Treaty of Nice, further extension of European power has been debated, but with little concrete result. Perhaps most significantly, ten new European member states were accepted into the EU in May 2004 (the Czech Republic, Estonia, Hungary, Latvia, Lithuania, Poland, the Slovak Republic, the Republic of Slovenia, Cyprus and Malta) followed swiftly by Romania and Bulgaria in 2007. Croatia and the Former Yugoslav Republic of Macedonia are the latest to have been officially labelled as candidates for future membership. These enlargements have naturally brought some benefits in terms of the continued development of European integration, not only in the greater political stability that they have engendered (van der Veen, 2005), but also in the adaptations to "structures, policy regimes and political dynamics" (Dinan, 2006, p. 289) that they have necessitated. However, while the most recent rounds of enlargement have undoubtedly widened the EU, it does not necessarily follow that they have also deepened the nature of integration within it. Further, some have suggested that it may have done the opposite: "Each enlargement gives the impression that the undertaking is being diluted, resulting in more weight given to national interests and less willingness to take the next integrative step" (Wyplosz, 2007, p. 6).

Even before the 2004 enlargement was completed, the need for fundamental changes to pre-existing European treaties was recognized. For 25 or more countries to be governed by decision-making processes originally designed for use by six countries at the most no longer seemed feasible. To this end, a European Union Constitutional Convention was held between 2002 and 2003 which aimed to reform previous treaties into a single simplified treaty operating under a single pillar structure, to amend provisions of the Nice Treaty that made it stringently difficult for new legislation to be passed under the rules of QMV as extended to 25 or more member states and to represent a stronger level of integration than previously seen. On 18 June 2004, these aims were realized in the agreement of a constitutional treaty by heads of state that summarized and simplified pre-existing treaties, deepened political integration, lowered QMV requirements, advocated an individual president for the EC and considerably furthered powers for the ECJ in terms of social policy (de Menil, 2007). Seemingly, irrevocable steps towards a federal EU were being taken, however, the constitutional treaty had to be ratified by all member states and, in the summer of 2005, both the French and the Dutch, via public referendum, refused to give their endorsements. The treaty was put on ice and a period of European integrative slowdown, not experienced since the "empty chair crisis", was hailed by those opposing the development towards a federal union.

While some degree of slowdown of European integration was obviously enforced due to the abandonment of the constitutional treaty, it did not, however, necessarily precipitate the crisis that many expected. In 2007, work began afresh on the development of a new treaty,

remaining remarkably faithful to the old constitutional treaty, but differing in terms of the removal of constitutional language, the provision
of a greater ability to opt out from decisions and a postponement of
changes to QMV. This treaty was signed by heads of state in Lisbon in
2007 and has become known as the Lisbon Treaty or the Reform Treaty.
A further setback was experienced in June 2008 when Ireland, the only
country to put the issue to a national referendum, failed to ratify the
treaty and once more appeared to stymie hopes of any advancement
towards a more federal Europe. Yet the move towards an "ever closer
union" has again proved enduring: after the negotiation of some concessions in the areas of abortion, taxation and military neutrality, Ireland
held a second, and this time successful, referendum. The Lisbon Treaty
was finally ratified by all 27 member states on 1 December 2009. Com-
mentators such as Wyplosz (2007) therefore continue to anticipate the
advent of an increasingly federalist Europe, postulating that it is natural
for such a process to go through periods of both acceleration and slowdown and that, as the most obvious steps of integration have already
been taken, these later ones will be more controversial and will therefore
take more time.

"Harmonization" is clearly a key policy concept within the EU and its
predecessors, and is recognized as such by the aim of providing an "ever
closer union". The original idea of a European supranational power was
first raised as a protection against nationalistic ideologies leading to the
possibility of war within Europe, and the powers granted in the area of
coal and steel have been gradually increased and extended. Originally
founded on areas of economic interest, such as coal and steel, agri-
cultural policy and monetary systems, powers have rapidly increased,
albeit minimally, in political, and social areas. These increases in power
have been complemented by increases in levels of institutional governance for the EU such as the introduction of a European Council and
a European Parliament. Since expansion into new areas of European
policy, control in these areas has steadily increased.

Subsidiarity, Multi-level Governance and Regional Policy

One highly important facet of European integration not so far mentioned is subsidiarity. Cary (1993, p. 45) has described subsidiarity as
"the 'best level' principle. Before lawmakers set to work there needs first
to be a consensus on the best level for deciding a given policy, and the
best level for implementing it." Subsidiarity is a two-pronged concept.
It encapsulates both the idea that decisions should be taken as closely
as possible to the citizen and that the EU should only intervene where

action cannot satisfactorily be left to member states. Subsidiarity as a notion was officially raised at a European level in the TEU (or Treaty of Maastricht). Article A of Title 1 enshrines the necessity of taking decisions as closely as possible to European citizens and Article 3b deals with the limited intervention of the EU in national affairs. "In areas which do not fall within its exclusive competence, the Community shall take action, in accordance with the principle of subsidiarity, only if and in so far as the objectives of the proposed action cannot be sufficiently achieved by the Member States and can therefore, by reason of the scale or effects of the proposed actions, be better achieved by the Community" (cited in Duff, 1993, p. 8). It has since become an important and often referred to concept related to European integration theory.

Subsequent to its inclusion in the TEU an Annex was held at Edinburgh to further define this notion. Duff (1993) describes the resulting criteria for EU involvement in policy. For a policy area to warrant intervention at the European rather than exclusively national level, a clear basis for involvement must be defined from the outset, the area must have transnational aspects, non-EU intervention must be perceived to be harmful and, additionally, EU action must be perceived as being desirable and beneficial. Once the need for EU intervention is recognized, resultant law should provide a framework for member states to work within, for example the setting of minimum standards, but the discretion for implementing arrangements should be left to national governments. Finally, a caveat has been issued declaring that the principle of subsidiarity must not be used to impede the decision-making process or lessen the power of the EC.

Although, at a first reading, subsidiarity may appear to be, in its entirety, a check on supranational and neo-functionalist theories, it is a more complicated concept than that. Gasoliba i Bohm (1993, p. 70), a Spanish MEP, puts the case for subsidiarity as a brainchild of those who support national sovereignty: "The aim of the introduction of subsidiarity into the Treaty has been to place a limit on the non-democratic extension of the future powers and responsibilities of the Community." However, subsidiarity can also be invoked by "Crusaders for European federalism ... [who] see subsidiarity as the very incarnation of the federal principle that powers should be clearly divided between different tiers of government" (Cary, 1993, p. 46). The rise of the principle of subsidiarity has therefore led to a subtle shift from government by those in power to governance which seeks the "involvement of stakeholders and civil society organisations besides government bodies and experts" (Garcia, 2006, p. 745).

Such a style of governance has been termed "multi-level governance" (Marks, 1992) due to its inclusion of actors at the civil, subnational and transnational level (Armstrong, 2002; Hooghe and Marks, 2001). Pertaining to the EU, it has been described as "a system of multi-level, non-hierarchical, deliberative and apolitical governance" (Hix, 1998, p. 54). Under such a system, independence no longer has to mean isolation for member states. However, the fact that large issues would be dealt with at the EU level while smaller issues would be dealt with at the local level could result in a certain lack of necessity to the national government (Marks and Hooghe, 2004). EU institutions would operate at a framework level producing policy guidelines while local authorities would have the power to implement initiatives that were most appropriate to the local environment. Thus, the EU would fulfil its aims of expanding harmonization and unity in European policy while national governments would be able to conserve important national differences (Carter and Scott, 1998). Multi-level governance therefore represents an opportunity for European integration to move beyond the fruitless supranational/intergovernmentalist divide (George, 2004).

However, the fact that the principle of subsidiarity is relied upon to sustain arguments both from supporters of increased recourse to national sovereignty and those who desire the implementation of an entirely federalist Europe can present problems in terms of its application. Subsidiarity has been defined as the necessity of deciding on and implementing policy at the "best level" but it can be difficult for officials, approaching subsidiarity from different integrative positions, to agree on what the "best level" is. There are further problems with subsidiarity as defined at the Edinburgh Annex. McCormick (2008) lists these as the fact that the principle of subsidiarity cannot be applied in retrospect to areas where the EU already holds powers, there is no official allocation of who should decide when and where subsidiarity is invoked and the fact that subsidiarity attempts to limit powers through decisions of competence rather than through any clarification of powers.

Although subsidiarity can be heralded as an advance of either realist or neo-functionalist ideals of integration, it is possible that it will provide the greatest stem to the development of supranational power since Charles de Gaulle. Article 3b of the Maastricht Treaty, relating to the limitation of EU powers in areas where national governments can satisfactorily legislate, is currently most heavily associated with subsidiarity. If the tendency of paying most attention to this part of the definition of subsidiarity continues, then the application of power at a supranational level may cease to develop at previous rates, despite warnings to avoid such a situation. However, serious attention to the second defining part of the principle of subsidiarity will prevent this occurrence.

The second part of the definition of "subsidiarity", legislated in Article 1 of the TEU, refers to the practice of ensuring that "Decisions should be taken as closely as possible to the citizens themselves, without endangering the advantages to be gained from common action at the level of the union as a whole" (Hantrais, 2007, p. 12). It is this aspect of subsidiarity in which neo-functionalists, aspiring to an eventual federal union, find their support. They observe that if this objective of subsidiarity is fully capitalized on, it will lead to "a general presumption of precedence of lower level over higher level governance, and ultimately a principle of laissez faire with respect to whatever lower units may do" (Streek, 1995, p. 426). In this version of integration, member states will both decentralize and integrate at the same time. Member states will gradually lose their own sense of national identity, becoming instead regions of a greater European power with relatively high levels of autonomy in policy making.

There is some evidence that such a practice is already developing within EU member states. Bongers and Chatfield (1993, p. 78) observe that "the creation of strong regional authorities has been a major political development in several European countries over the last 25 years". Gasoliba i Bohm (1993, p. 72) also notes this trend: "Since the creation of the European Community in the 1950s, a slow but sure process of political and administrative decentralization has been taking place in several Member States in favour of Länder, nations, autonomous communities and regions with the power to make laws." In the United Kingdom, in 1997, for example, power was decentralized in an act of devolution to the principalities of Scotland, Wales and Northern Ireland.

The EU itself has recognized this trend and has developed regional and cohesion-based policies. There is a growing acceptance of the fact that cultural differences between different communities will ensure that different approaches are taken to common problems (McCormick, 2008). EU regional and cohesion policy is therefore primarily aimed at reducing any disparities that may exist between various regions in terms of economic and social progress. Gasoliba i Bohm (1993) describes the importance of regional policy within the EU. If successfully developed, it will provide better information about the EU and increased citizen participation in international policy making. Respect for the EU will also increase and a regional input in implementing EU law will guarantee that it is done correctly. However, many people have expressed a fear that important cultural differences between member states will disappear as supranational powers increase. In fact, regional policy offers an opportunity to ensure the preservation, and possible increase, of diversity within Europe. Regions will not necessarily respect national borders and minority groups within member states will find, in regional policy, an expression for their beliefs and policy ideals.

Currently, regional policy within the EU has numerous objectives. It provides aid, through the European Structural Fund, for poorer EU countries and specific regions with high unemployment and industrial decline. Specialized social programmes have been developed for disadvantaged areas and programmes aimed at reducing long-term unemployment and helping young people have been implemented (McCormick, 2008). However, Dinan (1994) has observed that it can be difficult to decide whether regional and cohesion policy is actually working. The divide between richer northern countries and poorer southern ones is closing, but the gap between individual regions is growing. Although the decentralized nature of the CEECs promoted regional policy on their accession, it also introduced many, considerably poorer, countries to the EU which further widened the gaps between different regions in Europe.

So far, the history and development of both the EU and integration theory have been described. From the first, ideas of increased unity in European policy have envisioned cooperation in a wide range of areas. However, in practice, unification has been much more limited. Originally, the ECSC modestly limited integration to the specifics of the coal and steel industries. Gradually these areas have been extended, first to other trading sectors and economics in general, and then to social and political policy. Understandably, harmonization has progressed furthest in the area of economic policy, both because this was the first area in which integration policy was pursued and because the advantages of coordinated economic policy are the most obvious. However, the development of economic integration has not been possible in Europe without some political and social cooperation. If a federal Europe, or a fully unified Europe, is ever to be achieved, social and political integration must achieve the same level of harmonization as enjoyed by the economic sector. Harmonization efforts will now be examined in each of these areas in turn.

Harmonization of Economic Policy

Economic integration was initially supported in Europe as European national powers saw the opportunity offered by integrated economic policy in the areas of coal and steel as a chance to create a trading market to rival those operated by the USA and Japan. The six powers involved in the ECSC (Germany, France, Italy and the Benelux countries) were keen to extend integration to all goods and created the European Economic Community (EEC), later known as just the European Community (EC), whose members were gradually extended from 6 to 12. Economic union, at this stage, meant that "the member states would, at most, cease to follow independent economic policies, and at least would follow co-ordinated policies" (George, 1996, p. 205). By seeking to extend the harmonization of trade in coal and steel to all other commodities, the member states were effectively intending to create a European Single Market. Although a truly single market in the limited areas of coal and steel had never been fully achieved, the goal of a single market for all goods was pursued with much more vigour and, indeed, success. In 1985, under the drive and support of Delors, an extensive list of all the changes necessary to effect the completion of the single market was created and a timetable ending with the completion of a single market in 1992 was produced.

Making a reality of the single market involved numerous adjustments to national policies. A single market implied the free movement of goods, people, services and capital in an area without internal frontiers. A great deal of difficulty was encountered in ensuring the free movement of people between countries. The implementation of such a measure required much harmonization of employment and benefit policy and thus inspired the EC to take a new interest in the harmonization of social policy. Many difficulties were also experienced with removing technical, trade-related barriers developed at a national level. It was difficult to incorporate integrated levels of legislation related to fields such as consumer standards, health and safety regulations and fluctuating exchange rates. In fact, eventually, member states had to implement a policy of mutual recognition whereby they agreed to accept products if they met the technical standards of the producer country in order to simplify matters (McCormick, 2008). It is debatable whether, even now, all the finer points relating to the creation of a truly free internal market have been satisfied, but the European Single Market has generally been successfully regarded as such for the past 15 years.

The creation of the Single European Market represented a great step forward for integrated economic policy. However, ambition in this area did not end there. Even in the days of Delors's presidency of the EC, the eventual goal of monetary union, or single currency, was desired. "Delors repeatedly described monetary union as 'indispensable' to the programme to free the internal market" (George, 1996, p. 223). Economic Monetary Union (EMU) could be construed as either the maintenance of fixed exchange rates between the currencies of differing member states or as the adoption of a single community currency. The issue of EMU implementation was officially included in the Treaty of Maastricht and it was here that it was decided to follow the road to the more ambitious creation of a single European currency.

It is a measure of great success for European economic integration that in 1999 EMU was achieved in the adoption of the euro by 12 of the 15 EU member states. McCormick (2008, p. 157) observes that this is an issue that "cuts to the heart of sovereignty and independence, because a state that relinquishes control over its national currency effectively relinquishes control over all significant domestic economic policy choices, such as the freedom to adjust interest rates". There are also many positive consequences of EMU, and more specifically, a single currency, for member states, at least in times of prosperity. The introduction of such a measure helps European citizens to feel more connected, increases stability and economic growth within participating member states, is good for business as protection charges against fluctuating exchange rates are removed and is useful to travellers.

However, these benefits must be balanced against powerful negative consequences. For example, the introduction of a new single currency is a risky venture and an unknown quantity as emphasized by the current recession sweeping across Europe, the fact that the barrier of language prevents true freedom of movement within Europe which may encourage the development of pockets of wealth and poverty, interest rates become inflexible and the one off change to adopt the euro was an expensive undertaking. Perhaps the primary negative consequences were the undoubted loss of national sovereignty to such a venture entailed as well as the considerable public resistance to such a measure that was encountered. In light of these factors it is perhaps surprising that the creation of a single currency occurred at all, but the road to its adoption was certainly not smooth.

Peterson and Bomberg (1999) have referred to a weakening of commitment to the completion of the single market in the 1970s as a general state of economic recession hit Europe. This weakening of commitment to integration by member states in the face of economic adversity was witnessed again in the 1990s; as European economies began once again to go into depression, so the fate of EMU and the adoption of a single currency suffered. However, the strength of the desire to create not, only a single market, but also a single currency capable of competing on an equal footing with Japan and the USA, coupled with a desire by member states to break their dependence on the dominant German Bundesbank, ensured that EMU was not overly neglected. In fact, the turmoil of national currency was eventually to cause member states to rally around the launch of a single currency as a possible panacea to their national problems.

Despite this continued desire for economic unity, the adoption of a single currency was by no means certain. Strict convergence criteria had been laid down for joining the EMU venture and it seemed unlikely that all countries would be able to meet these requirements. In order to be part of EMU, countries had to show that they had price stability and low inflation, they must have budgetary discipline and no excessive budgetary deficit, their national currency must be stable and they must have shown convergence on interest rates (Dinan, 1994). It was unlikely that countries such as Spain, Greece and Portugal, although very much wanting to join EMU, would be able to meet these requirements. However, in 1999, 12 European member states did adopt the Euro and the countries that did not (Britain, Denmark and Sweden) opted out for reasons other than inability to meet the criteria.

Dinan (1994) has speculated that monetary unity occurred despite some countries not fully meeting the membership criteria. He observes that the determination of France and Germany to succeed in this venture, national economic recovery in the late 1990s, a rise in public popularity of economic integration and the seriousness with which the venture had been regarded from the outset ensured EMU would occur and occur on time. This is a strategy that may come back to haunt those involved in its implementation now that Europe as a whole once again faces recession, with particular economic crises in countries like Greece, which were judged to be economically weaker at the time, threatening the European economy as a whole.

Since the tentative proposals of a united coal and steel industry, European economic integration has followed an incredible journey. In 1968, a customs union was formed, followed by a single market in 1993 and a single currency in 1999. Changes since 1999 have not been so dramatic, but results show a deepening of harmonization as trade integration within the eurozone increases (Hix, 2005; Wyplosz, 2007) and the desire to further stimulate EU productivity is expressed (de Menil, 2007). Integration theorists have observed that single market and monetary union is the most advanced form of economic integration between sovereign states (Dinan, 1994). It is also the most advanced form of integration within the EU. As increasing integration of economic matters have been implemented in the EU, it has been impossible to ignore the issues of social and political integration and some concessions to unity have had to be made in these areas by member states. However, integration in these areas is far from the comprehensive, advanced and well-developed entity that is European economic integration.

Harmonization of Political Policy

When Jean Monnet, the "father of European integration", first envisaged unity in Europe, he prescribed that the need was "political as well as economic" (Monnet, 1998, p. 21). The benefits of economic integration, in the perception of national member states, however, far outweighed the benefits of political integration, at least at the beginning. In theory, the idea of an integrated Europe, preventing recourse to disagreement and possible war, was attractive to member states. The proposal of united coal and steel industries, and later of a single European market eventually leading to the adoption of a single European currency, represented benefits in terms of national economies and trading power. Some loss of national sovereignty was considered a small price to pay by most governments. However, this willingness to accede national sovereignty to the development of a supranational power did not extend to other areas. The benefits of integrated political and social policies were much more negligible at a governmental level and required a much heavier commitment to the development of power at a supranational level and at the expense of national sovereignty.

The development of political integration at a European level has most commonly been associated with the creation of a Common Foreign and Security Policy (CFSP). The foundations of a policy of this type were first suggested by President Pompidou in 1969 in a European summit at The Hague. He termed this policy European Political Cooperation (EPC) and, throughout the 1970s, integration developed relatively successfully in this area of high politics. This is perhaps surprising as areas of low politics were enjoying less integrative success at this time due to the economic problems facing Europe in general. At this stage, however, cooperation was very much of an intergovernmental nature rather than a supranational one (Dinan, 1994). National governments showed willingness to share information and closely coordinate on policy options, but did not go so far as to hand over traditionally national powers to European control.

EPC enjoyed several early successes, leading to a sense of optimism about its further development and expansion. Governments of the EC managed to develop and present a common position on policy towards affairs in the Middle East, they were able to present a united position at the Conferences on Security and Cooperation in Europe (CSCE) and achieved unity in position within the UN. Minor failures in terms of EPC had also been observed. For example, member states had found it difficult to find a common position on the 1979 invasion of Afghanistan by the Soviet Union and had been unable to satisfactorily agree on a policy incorporating the adoption of sanctions against South Africa. In general, however, at this stage, EPC was considered a moderate success with every possibility of development in the future.

The Gulf crisis occurring in the early 1990s shattered these optimistic expectations. Iraq's invasion of Kuwait in 1990 initially elicited a unanimous European response. The attack was condemned and economic sanctions were imposed. Subsequently, however, countries found it difficult to agree on policy strategies. Other countries, in particular America, but also international organizations like the UN, looked to Europe to provide a united, and thus powerful, voice. Instead, the reality of the fragmentation of political opinion within Europe was dramatically revealed. Third parties trying to deal with Europe found there was no essential "European voice". "Back in the 1970s, a frustrated Henry Kissinger was said to have asked, 'When I want to speak to Europe, whom do I call?'" (cited in Branegan, 1996). At the time of the Gulf crisis in the early 1990s the situation was no different. The French wanted to find a peaceful resolution to the crisis. Britain, Germany and the Netherlands, on the other hand, supported a military solution, despite the fact that no European army, as such, existed.

Divisions were further revealed in European political action in the break-up of the former Yugoslavia, also in the early 1990s. Again, a unified policy was followed, initially at least, comprised of sanctions and peace talks. However, this policy strategy fell apart when Germany supported the recognition of Croatia and Slovenia due to its Slavic links. The disintegration of Yugoslavia highlighted the fact that European member states have different historical links with former colonies that may lead to incompatible foreign policy objectives.

Despite these not inconsequential factors, the TEU committed EU member states to the development of a proper Common Foreign and Security Policy to replace the now redundant EPC. Affairs that had previously been included in EC policy making were retained under the first pillar of the Maastricht Treaty. A second pillar was developed to deal with CFSP and the development of a Common European Security and Defence Policy (CESDP) and a third to deal with JHA. Yet, as emphasized by the radically different political stances taken by various European countries in the 2003 invasion of Iraq, political agreement has remained elusive. Countries such as Britain, Italy and Spain were eager to enter into the use of military force while France, supported by Germany, once again dug her heels in and sought to engender a peaceful resolution to the conflict.

European enlargement, despite the fact that it can be seen as a certain success for foreign policy in itself, has also presented problems for the development of political unity in adoption of new EU borders and an increase in the number of competing national allegiances already experienced within the Union. Nevertheless, a unified political policy continues to remain a priority for the EU as evidenced by its desire to engage in the war on terrorism as recognized within the Lisbon Treaty and its Headline Goal for 2010 to be able to respond to crisis with rapid and decisive action (Hill and Smith, 2005). Political cooperation within Europe can therefore be described as a constant conflict between the desire for national governments to be part of a greater group power and the desire for them to protect their national interests and sovereignty. The desire for increased security against foreign invasion is great. This is evidenced by the fact that no member state sought an opt-out clause for CFSP in the TEU (Sassoon, 1996) and that it continues to be a priority in the latest treaties. However, no matter how great this desire is, national governments have been so far unable to transfer significant power to a supranational level and the CFSP of the EU therefore "continues to lack credibility" (Hill and Smith, 2005, p. 58).

The EU, in its present form, has greater powers than any other international organization and is an extremely powerful economic entity. Third parties have often tended to extend this powerfulness to influence in areas of foreign affairs. This extension is not, however, warranted. Member states have shown a high degree of commitment towards developing a fully harmonized policy in theory, but have so far, in practice, not been able to act in unity. While economic European integration deserves to be called "supranational" in every sense of the word, political integration has remained strictly intergovernmental leading to the popular cliché that the EU is an "economic giant but a political dwarf". Recent efforts to continue to develop the powers of the EU in this area have not yet resulted in significant success and the policy remains a reactive one "responding to events rather than shaping them" (Hix, 2005, p. 398).

Harmonization of Social Policy

McCormick (1999, pp. 66–7) has commented that "For a long time social policy was a poor relation to economic and political integration. Although the EEC Treaty provided for the development of an EEC social policy, this was left in the hands of member states and was very narrowly defined." Social policy is probably the area of European integration which national governments find the most difficult to view in a beneficial light. While Europeans themselves may welcome European wide standards in areas of social policy, governments have typically approached supranational policy making attempts in these areas with caution. European agencies are seen as interfering in domestic concerns and different member states have raised concerns about either the sharp rise in their standards that would be required or the possible decline in national standards that would ensue, were European wide standards to be introduced.

Nevertheless, as economic integration has advanced it has been increasingly necessary to introduce and develop some social integration (Ross, 1995). The Treaty of Rome forming the EEC did mention social policy, but defined its sole purpose as an actor in the construction of a European wide labour market. Harmonization in this area was not an aim – rather the EEC limited itself to the removal of obstacles related to the mobility of manual workers among national labour markets (Streek, 1995). A relationship did exist between economic and social policy objectives, but "the dominant partner was undoubtedly the economic dimension" (Hantrais, 2007, p. 240) leaving social policy a mere "prerequisite and a support for economic integration, rather than an equal partner" (Hantrais, 2007, p. 241).

Although social integration may have gained some support in the years after the Treaty of Rome, it suffered, along with all integrative efforts, in the "doldrum years" of the 1970s. When Delors ascended to the Commission presidency in the 1980s, revitalizing the integrative drive within Europe, he was motivated by economic rather than social concerns (Springer, 1992). Therefore, social policy remained a very much subservient partner to economic policy at this time. The SEA, outlining the plans and timetable for the creation of a single European market, spurred the drive for increased European social integration, however, this was very much in order to facilitate economic integration rather than to further social integration for its own merit.

The creation of a single European market necessitated the free movement of people, goods, services and capital within Europe. In order to facilitate the free movement of people, social integration had to be achieved in a number of areas. For example, issues such as living and working conditions, rights for migrant workers, fair wages, social protection and benefits, vocational training, gender equality, health and safety in the workplace, minimum working ages, pensions and disabled workers had to be approached, within member states, on an equal footing. In reality, it proved difficult to effect these changes, with the only area approaching full harmonization being that of health and safety in the workplace. The drive to implement social integration extended as far as it was perceived to be beneficial in facilitating economic integration and no further. "While the SEA constitutes a major step toward economic integration, it adds only a tentative half step toward a European social policy" (Springer, 1992, p. 40). The will from national governments to further pursue integration in this area simply did not exist.

However, the need to engender some social integration to facilitate the completion of the single market, coupled with the relatively advanced structure for social integration limited to the area of workers' rights launched by Delors's 1989 Social Charter, did advance social integration within Europe to some extent. These tentative foundations were developed to a greater extent throughout the 1990s. The early 1990s can be characterized as a period of depression with reference to European economies in general. Hantrais (2007) cites persistently high levels of unemployment and the prospect of population decline and ageing as promoting the modernization of national social protection systems, with a view to increasing harmonization in this area within Europe. Plans for EMU and enlargement to Central and Eastern Europe provided further impetus for a regeneration of integrated European social policy. This impetus has not, however, been fully borne out.

In terms of enlargement itself, this practice has once again brought further diversity to the EU policy making process, with Hantrais (2007, p. 37) designating harmonization of social policy an ever "more distant goal". Employment policy has formed the latest jewel in the crown of EU level social policy and has featured prominently in both the (now defunct) constitutional treaty and in the Lisbon or Reform Treaty. Expressions of EU level power in other areas of social policy, however, have remained limited. While a 2005 Social Agenda provided a roadmap for social policy until 2010, it was still underpinned by justification on economic grounds. "Social learning and best practices are hallmarks of the new social policy" (Roberts and Springer, 2001, p. 43) and coop-eration, in the form of the exchange of good practice, is now given more weight than harmonization. The power to act in this area is firmly governed by the principle of subsidiarity: "the right of Member States to define the fundamental principles of their Social Security Systems and ensure their financial equilibrium would be left intact" (Hantrais, 2007, p. 18).

Social policy in the EU is thus obviously not developing at a rate, or in a manner, commensurate with economic policy. It lacks the impe-tus of economic policy in that it does not contain an objective to rival that of the creation of an influential and powerful trading entity. Pol-icy implementations in this area therefore do not tend to be of as concrete and well-structured a nature as those relating to economic matters. Political policy has not been as successful as economic pol-icy in Europe but the commitment to continue to strive for integration in this area is there. Social policy, however, remains the poor relation for which the seeds of hope may lie in the application of multi-level governance (Barnard, 2002; Kleinman, 2002). Scott and Trubek (2002) have suggested that this system of governance can prove a beneficial style wherever an issue appears particularly complex without apparent uniformity of solution.

A unique character of European social policy is that it has not devel-oped towards the creation of EU institutions and legislation as the replacement for national governments' social policy regimes. Rather, its limited promotion has allowed the EU to obtain a regulatory role over-seeing, and making small adjustments to, national policies. It has been described as "a multileveled, highly fragmented system in which policy 'develops' but is beyond the firm control of any single political author-ity" (Pierson and Liebfried, 1995, p. 433) and Geyer (2000, p. 212) has further suggested that "Instead of harmonizing national-level social pol-icy regimes, EU social policy may actually encourage them to diversify." The implementation of supranational power has therefore traditionally been granted at the economic level, desired, at least by some, at the political level and ignored at the social level. However, it may be that integrative social policy will come into its own under the notion of multi-level governance. The path towards a fully fledged European social policy now resembles the path towards a fully fledged federal Europe. A working European social policy requires the need for different issues to be resolved at different levels and by consultation with local citi-zens. Certain issues will be divided into regional areas rather than those following traditional national borders. The development of a European social policy and the development of multi-level governance therefore go hand in hand.

Harmonization of Illicit Drug Policy in Europe

To return to the field of drug policy, considerable drive to unify national drug policies within EU member states was made, consistent with the developing popularity of functionalist theories of integration. The issue of European illicit drug policy could, like many other issues, be said to be bound up with the fate of the single market. The free movement of people in Europe, one of the four freedoms ensured by the single market, raised serious questions about the free movement of international criminals and drug traffickers. Towards the prevention of free movement in these instances, officials sought unity in response to illicit drugs.

However, the introduction of the principle of subsidiarity had a sobering effect on progression towards harmonization in this area. Strong national divisions in drug policy had been revealed, divisions which had spread to European institutions themselves. While member states were in agreement on the need to present a unified front in the fight against international drug trafficking, they were not so willing to be united in their responses to drug use and drug users. Faced with such deep divisions, illicit drug policy was declared an area in which policy was best decided at a national level – in other words, an area in which the principle of subsidiarity was to be invoked. Since this decision, hard work has been put into harmonizing interventions against drug traffickers and large-scale suppliers with some success. At the level of drug users and drug use, however, diversity between member states has remained the order of the day, but it may be that multi-level governance, with its emphasis on the sharing of information and instances of best practice, provides a new vision for harmonization in this area. These ideas will be further explored in the next chapter.

2
Drug Policy in the European Union

The last chapter dealt with theories of harmonization within the EU in general. This chapter examines harmonization of drug policy in particular. Since the beginning of the twentieth century, attempts have been made to harmonize drug policy on a worldwide basis. More recently, however, the EU has declared drug policy an area of subsidiarity – one in which countries have been unwilling to surrender their national sovereignty. Harmonization of drug policy resembles attempts to cooperate in areas of social policy discussed in the last chapter. National governments have maintained control while EU institutions have accepted a guiding and advisory role in this area. However, drug policy also has important attachments to the area of JHA under the third pillar of the TEU. There is an important impetus to harmonize national laws and police forces working in the area of control of organized crime and international drug trafficking. European integration in the area of drug policy has therefore not been abandoned, although it is focused on dealing with international traffickers rather than drug users themselves. This chapter examines the history of drug policy within the EU and considers continuing attempts to achieve a closer unity in national policy making.

International drug policy

Drug policy has long been an area subject to international as well as national control. Until the early 1900s, few European countries had any form of national drug legislation, but this situation was to radically change from the date of the first Opium Convention held at Shanghai in 1909. Thirteen powers met at this convention, although it is generally recognized that America provided the main driving force behind the meeting, and formed an aim to make international drug policy subject to stricter control measures. This aim was realized three years later at the Hague Opium Convention in 1912 which saw the birth of an international approach to drug policy as well as the emergence of prohibition style policy as the accepted way to deal with drug problems (Bruun *et al.*, 1975). The 1912 Hague Convention also led to the creation of an Advisory Committee on Traffic in Opium and other Dangerous Drugs and designated the general supervision of opium trafficking to the League of Nations.

Between the 1912 Hague Convention and the famous 1961 Single Convention on Narcotic Drugs, numerous drug-related international meetings were held, and further international commitments were made by individual countries. In 1925, regulation of drug distribution was organized at the Geneva Convention and, in 1931, a Limitation Convention was held to specify the limitation of opium manufacture to the amounts required for scientific and medical purposes. Further working bodies were also created to deal with the increasing regulation of the drug trade at this time. 1929 saw the creation of a Permanent Central Narcotics Board (PCB), a Drug Supervisory Body (DSB), the International Health Office in Paris and the Health Committee of the League of Nations.

After the Second World War, the United Nations (UN) took over primary responsibility for drug control from the League of Nations. It was decided that, to simplify the wealth of international cooperation and legislation that now existed in the matter of drug control, a single Act was needed to encapsulate international commitment in this area. The Single Convention on Narcotic Drugs 1961 is a weighty treaty committing signatories to the recognition that "addiction to narcotic drugs constitutes a serious evil for the individual and is fraught with social and economic danger" (United Nations, 1961, p. 1). This convention bound its signatories to a prohibitive approach towards controlling the drug problem and made them acknowledge the need for international cooperation in combating this problem. Today, all EU member states are committed to formulating their national drug policies within the boundaries of this convention and commitment to the convention is a prerequisite for countries seeking to join the EU.

Since the implementation of the 1961 Single Convention on narcotic drugs, EU member states have continued to extend international cooperation in the field of illicit drugs under the guidance of the UN. In 1971, the Convention on Psychotropic Substances was adopted, extending existing policy to synthetic psychotropic substances like amphetamines and ecstasy. Again, in 1988, a further international drug control convention against Illicit Traffic in Narcotics and Psychotropic Substances was held in Vienna. At this international convention a commitment to focus on the demand side of the drug problem, as well as on the more traditional supply side, was made (Leroy, 1995).

The 1988 convention was the first to require states to establish the offence of possession for personal use under criminal law, which could be viewed as an extension of harmonization from the trafficking of drugs to the possession of drugs for personal consumption. However, the requirement in relation to possession of drugs is not as strict as for drug trafficking. It is subject to the proviso of constitutional limitations of the state or, in other words, subsidiarity (Dorn and Jamieson, 2000). It is possible to avoid the imposition of criminal sanctions on those possessing drugs purely for personal use by arguing that, as existing legal systems do not provide sanctions for drug use, it would be inappropriate to provide them for possession for personal use. Equally, where criminal sanctions do exist, it can easily become the norm to divert those possessing drugs for personal use to treatment or social facilities (Dorn and Jamieson, 2000).

Despite this wealth of international cooperation existing in the area of drug policy, the EU itself was slow to adopt drug policy as an area for supranational intervention. Early attempts to define the appropriate measures for dealing with the problem of illicit drugs within the EU resulted in confusion and failure to find universal support for either restrictive or tolerant methods. Since then, drug policy has become increasingly important within the EU, but any aims to harmonize national policy in this area have been outwardly abandoned. This chapter will examine the reasons behind this EU decision as well as the history of EU drug policy in general.

A European Union drug policy – liberal or restrictive?

The EP is the traditional arena of debate within the EU and was the first institution to approach the problem of illicit drug control on an EU-wide basis. In order to facilitate EU intervention in this area, the EP launched two commissions to seriously consider the most appropriate response to the problem of illicit drugs in the 1980s. At this time, two broad ideologies concerning drug policy were in existence in Europe. Some member states subscribed to tolerant policies towards drug users or towards drugs like cannabis, whereas others operated a much more prohibitive and restrictive policy in all areas of drug control.

The EP commissions were charged with investigating these two approaches to dealing with the drug problem and were asked to produce a report advising on the appropriate nature of a European drug policy. In 1995, the President of the European Parliament reported that "This Parliament has been at the forefront in demanding measures to deal with drugs...since 1986 when it set up a full committee of inquiry into the drugs problem" (Hansch, 1995, p. 1). The committee he is referring to is the first parliamentary commission, headed by Stewart-Clark and undertaken in 1986. This was complemented by the subsequent parliamentary commission headed by Cooney and undertaken in 1991. The reports of both these commissions are extensively discussed by Blom and van Mastrigt (1994).

The first commission, headed by Stewart-Clark, was charged with investigating the nature of the drug problem and deciding whether liberal or restrictive strategies were more effective and/or desirable in combating this problem. However, when the commission presented their conclusions, they were divided between majority/minority positions within the group of members. Overall, they agreed that large-scale dealing should be treated with a strict enforcement policy, but elsewhere no conclusive recommendations had been reached.

The majority position held that a repressive approach should be maintained in drug control problems. They cited brief periods of legalization in Spain and Sweden as a failure, resulting in an increased number of drug dependents. They also criticized the contradictory policy operating in the Netherlands whereby trade and supply in cannabis was illegal but sale and small-scale possession was not a criminal offence. In contrast, the minority position linked large-scale organized drug trafficking to repressive policies and allowed for the possibility that legalization could be an effective tool in controlling trafficking. They concluded that Dutch policies made sense and favoured the decriminalization of use, possession and small-scale dealing. They found it inconsistent that some drugs, such as alcohol and nicotine, were legal but others were not.

When the Stewart-Clark commission presented its report to the EP, there was little choice but to judge the findings inconclusive. The considerable split in opinion on how to tackle the problem of illicit drugs was then neatly sidestepped by the EP as they refrained from upholding the opinion of either side, instead implementing recommendations endorsed by both sides such as the establishment of research centres and the improvement of national and international coordination. It was not until 1991 that the Parliament authorized another investigation into the nature of the drug problem and the relative suitability of either liberal or repressive strategies in dealing with it. This time, the commission was headed by Cooney who was given a similar brief to the 1986 commission: to determine the most effective and/or desirable approach in tackling the problem of illegal drugs.

Again, when the commission made its report to the EP, opinions were divided, but this time the majority group was in favour of liberal methods and it was the minority group that remained dedicated to restrictive measures. Dutch policies had been more closely researched and, this time, were judged in a much more favourable light. The distinction between soft and hard drugs, the high priority placed on prevention projects, the general assistance of dependent users and, in particular, programmes implementing free treatment, needles and substitute drugs were upheld by the majority group.

They were also impressed by the growing view that drug problems should be dealt with in the public health sphere and possession of drugs for personal use should not be regarded as a criminal offence. However, they did maintain that legalization should be rejected as the EU should follow the UN in its aim to minimize the use of drugs. Meanwhile, the minority group protested that possession should stay illegal and be punishable by criminal sanctions, and the illogical policy adopted by the Netherlands (legalizing sale and small-scale possession of drugs in an overall system where trade and supply was still illegal) should be eradicated.

The confusion over how best to deal with illicit drugs was clearly high as neither parliamentary commission had been able to reach an overall conclusion on the matter, and even the majority of opinion of the two reports was not the same. Nevertheless, when the Cooney report was presented to Parliament, the minority position was upheld at the expense of the majority one, possibly due to pressure from the USA (Blom and van Mastrigt, 1994). Obviously, opinion within the EP, and by extension the EU itself, is very divided in the area of illicit drug control. A predominantly prohibitionist front, however, has consistently been followed, with any possibilities for legalization within the EU being denied.

Since the 1991 Cooney report, the EU has withdrawn from attempts to judge the desirability of one method of drug control over another. The principle of subsidiarity has been invoked in the area of illicit drug control and the EU has been content to promote vague aims of cooperation and coordination between member states at the expense of concrete policy interventions in this area (Chatwin, 2003). Provision has been made for the coordination of law enforcement agencies and strategies across the Union, as well as for the collation and dissemination of data relating to the problem, but the aim of harmonization within the EU, with reference to the area of drug control and prevention, has not so far materialized. It remains an area in which the national governments of member states have ultimate control.

The necessity of this decision to declare drug policy an area of subsidiarity can be observed by the fact that some member states have aligned themselves strongly with one or other side of the debate. An obvious example is the Netherlands as a promoter of liberal policies, incorporating distinctions between different drugs and the practice of normalizing the dependent user. Another is Sweden, a country loudly critical of policies tolerant to the drug-dependent user in its moral aim to eradicate all drugs from its own society. This situation is amplified by the fact that within member states there also exists a division of opinion on how to tackle the illicit drug problem.

In many European countries some aspects of drug control fall to local authorities and there may be local differences in the way national policy is implemented and practiced. For example, in Germany, where drug control is a federal matter but implementation of policy is left up to individual states (Länder), northern states originally adopted a liberal position while southern states were still very much pursuing repressive policies (Albrecht and van Kalmthout, 1989). This provides evidence for the implementation of the principle of subsidiarity in its full multi-level governance context. Not only should the area of drug policy be left to national governments, but perhaps it should be further broken down to governance by local authorities with an increased role for citizen participation.

This phenomenon is further illustrated by the foundation of two networks of European cities that are radically different in their opinion of how best to approach the drug problem. These European city networks are extensively discussed by Kaplan and Leuw (1996). In November 1990, the Frankfurt resolution was signed forming a network of European cities devoted to the problem of drug control, known as European Cities on Drug Policy (ECDP). Originally, this agreement was signed by Amsterdam, Frankfurt am Main, Hamburg and Zurich, all of whom agreed to work towards the principles of "legalisation, liberalisation and harm reduction", whatever the nature of their respective national drug policies. Authorities, at a city level, are embroiled in the debate over the best approach to combating illicit drugs to such an extent that they will commit to aims such as reintegrating drug-dependent users into society, offering them treatment rather than punishment, working towards the legalization of cannabis and sharing the drugs problem equally between the police and welfare groups, even where these aims may not be subscribed to by their own national governments.

The restrictive side of the drug debate has not lost out here as, in direct response to ECDP, the Stockholm resolution was signed in April 1994, forming the network of European Cities Against Drugs (ECAD). The signatories to this resolution dedicate themselves to "prohibition, zero tolerance and a war on drugs", in direct contradiction to the aims promoted by the ECDP. In several cases, cities from the same countries have signed up to either ECDP or ECAD, and there is even one city from the Netherlands (Hulst), a country traditionally strongly liberal in the area of drug policy, that has signed the Stockholm resolution promoting a "war on drugs" (Kaplan and Leuw, 1996).

The irresolvable divide in opinion on the best approach to the drug problem that is present in the EP and, by extension, the EU itself, is reflected at national and local levels. Instead of becoming hopelessly entangled in this lively debate, the EU has allowed control thus far to stay in the hands of member states. It has restricted its interventions towards achieving a better understanding of the drug problem and towards making information on the nature of the problem and possible policy solutions widely available. However, an EU role in drug policy is very far from having been abandoned. From the instigation of the Stewart-Clark report in 1986, EU interest and control in the area of drug policy have continually increased. This chapter will now consider the management of drug policy at a European level and evidence that international cooperation in the field of drug policy continues to be an EU priority.

A brief history of drug policy development at a European Union level

Prior to the 1990s, the issue of an illicit drug problem was scarcely mentioned within the official legislation of the EU. It was not referred to specifically in either the 1957 Treaty of Rome, which was instrumental in the creation of the European Community(EC), or the 1987 SEA (Boekhout van Solinge, 2002). However, the first signs of an EU interest in the illicit drug problem began to emerge during the late 1980s via the Stewart-Clark commission discussed above. A further issue being heavily debated at the time also held consequences for the nature of the illicit drug problem. For some time, discussion over the opening of borders and the creation of an area of freedom of movement had been held. In 1985, the Schengen Agreement was entered into by France, Germany, Belgium, Luxembourg and the Netherlands in an effort to create a territory without any internal borders. This agreement can be regarded as the first time that the idea of formal cooperation of this nature between member states was expounded (Commission of the European Communities, 2001a).

Throughout the 1980s, a debate had opened up within the EC about the meaning of the concept of "free movement of persons": the Schengen Agreement recognized the aim of freedom of movement and paved the way for the creation of a "Schengen Area" in which internal borders would be abolished (EUROPA, 2002). The creation of such an area raised questions and concerns about criminal organizations, including illegal drug traffickers, capitalizing on the subsequent ease of crossing international borders. For the first time, the negative effects of international crime, such as drug trafficking, were raised on an EC-wide level and cooperation across Europe in this area was considered.

The Schengen Agreement was rapidly followed by the ratification in 1987 of the SEA which increased cooperation between individual member states in a number of areas. Although the areas of drug control and prevention were not specifically mentioned in this treaty, it is generally recognized as "the most important and successful step in the process of European integration since the Treaty of Rome" (McCormick, 2008, p. 77), and gave the EC responsibility over new policy areas as well as increasing the powers of the ECJ. Cooperation was still largely confined to economic areas, but the need for cooperation in other areas, as well as the need for bodies governing international crime, had been recognized.

In terms of drug policy, the first EU institution developed for dealing specifically with this issue was the Comite Europeen de la Lutte Anti-Drogue (CELAD), a coordination group on drugs. It was set up in 1989 with the aim of coordinating activities in the field of drugs and ensuring a place on the agenda for the problems of drug control and prevention. CELAD was responsible for implementing several useful strategies in terms of EU drug policy. It has since been dissolved and replaced by the coordinating K4 group, named for the Article of the TEU under which they acted, Article K.4(3), and comprised of senior civil servants. In turn, the K4 group is now often known as the Article 36 Committee in reference to the fact that it now acts under Article 36 of the Amsterdam Treaty.

CELAD was directly responsible for proposing the first EU Action Plan to Combat Drugs which was adopted at the Rome European Council in 1990, and has been updated at four yearly intervals ever since. The Action Plan is a tool used by the EU to state their aims in terms of drug policy and to guide individual member states in areas in which it is felt possible for them to work together against the illicit drug problem, without compromising rights to national subsidiarity. It was also responsible for creating the Reseau Europeen d'Information sur les Drogues et les Toxicomanies (REITOX), a European Information Network on Drugs and Drug Addiction, in 1993, which later led to the development of its coordinating and governing body, the European Monitoring Centre for Drugs and Drug Addiction (EMCDDA) in 1995.

These bodies are concerned with the collation and dissemination of data regarding the extent and nature of the drug problem across EU countries. They also provide information on interventions that are in practice against the drug problem, without ostensibly offering judgement on the moral or practical desirability of those interventions. REITOX is a computer network at the heart of the collection and exchange of drug information and documentation in Europe. It stores national statistics on drugs from each member state of the EU and is represented by a national focal point in each country. In 1995, these national focal points were appointed a coordinating and governing body in the form of the EMCDDA, whose main objective is to collect and analyse information relating to drugs by carrying out surveys, studies and pilot projects, and to make this information available to a wide audience (EMCDDA, 1998). Its main priorities have been identified as the reduction of the demand for drugs, international cooperation, the control of trade and an examination of the implications of the drugs phenomenon for producer, consumer and transit countries (EMCDDA, 2001a).

CELAD, however, was only responsible for the initial foundation of the REITOX network and much of the EMCDDA's work has been developed since its dissolution and in light of the Maastricht Treaty (1993) and the Amsterdam Treaty (1997). The Maastricht Treaty, symbolizing the next stage in the process of European integration, expanded areas of EU policy intervention under a new three pillar system of policy decision-making. For the first time, drugs were specifically mentioned as an area for EU concern, although the governance of this problem was a matter of confusion as the discussion of illicit drugs came under all three pillars of the new policy foundation (Boekhout van Solinge, 1999).

The first pillar dealt mainly with the traditional economic policy of the EU, however, Article 129 of this pillar stipulated a responsibility of the EU to deal with the "prevention of diseases, in particular the major health scourges, including drug dependence", although it was left up to the individual member states to coordinate their own policies and programmes to achieve this objective. The second pillar, dealing mainly with Common Foreign and Security Policy (CFSP), covered cooperation in external relations and dealt with drugs in terms of supply reduction and the fight against drug trafficking. The third pillar regulated cooperation in JHA and therefore dealt with many of the important decisions being made on drug issues. Drug issues can therefore be said to come under all three pillars. This has made their regulation somewhat difficult.

In addition to adopting the problem of drug control and prevention as an issue with important relevance to EU policy making, the TEU also created a European police intelligence agency (Europol) to combat organized crime and drug trafficking. While the provision of Europol as a body designed to provide a structure for developing police cooperation between member states in preventing and combating serious forms of international crime, including terrorism and drug trafficking (EUROPA, 2001), was originally envisioned in the TEU, Europol itself did not formally fully come into existence until 1999. Before this, a temporary Europol Drugs Unit (EDU) was established to combat drug trafficking and associated money laundering. The early creation of this unit emphasizes the importance and urgency attached to coordination of police policy in the area of drug control.

Prior to the signing of the TEU, drugs were hardly ever discussed within institutions of the EU, largely because they were not a European political issue. Therefore, one of the important consequences of this treaty was the adoption of drugs as a problem for the EU, along with many other changes in the European political landscape (Boekhout van Solinge, 2002). However, despite the creation of numerous policy governing bodies, this treaty was largely unsatisfactory in organizing drug policy as it failed to lay down sufficient provisions for international cooperation, and for effective methods for dealing with the drug problem in Europe. Individual member states were left to fight international crime relatively informally, much as they had been doing for the previous 20 years.

In 1997, another important EU treaty was signed at the Amsterdam European Council, which is therefore known as the Amsterdam Treaty. In terms of the EU as a whole, this treaty is not as important as either the SEA or the Treaty on European Union but, in terms of drug policy, it signified a major step forward in recognition of the problem by the EU. It officially recognizes that crime extends beyond national borders and the only effective way to fight the international networks that have formed is through closer international cooperation (EUROPA, 1998). The main aim of the treaty is to enable the EU to deal with the globalization and evolution of the international situation (EUROPA, 1998). Within its broad objective to ensure freedom, security and justice throughout Western Europe, the fight against drugs is given special attention and has, to some extent, been reorganized within the EU by this treaty. In addition to the pillars' organizing policy within the EU that already existed, the Amsterdam Treaty incorporated the use of Titles to further organize and regulate policy issues on an EU-wide scale.

Title XIII, Article 152 of the Treaty of Amsterdam, deals with drugs as a public health priority. It stipulates that "a high level of human health protection shall be ensured in the definition and implementation of all Community policies and activities" as well as specifically mentioning the need for action "in reducing drugs-related health damage" (Commission of the European Communities, 1999, p. 9). Title IV of the Amsterdam Treaty is also relevant to the issue of illicit drugs as it deals with checks at external borders and judicial cooperation in criminal matters. It aims to make freedom of movement easier while, at the same time, building up effective international cooperation against organized crime in general and illicit drug trafficking in particular.

Title VI is the main part of the Amsterdam Treaty which covers policy in the areas of drug control and prevention as it deals with JHA. It refers specifically to drugs in two areas: Article 29 mentions "preventing and combating crime at the appropriate level, organised or otherwise, in particular... illicit drug trafficking" and in Article 31 (e) "the adoption of measures establishing minimum rules relating to the constituent elements of criminal acts and to penalties in the fields of organised crime, terrorism and illicit drug trafficking" is encouraged (Commission of the European Communities, 1999, pp. 10–11). This treaty has focused on international cooperation and may allow more effective methods of drug control to be developed, although it does not affect the right of the member states to exercise their own responsibilities for maintaining law and order and safeguarding internal security (EUROPA, 1998). Instead, the new organization is aimed at improving the coordination of action and collaboration of ideas in the areas of drug prevention and control between member states.

As the area of drug control and prevention still falls under all three pillars of the TEU, as well as several Titles of the Amsterdam Treaty, a Horizontal Drugs Group (HDG) was set up in 1997 to monitor and coordinate all cross-pillar activities in the field of drugs and report back to the Committee of Permanent Representatives (COREPER). The HDG is the main group currently responsible for overall coordination in the field of illicit drugs within the EU. It is indicative of the importance now attached to the issues of drug control and prevention within the EU that so many other groups have been founded to deal with different aspects of the problem. The many responsibilities of these different drug-related groups have now been subsumed by the HDG.

The Commission of the European Communities (1999) describes the functions of these policy bodies and groups dealing with drug issues that are now part of the HDG. Two of the most important of these are The Common Foreign and Security Policy Council Working Group on Drugs (CODRO), which coordinates foreign policy initiatives related to drug control cooperation with third countries and the K4 (or Article 36) group which took over from the dissolute CELAD. There is also a Health Group examining issues linked in particular to the Community Action Programme on the Prevention of Drug Dependence, the Economic Question Group examining issues linked to the control of chemical precursors and various working groups set up under Title VI of the Amsterdam Treaty: for example, the customs cooperation group and the police cooperation group.

Several bodies have also been initiated to deal with cross-border trafficking of illegal drugs and are described in a 1996 EP document – "The Fight Against Drugs". As previously mentioned, Europol was set up, in part, to obtain information about drugs and drug trafficking with the ability to analyse this information and to initiate investigations resultant from it. In addition to Europol, the Trevi Group was also set up relatively early on in the history of the EU in 1976 to fight international terrorism. Its activities have since been extended to cover drug policy and, more recently, this group has been charged with coordinating and developing a system of Drugs Liaison Officers (DLOs) from national customs and police, posted in producer or transit countries. A project (OISIN) to enhance cooperation in general between law enforcement agencies at an EU level and a World Customs Organization has also been founded.

The most recent European Treaty to have been ratified, the Lisbon Treaty, finally implemented in 2009, has further contributed to the complexity of drug policy making at the European level. While making little direct reference to illegal drugs – Article 168 is concerned with the improvement of public health in general, but also specifically makes provisions for reducing drug-related health damage – some significant key powers are extended that will have a knock-on effect on the field of drug policy. For example, the treaty makes the EU charter of fundamental rights binding, which makes decisions on issues like trial by jury, euthanasia and the legalization of hard drugs a European concern. In addition, minimum rules surrounding the definition of crimes and their punishment and an extension of the power of the European Prosecutor's court have been implemented in an attempt to increase efforts against terrorism and international trafficking, whether it be of drugs, arms or women.

Drug policy can therefore be seen to have been a steadily increasing concern for the EU. As the years have gone by an increasing number of groups charged with tackling the issue have emerged and each European Treaty has added to the complexity and depth of policy making in this area. The importance of the issue to the EU itself can be further inferred by its affiliation to each of the major power structures of the EU: the Commission, the Council and the Parliament. As outlined above, the EP has been interested in the question of the illicit drug problem and has been active in this field, at least in the initial stages of the definition of the problem. Early on in the recognition of drugs as a problem for Europe, the EP was influential in trying to define the nature of the problem by commissioning two reports into the issue. The EP, however, has been fundamentally split over the most appropriate approach to the problem and possible solutions to it, and has therefore advised EU-wide drug policy to be content with producing guidelines and conducting data analysis, rather than giving concrete direction.

Boekhout van Solinge (2002) describes how the Commission and the Council have also been, at least to some extent, involved in the formulation of EU drug policy. The Commission's control lies in the area of first pillar matters which are mainly health related, so, in relation to drugs, their predominant concern is with prevention. Recently the Commission has played a strong role in external relations and has consistently raised the drugs question with applicant countries to the EU. The European Union Action Plan is also a document produced by the Commission.

The Council is also involved in debating drug policy with applicant countries to the EU and governs the HDG, thus monitoring the question of drugs across all three pillars. An important drug-related group attached to the Council is the Pompidou group. Set up in 1971 at the instigation of French President Georges Pompidou, this was originally an informal group whose members debated drug policy. In 1980, it became part of the European Council. Its members are countries rather than individuals and it provides a forum for international specialists, officials and professionals to cooperate and exchange information. Its main aims are to stimulate and facilitate the exchange of knowledge in the area of illicit drug control, to promote comprehensive drug strategies at a national, regional and local level and to improve data collection systems and monitor emerging trends in the field of illicit drugs.

The drugs issue thus permeates all main policy pillars and titles of EU governance and attracts the attention of all three power structures within the EU. An impressive range of tools has been developed in connection with the regulation of the drug problem ensuring that drug issues stay firmly on the international policy agenda, although they must remain, for the moment at least, an area of national subsidiarity for EU member states. An examination of more recent policy developments in this field reveals an increasing emphasis on coordination of drug policy wherever and whenever possible.

Harmonization of drug policy in the European Union

An examination of the decision-making processes and recently produced drug-related documents of the EU reveals a slow-burning commitment to deepening cooperation in this controversial area. Since the early 1990s, and CELAD's inauguration of the EU Action Plan on Drugs and the European Anti-Drugs Strategy, a vision of drug policy has existed at a European level. Since their inception, the EU Action Plans, developed at four-year intervals, have aimed to reduce demand and supply of drugs and to increase international cooperation and coordination at national and EU level. Additionally, they have consistently emphasized the importance of collecting, analysing and disseminating data on the drug phenomenon in the EU.

Up until 2004, the making and implementing of EU Action Plans on drugs passed with relatively little controversy. Many countries incorporated the goals and objectives wholesale into their national policies, especially the general principles of fighting demand and supply while increasing international cooperation. These documents served as recognition of the common nature of the drug problem within individual member states. They inferred that appropriate solutions could be very similar although, rather than defining these solutions, they presented themes and strategies that all member states could follow while remaining faithful to their national policies. Rather than dictating the major policy tools a member state must employ in dealing with drug problems within their own countries, the Action Plans served as a guiding path to cooperation and interaction.

To an extent this is still true, but an element of controversy entered the process in 2004 with the production of the "Catania Report" (European Parliament, 2004), named after MEP Giusto Catania, "a set of recommendations towards future EU drug policy... [which] proposes a radical change in EU drug policy and advocates harm reduction and a scientific and balanced approach instead of maintaining drug prohibition" (ENCOD, 2007, p. 1). An evaluation of the 2000–04 Action Plan suggested that "no strong evidence exists to support the contention that the goal... to significantly reduce drug use prevalence has been achieved, or that fewer young people are using drugs... similarly, the available information does not suggest that the availability of drugs has been reduced substantially.... This final evaluation should be taken into account in the development of the new EU Drugs Strategy 2005–2012" (Commission of the European Communities, 2004, pp. 12–13).

Giusto Catania's report seized upon this apparent failure and further intimated that none of the six overarching objectives of the European Anti-Drugs Strategy had been achieved (ENCOD, 2007). His report suggested this failure of European drug policy indicated that the time was ripe for a change in overall strategy and that future European drug policy must be based on harm reduction rather than prohibition. In December 2004, to considerable surprise, the report was approved by the EP, however, in 2005 a new European Anti-Drugs Strategy (2005–12) and a new European Action Plan on Drugs (2005–08) were implemented. Despite the public acceptance of the Catania report, these new documents were virtually indistinguishable, in terms of overall aims and objectives and in terms of the recommendations they made with reference to the development of drug policy, from their predecessors.

This seemingly hypocritical approach, whereby failure had been acknowledged and the need for alternative solutions admitted at the same time as new documents committing to the old strategies had been produced, attracted some criticism. The European Coalition for Just and Effective Drug Policies (ENCOD) sent a communication to the Horizontal Working Party on Drugs urging them to "cancel the approval of the new Action Plan" (ENCOD, 2005, p. 1) suggesting that "a policy is being continued which has been shown to be ineffective.... Authorities responsible for drug policies are thus ignoring the evidence that their policies do not work" (ENCOD, 2005, p. 1). While the EU Drugs

Strategy and Action Plan continue to be based around drug demand reduction, drug supply reduction and international cooperation, there is some evidence that individual targets including "the attainment of a high level of health protection, well-being and social cohesion by preventing and reducing drug use, dependence and drug-related harm to health and society" (*Official Journal of the European Union*, 2007, p. 1) have been added. The key here is in the final phrase dealing with drug-related harm to health and society, which some have taken to be an endorsement of an increasing turn towards harm reduction principles at the expense of prohibition.

The most recent EU Action Plan on Drugs (2009–12) reinforces the ever-present aims of demand reduction, supply reduction and international cooperation, but has been marketed as being "more pragmatic, focused and targeted than its predecessors" (Rhodes and Hedrich, 2010, p. 7). The principle of harm reduction has gained a stronger foothold with an increased presence in the detailed objectives of the plan (Rhodes and Hedrich, 2010). One further relevant concept to have emerged from the latest collection of aims is an increased emphasis on civil consultation and citizen involvement in drug policy making which echoes some of the principles of multi-level governance outlined in Chapter 1. The Commission of the European Communities (2004, p. 4) has declared that "National drugs coordination needs to be extended to all areas of drug policy, including regular consultation with civil society" and the Council (*Official Journal of the European Union*, 2008, p. 2) has proposed "an alliance between citizens and the institutions created by them and for them ... to put the people of Europe at the centre of policy in this field and to get Europe's citizens more involved".

One of the principles consistently enshrined in all the existing Action Plans and Drug Strategies has been the call for increased international cooperation in this field, despite the previous decision to make this an issue of national subsidiarity. Traditionally, this has involved individual member states developing their own national policy while participating in interaction with the policies of other member states. "Not everyone has to fight on the same fronts at the same time but coordination and interaction of players and approaches must be ensured to reach maximum efficiency" (EUROPA, 1999, p. 2). Careful assurances of the continuing need for individual autonomy in defining drug policy have always been offered to countries whose policies diverge somewhat from the guiding principles. "Countries and regions have sufficient room to experiment and find out which approach works best. Such differentiation must be respected within the general framework of

European Union policy" (Hellenic Presidency of the European Union, 2003, p. 3).

The most recent Action Plan, and communications within the EU generally, however, reveal an increase in emphasis on the benefits of coordination. The latest Drug Strategy unveils more specific aims in this area: to adopt EU common positions on drugs in international fora and to promote an EU approach to the illegal drug problem (Horizontal Working Party on Drugs, 2005). The Council has declared coordination "key to the establishment and conduct of a successful strategy against drugs" (Council of the European Union, 2004, p. 8) and recommends that this be achieved through the Horizontal Drugs Group. While consensus on coordination may have been achieved, implementing it still proves problematic as a question mark hangs over the content of such a policy. "Drugs are a sensitive and highly political issue. The debate is often polarized between a more enforcement-oriented approach focusing on measures to combat trafficking and a more tolerant approach that focuses on prevention and reduction of drugs-induced health disorders. The dichotomy is visible both within all the member States and also between them" (Commission of the European Communities, 2003, p. 4). Nevertheless, international observers have reported that the EU is beginning to speak with one voice as regards drug policy (Reuter, 2009).

So, on paper at least, European commitment to developing a European drug policy, communicated through the Action Plan and Drug Strategy, endures, and the will to take this cooperation to the next level is openly declared. Yet the various power structures of the EU have remained unable to reach a consensus on the overall style of a European drug policy: prohibition or tolerance, at least towards drug use and drug users. Instead, the EU has continued to steer a "middle road" between the two paradigms of drug control. Evidence that this commitment to a European policy goes beyond EU-produced documents and strategies and successfully translates into national policies will now be examined.

Overwhelmingly, the easiest area in which to engender international coordination of drug policy has been in relation to drug trafficking and drug traffickers. Measures focused against trafficking make up a large part of the content of the Action Plans and Drug Strategies; for example, two joint actions on drugs have been passed, largely due to the efforts of the K4 (Article 36) group. One was a largely academic document making slight adjustments to national legislation in order to make EU member states more similar in their drug laws and practices, and the other created an early warning system for new synthetic drugs (Boekhout van Solinge, 2002).

Recently, the EU also made important inroads into developing a united European policy against drug trafficking. The Commission of the European Communities proposed a framework decision (2001b) on combating terrorism in which a recommendation to introduce EU-wide minimum penalties in the area of organized crime and terrorism was made. One of the areas of proposed introduction of these aims was that of illicit drug trafficking. A recommendation was made to adopt a minimum penalty of five years' imprisonment which must be imposed in all cases of drug trafficking, and a minimum penalty of eight years' imprisonment to be imposed in all cases of serious drug trafficking (Oostlander, 2001). In 2004, this recommendation was realized in Council Framework Decision 2004/757/JHA (*Official Journal of the European Union*, 2004) marking the beginning of EU-wide legal policy on drug control. Furthermore, in addition to the control of drug trafficking as a strong area of restriction within EU policy, it is still the case, with notable exception, that prohibition of possession of drugs is the basic precept followed by all EU countries. While decriminalization of some drugs may be gaining ground in Europe, legalization is not currently considered a serious option in any member state, although there is consistent evidence of awareness that prosecution and imprisonment of individuals with drug problems can lead to escalation of their problems.

The other instantly observable trend in drug policy within the EU has been towards the principle of harm reduction referring to the desire, through policy interventions, to reduce the amount of harm done to drug users; for example, providing access to clean needles to heavily addicted heroin users to limit the amount of suffering they cause both to themselves and to society in the pursuit of their drug habit. It is also associated with the idea that drug-dependent users should be viewed as patients rather than criminals. This principle of therapy over punishment has been adopted in the general guidelines of drug policies in a growing number of countries. Some member states have consolidated social and medical support towards drug-dependent offenders and, increasingly, the first contact with law enforcement authorities is being used as a door to treatment or counselling activities throughout the EU (Flynn, 2001).

In terms of the most established harm reduction innovations, such as the provision of needle exchange services and substitution treatment programmes for heroin users, "controversy has to a large extent been replaced by consensus" (Rhodes and Hedrich, 2010, p. 9). Additionally, the European Legal Database on Drugs (ELDD) (2001) records some trends in national drug laws which may be indicative of an increasing acceptance of relatively liberal ideas towards drug users and drug use. For example, in many EU countries, personal consumption of a drug no longer leads to imprisonment but is instead dealt with by means of social and/or medical interventions, particularly when dealing with those seriously dependent on illicit drugs. As a reflection of this trend, most EU countries are starting to distinguish between personal use and other drug offences. Some countries are beginning to discuss the validity of determining between a selling offence in general and an offence often known as "social dealing" whereby an individual is buying and disseminating drugs on behalf of a group of friends. Nevertheless, MacGregor and Whiting (2010) caution against overstating the role of harm reduction in the development of European drug policy. Newer harm reduction initiatives, such as rooms where users can safely consume their drugs and the official provision of heroin to heroin users, enjoy far less unanimity of acceptance and there are significant countries that remain wedded to the ultimate eradication of drugs from society.

The desire for increased harmonization of drug policy at the European level, at least by the power structures of the EU itself, could not be clearer. The sticking point remains the inability to provide a fundamental judgement between the minority and majority positions of the Stewart-Clark and Cooney commissions or, more recently, the aims of the Catania report or those of the official European Anti-Drugs Strategy. Should a European drug policy be based entirely on repression and prohibition, as it clearly is when it comes to drug trafficking and drug traffickers, or should it encompass tolerance and liberalization, at least with regard to drug use and drug users? The challenge is deciding on this content and convincing all member states that the correct approach has been inarguably arrived at. The role of the EMCDDA, since its inception in the 1990s, has been to collate data on the state of the drug problem in individual member states and to amass examples of best practice in the field of drug policy interventions. The EU itself has thus far refrained from drawing conclusions from this data, but the next chapter of this book will examine the possibilities for doing so.

3
Statistical Information on the Drug Problem in the European Union

The European Monitoring Centre for Drugs and Drug Addiction's EMCDDA's purpose in collating data on the illicit drug problem in Europe has never been to offer an ultimate judgement on the best overall policy style for Europe as a whole. Rather, the role of the EMCDDA is a scientific one: information is collected and analysed and the results are presented; however, it is up to individual member states to draw their own conclusions from the data the EMCDDA has made available. This stance ensures the continued cooperation of all EU member states in providing data and remaining committed to the idea of increasing harmonization where possible. However, were the data collected by the EMCDDA to be reliable and were it to point clearly towards the success of one style of drug policy over another, this would obviously be very useful in developing opportunities for harmonization. This chapter will seek to explore the reliability and usefulness of EMCDDA data in removing barriers to the harmonization of European drug policy.

The problematic nature of cross-national comparative research

The first issue to be dealt with here is the extreme difficulty of cross-national comparative research conducted on the scale achieved by the EMCDDA. Galtung (1990, p. 107) encapsulates the problems associated with research depending on the collation of data from many different countries as trying to create a universal social science, "a social science transcending geography and history with all that implies of structural and cultural diversity". There are many difficulties with creating this "universal social science" that are relevant to comparative, statistical-based, studies in the drug policy field. Hakim (2000) highlights the difficulties in drawing reliable conclusions from studies where there may be hidden agendas subscribed to by the institution undertaking the research, where there are cultural differences in styles of work (although these can also exist at a national level), or where scholars from different countries involved in the research may come from different disciplinary perspectives. All these problems are encountered in the drugs field.

There are cultural differences to be observed in styles of both data collection and presentation between countries. Data is also often provided by different departments in each member state. While the EMCDDA posits itself as an independent and objective body compiling statistics on the drug problem in individual member states without passing judgement or seeking to guide policy, it is not impossible that it, and by extension the EU, has a hidden agenda regarding eventual EU control on the drugs issue. Flynn (2001, p. 4) has raised a further obstacle to the interpretation of statistics gathered by the EU: "Measuring the comparative success of drug policies is, of course problematic. There are no universally accepted criteria for success, for example, by which competing drug policies can be assessed." While member states continue to maintain widely differing national drug policies, such criteria are not likely to be developed, ensuring the interpretation of statistics remains relatively meaningless.

Nevertheless, the statistics on the nature of the drug problem collected by the EMCDDA are a useful starting point in understanding the problems which face the implementation of a unified European drug policy, as well as the desirability of that implementation. The statistics collected from national focal points in each country are relatively useless in determining which countries have developed the most effective strategies in dealing with the drug problem. However, they are helpful in exposing the fact that the nature of the drug problem is relatively similar in each member state.

The questions asked by the EMCDDA about numbers of problem drug users, numbers of drug-related deaths and numbers of HIV positive intravenous drug users, for example, can be answered by all member states indicating that these are problems for them all. The extent of the problem may vary to a greater or lesser degree, but the simple truth is that the problems experienced in the field of illicit drugs are universal: it is only the solutions which are not. This chapter will examine some of the most recent statistics compiled by the EMCDDA in an effort to illuminate the problems of interpretation that face researchers who depend on this type of information. It will also emphasize the relative similarity of the nature of the drug problem across Europe.

The EMCDDA collects information on many and detailed aspects of the drug problem; however, for the purposes outlined above, it is necessary only to include an examination of a selection of statistics taken from all areas covered by the EMCDDA. The selection presented here includes statistics drawn from sections on the prevalence of drug use, the extent of problem drug use, drug-related infectious diseases, drug-related deaths, drug-related crime and drug markets and availability.

Prevalence of drug use

Prevalence of drug use is measured by the EMCDDA in two ways: within the general population and among school children. Most countries conduct national population surveys of both these populations, with some also conducting them within the population of army conscripts. However, not all of the countries conduct national population studies in each of these areas, so comparisons on the prevalence of drug use are not complete. In addition to this, national surveys may ask about lifetime prevalence of drug use (for example, have you ever used a certain drug?), last year prevalence of drug use (for example, have you used a certain drug in the last 12 months?) and last month prevalence of drug use (for example, have you used a certain drug in the last 30 days?).

Again, some countries ask all of these questions, but not all of them do. Last 12 months and last 30 days prevalence reports enrich lifetime prevalence statistics and help to capture the current situation, but are by no means universal. Finally, where countries have conducted national surveys regarding prevalence of drug use in the general population, these statistics have been broken down by the EMCDDA to include general prevalence and prevalence among "younger adults", which is usually much greater. Further comparability problems emerge when you consider that different countries have used different age range samples in general and in their consideration of "younger adults".

A full breakdown of the most recent available statistics on lifetime and last 12 months prevalence of drug use for adults and younger adults is presented in Tables 3.1–3.4. Examination of these statistics reveals that cannabis continues to be the illegal substance most commonly used in all EU countries. Lifetime experience of cannabis is the most common, being reported by 2–39 per cent of European adults and 3–50 per cent of European younger adults. Cannabis use in the last 12 months has been reported by 0.5–15 per cent of adults and 1–28 per cent of younger adults. Use of other drugs is reported much less frequently than

Table 3.1 Lifetime prevalence all adults: last survey available for each member state (from 2000 onwards)

Country	Method			All adults %			
	Year	Data coll.	Sample	Age range	Cannabis	Cocaine (1)	Amphet amines (2)	Ecstasy (3)
Belgium	2004	Interview		15–64	13.0			
Bulgaria	2008	Interview	5,139	15–64	7.3	1.7	2.1	1.7
Czech Republic	2008	Interview	4,500	15–64	34.2	2.0	4.3	9.6
Denmark	2008	Mail/web	3,408	16–64	38.6	4.7	6.3	1.9
Germany	2006	Mail	7,912	18–64	23.0	2.5	2.5	2.0
Estonia	2008	Mail	1,401	15–64				
Ireland	2006–07	Interview	4,967	15–64	21.9	5.3	3.5	5.4
Greece	2004	Interview	4,351	15–64	8.9	0.7	0.1	0.4
Spain	2007–08	Interview	23,715	15–64	27.3	8.3	3.8	4.2
France	2005	Phone	25,879	15–64	30.6	2.6	1.4	2.0
Italy	2008	Mail	10,940	15–64	32.0	7.0	3.2	3.0
Cyprus	2006	Interview	3,504	15–64	6.6	1.1	0.8	1.6
Latvia	2007	Interview	4,500	15–64	12.1	3.3	3.3	4.7
Lithuania	2008	Interview	4,777	15–64	11.9	1.6	1.6	2.1
Luxembourg								
Hungary	2007	Interview	2,710	18–64	8.5	0.9	1.8	2.4
Malta	2001	Interview	1,755	18–64	3.5	0.4	0.4	0.7
Netherlands	2005	Interview	4,516	15–64	22.6	3.4	2.1	4.3
Austria	2008	Interview	3,761	15–64	14.2	2.2	2.5	2.3
Poland	2006	Interview	2,859	15–64	9.0	0.8	2.7	1.2

Portugal	2007	Interview	12,202	15–64	11.7	1.9	0.9	1.3
Romania	2007	Interview	6,797	15–64	1.5	0.1	0.0	0.3
Slovenia	2007	Interview	1,724	15–64				
Slovakia	2006	Interview	1,305	15–64	16.1	1.2	1.2	4.3
Finland	2006	Mail	2,802	15–64	14.3	1.1	2.2	1.6
Sweden	2008	Mail/web	22,095	15–64	21.4	3.3	5.0	2.1
Sweden	2008	Mail	8,343	16–64	11.2			
UK (E&W)	2008–09	Interview	28,407	16–59	31.1	9.4	12.3	8.6
UK (NI)	2007–08	Interview	2,731	16–64	17.8	3.9	5.6	6.4
UK (S)	2006	Interview	3,157	16–59	32.9	8.9	14.1	9.9
UK (UK)	2006			16–59	30.2	7.7	11.9	7.5
Croatia								
Turkey								
Norway	2004	Interview	2,669	15–64	16.2	2.7	3.6	1.8

Table 3.2 Lifetime prevalence young adults: last survey available for each member state (2000 onwards)

| Country | Method | | | Age range | Younger adults % | | | |
	Year	Data coll.	Sample		Cannabis	Cocaine (1)	Amphet amines (2)	Ecstasy (3)
Belgium	2004	Interview	2,164	15–34	23.7	3.0	4.4	3.6
Bulgaria	2008	Interview	2,079	15–34	14.3	3.6	7.8	18.4
Czech Republic	2008	Interview	1,744	15–34	53.3	9.5	10.5	4.5
Denmark	2008	Mail/web	3,306	16–34	48.0	4.9	5.1	5.6
Germany	2006	Mail	545	18–34	37.5			
Estonia	2008	Mail	2,620	15–34	28.6	8.2	5.1	9.0
Ireland	2006–07	Interview	9,843	15–34	10.8	1.0	0.2	0.6
Greece	2004	Interview	10,855	15–34	37.3	11.8	5.5	7.1
Spain	2007–08	Interview	6,398	15–34	43.6	3.5	1.3	3.7
France	2005	Phone	1,753	15–34	37.5	7.6	3.4	3.8
Italy	2008	Mail	2,497	15–34	9.9	1.4	0.8	2.4
Cyprus	2006	Interview	2,152	15–34	21.7	4.0	6.1	8.5
Latvia	2007	Interview		15–34	21.2	0.7	2.5	3.9
Lithuania	2008	Interview	1,111	15–34				
Luxembourg			640					
Hungary	2007	Interview	2,558	18–34	19.1	1.8	4.0	5.1
Malta	2001	Interview	2,031	18–34	4.8	0.9	0.7	1.4
Netherlands	2005	Interview		15–34	32.3	4.9	3.0	8.1
Austria	2008	Interview		15–34	19.2	2.8	3.1	3.3
Poland	2006	Interview		15–34	16.1	1.3	4.8	2.1

Country	Year	Method	N	Age				
Portugal	2007	Interview	4,765	15–34	17.0	2.8	1.3	2.6
Romania	2007	Interview	2,262	15–34	2.9	0.1	0.1	0.6
Slovenia	2007	Interview	691	15–34				
Slovakia	2006	Interview	556	15–34	28.6	2.0	2.4	8.4
Finland	2006	Mail	1,387	15–34	22.1	1.7	4.7	3.6
Sweden	2008	Mail/web	16,271	15–34	19.2	4.6	5.7	3.7
Sweden	2008	Mail	2,546	16–34	16.2			
UK (E&W)	2008–09	Interview	9,683	16–34	40.5	14.9	15.4	13.8
UK (NI)	2007–08	Interview	919	16–34	28.8	7.7	10.5	13.2
UK (S)	2006	Interview	1,115	16–34	49.6	15.5	22.1	19.4
UK (UK)	2006			16–34	41.9	12.8	16.8	13.5
Croatia								
Turkey								
Norway	2004	Interview	1,238	15–34	25.5	4.3	5.9	3.6

Table 3.3 Last 12 months prevalence all adults: last survey available for each member state (2000 onwards)

| Country | Method | | | | All adults % | | | |
	Year	Data Coll.	Sample	Age Range	Cannabis	Cocaine (1)	Amphet amines (2)	Ecstasy (3)
Belgium	2004	Interview		15–64	5.0			
Bulgaria	2008	Interview	5,139	15–64	2.7	0.7	0.9	0.7
Czech Republic	2008	Interview	4,500	15–64	15.2	0.7	1.7	3.7
Denmark	2008	Mail/web	3,408	16–64	5.5	1.4	1.2	0.4
Germany	2006	Mail	7,912	18–64	4.7	0.6	0.5	0.4
Estonia	2008	Mail	1,401	15–64	6.0	0.7	1.1	1.2
Ireland	2006–07	Interview	4,967	15–64	6.3	1.7	0.4	1.2
Greece	2004	Interview	4,351	15–64	1.7	0.1	0.0	0.2
Spain	2007–08	Interview	23,715	15–64	10.1	3.1	0.9	1.2
France	2005	Phone	25,879	15–64	8.6	0.6	0.1	0.4
Italy	2008	Mail	10,940	15–64	14.3	2.1	0.4	0.7
Cyprus	2006	Interview	3,504	15–64	2.1	0.6	0.3	1.0
Latvia	2007	Interview	4,500	15–64	4.9	0.5	0.9	1.5
Lithuania	2008	Interview	4,777	15–64	5.6	0.2	0.7	1.0
Luxembourg								
Hungary	2007	Interview	2,710	18–64	2.3	0.2	0.5	0.5
Malta	2001	Interview	1,755	18–64	0.8	0.3	0.0	0.2
Netherlands	2005	Interview	4,516	15–64	5.4	0.6	0.3	1.2
Austria	2008	Interview	3,761	15–64	3.5	0.9	0.5	0.5
Poland	2006	Interview	2,859	15–64	2.7	0.2	0.7	0.3

	Year	Method	N	Age				
Portugal	2007	Interview	12,202	15–64	3.6	0.6	0.2	0.4
Romania	2007	Interview	6,797	15–64	0.4	0.0	0.0	0.1
Slovenia	2007	Interview	1,724	15–64	3.1			
Slovakia	2006	Interview	1,305	15–64	6.9	0.6	0.3	1.6
Finland	2006	Mail	2,802	15–64	3.6	0.5	0.6	0.5
Sweden	2008	Mail/web	22,095	15–64	1.2	0.5	0.8	0.1
Sweden	2008	Mail	8,343	16–64	1.9			
UK (E&W)	2008–09	Interview	28,407	16–59	7.9	3.0	1.2	1.8
UK (NI)	2007–08	Interview	2,731	16–64	4.8	1.6	0.8	1.4
UK (S)	2006	Interview	3,157	16–59	11.0	3.8	2.2	3.2
UK (UK)	2006	Interview		16–59	8.4	2.7	1.4	1.9
Croatia								
Turkey								
Norway	2004	Interview	2,669	15–64	4.6	0.8	1.1	0.5

Table 3.4 Last 12 months prevalence younger adults: last survey available for each member state (2000 onwards)

Country	Method				All adults %			
	Year	Data Coll.	Sample	Age Range	Cannabis	Cocaine (1)	Amphet amines (2)	Ecstasy (3)
Belgium	2004	Interview		15–64	11.3	1.5	2.1	1.6
Bulgaria	2008	Interview	5,139	15–64	6.0	1.6	3.2	7.7
Czech Republic	2008	Interview	4,500	15–64	28.2	3.4	3.1	1.1
Denmark	2008	Mail/web	3,408	16–64	13.3	1.6	1.6	1.2
Germany	2006	Mail	7,912	18–64	11.9	1.3	2.5	2.3
Estonia	2008	Mail	1,401	15–64	13.6	3.1	0.8	2.4
Ireland	2006–07	Interview	4,967	15–64	10.4	0.2	0.1	0.4
Greece	2004	Interview	4,351	15–64	3.2	5.5	1.7	2.3
Spain	2007–08	Interview	23,715	15–64	18.8	1.2	0.2	1.0
France	2005	Phone	25,879	15–64	16.7	2.9	0.6	1.0
Italy	2008	Mail	10,940	15–64	20.3	0.7	0.3	1.3
Cyprus	2006	Interview	3,504	15–64	3.4	1.0	1.9	2.7
Latvia	2007	Interview	4,500	15–64	9.7	0.3	1.1	1.9
Lithuania	2008	Interview	4,777	15–64	9.9			
Luxembourg								
Hungary	2007	Interview	2,710	18–64	5.7	0.4	1.2	1.0
Malta	2001	Interview	1,755	18–64	1.9			
Netherlands	2005	Interview	4,516	15–64	9.5	1.0	0.7	2.7
Austria	2008	Interview	3,761	15–64	6.6	1.2	0.9	1.0
Poland	2006	Interview	2,859	15–64	5.3	0.3	1.3	0.7
Portugal	2007	Interview	12,202	15–64	6.7	1.2	0.4	0.9

Romania	2007	Interview	6,797	15–64	0.9	0.1	0.1	0.2
Slovenia	2007	Interview	1,724	15–64	6.9			
Slovakia	2006	Interview	1,305	15–64	14.7	1.3	0.7	2.7
Finland	2006	Mail	2,802	15–64	8.0	0.8	1.7	1.3
Sweden	2008	Mail/web	22,095	15–64	4.9	1.2	1.5	0.2
Sweden	2008	Mail	8,343	16–64	4.5			
UK (E&W)	2008–09	Interview	28,407	16–59	14.4	6.2	2.3	3.9
UK (NI)	2007–08	Interview	2,731	16–64	10.1	3.8	1.6	3.3
UK (S)	2006	Interview	3,157	16–59	20.4	8.0	4.1	6.9
UK (UK)	2006			16–59	15.9	5.6	2.8	4.1
Croatia								
Turkey								
Norway	2004	Interview	2,669	15–64	9.6	1.8	20.0	1.2

Notes: (1) cocaine, any form. (2) For Belgium National 2001 and for Metropolitan France 1995: amphetamine and ecstasy. (3) For Spain: ecstasy and other synthetic drugs. This table aims to provide an overview of national surveys. Exceptionally, some relevant regional surveys are presented. Some city surveys reported by countries were not included as they tend to produce higher prevalence estimates, which are not comparable with estimates for whole countries (or large regions with both urban and rural areas). Athens was included as a reference point for the 1993 survey. In surveys with small sample sizes results should be interpreted with caution. Countries were asked to report results using, as far as possible, EMCDDA standard age groups (all adults: 15–64, young adults: 15–34). In countries where age ranges are more restrictive, prevalence estimates may tend to be slightly higher. Some countries have recalculated their prevalence figures using the EMCDDA standard age groups.
Source: EMCDDA, *Statistical Bulletin 2010.*

cannabis, with between 0 per cent and 14 per cent of all European adults reporting having used amphetamines, cocaine or ecstasy. For younger adults, 0–15 per cent had ever used cocaine, 0–22 per cent had ever used amphetamines and 0.5–19 per cent had ever used ecstasy. In the last 12 months 0–6 per cent had used cocaine, 0–4 per cent amphetamine and 0–8 per cent ecstasy.

The issue of drug prevalence within a society has many cross-national similarities. In all countries cannabis is the most commonly used drug and in all countries drug use in general is more prevalent among younger adults than among adults. The actual rate of drug use in a population may vary to a certain degree, but, whatever the size of the problem, it is of the same basic shape. When compared with statistics collected from previous years, findings show that cannabis use increased during the 1990s and early 2000s in most EU countries (EMCDDA, 2002) while more recent data shows a stabilizing, or even decreasing, situation (EMCDDA, 2009). This provides evidence that not only is the nature of drug prevalence similar across EU countries, but also that it is influenced by international trends that affect all countries in roughly the same way and at roughly the same time.

While the statistics presented in Tables 3.1–3.4 can show us that the nature of the drug problem is similar across EU member states, they are not very helpful in providing a deeper cross-national comparison. Matters are limited by the fact that not all countries are included in the prevalence data sets. Of the countries that have reported, not all have information on all illegal drugs and not all have collected information from all age ranges. These factors make deep level comparisons rather fruitless and frustrating. To further complicate matters, methods of collecting the data presented have varied widely from country to country. For example, information has been collected in different years, through different mediums (telephone, face to face interview or mail/web) and from different sample sizes. These problems invalidate the scientific accuracy of interpreting the statistics, but there are other, less concrete, problems as well.

When the statistics are presented here, devoid of the national strategies that underpin them, concepts that may be important in determining them are lost. For example, in a country where harm reduction principles are generously employed and policies that are acceptant of drug users as part of society are practiced, drug users are fairly willing to come forward and report themselves as such. On the other hand, in a country where the eradication of drugs from society is an acknowledged aim and drug users are subject to strict penalties, they may be far less willing to come forward and report themselves as drug users. Such a phenomenon may lead to important differences in levels of reported drug use within different societies that distort the presentation of the drug problem as provided by EMCDDA statistics.

Problem drug use

"Problem drug use" is defined by the EMCDDA (2002, p. 14) as "injecting drug use or long-duration/regular use of opiates, cocaine and/or amphetamines". Again, difficulties in comparing statistics across countries are numerous. There are several different methods employed in the national calculation of problem drug users. These include collecting information on the number of drug users seeking treatment for serious drug use, the number of drug users arrested for serious drug use (or discovered to have serious drug use on arrest), the number of drug users who die for reasons related to their habit and the number of people that have AIDS or are HIV positive that are drug users. Where different methods of collection have been used, results are not comparable. Denmark, for example, includes some cannabis users in its estimations of problematic drug use; Malta, in stark contrast, only includes daily heroin users in its estimations. This disparity is further demonstrated by the fact that within countries, where more than one method of collection has been used, the given figures vary widely.

The most recent available statistics shown in Table 3.5 are complex and difficult to generalize. What can be inferred is that estimates of problem drug use are all between 0.5 and 10 cases per 1000 members of the general population aged between 15 and 64. Little more can be revealed due to the fact that each country has estimated their report of the number of drug users in a different way, resulting in a situation where it is possible to observe the huge variations in figures given within countries when different methods are used. For example, in France, where a variety of sources for collecting data on problem drug users exists, estimations of the rate per 1000 members of the general population vary from 3.7–9.5.

As with figures on prevalence of drug use within a national population, factors that are outside the scope of statistical data collection by the EMCDDA may have an important part to play in the final figures presented. In countries where drug users are tolerated to a greater extent they will presumably be more visible to society and therefore reported numbers will necessarily be higher than in countries where restrictive policies are practiced, resulting in the reluctance of drug users to admit to their habits.

Table 3.5 Estimates of prevalence of problem drug use at national level, summary 2003–08, rate per 1000, age 15–64

Country	Year	Central rate/1000 Ages 15–64[1]	Lower and upper rates/1000	Estimate no. of users	Lower and upper prevalence estimates[1]	Target group: data sources and estimation methods
Belgium						
Bulgaria						
Czech Rep.[1]	2008	4.4	4.1–4.7	32,500	30,400–34,700	Problem opioid and stimulant users. Low-threshold facilities. Treatment Multiplier.
Denmark[1]	2005	7.5	7.1–8.0	26,979	25,390–28,568	Drug abusers having a persistent use of illegal drugs including cannabis. The National Patient Register. National Register of Drug Abusers Undergoing Treatment. Capture–recapture.
Germany[2*]	2006	n.a.	3.0–3.6	182,500	167,000–198,000	Problem opioid, cocaine and amphetamine users. National treatment statistics. Treatment Multiplier
Estonia						
Ireland						
Greece[1]	2008	2.7	2.3–3.1	20,181	17,502–23,391	Problem drug users. Drug treatment data. Capture–recapture.
Spain	2006	1.4	1.3–1.4	41,036	38,719–43,649	Problem opioid users. Drug treatment and surveys data. Treatment Multiplier.

Country	Year	Rate	Rate range	Estimate	Estimate range	Description
France[1]*	2008	6.8	3.7–9.5	255,500	144,000–367,000	Problem drug users. Health and socio-economic indicators. Drug treatment, surveys, CJS, emergency services, GPs, low-threshold services, hospitals, social services, methadone progs. Multivariate indicator method. Treatment and Police Multiplier
Italy[1]	2008	9.8	9.5–10.1	385,000	375,000–395,000	Problem stimulant and opiate users. Treatment data. Treatment multiplier
Cyprus[1]	2008	2.0	1.6–2.4	1,087	907–1,337	Problem opioid and stimulant users. Treatment data. Truncated poisson
Latvia*	2006	n.a.	3.1–6.2	7,191	4,794–9,588	Problem drug users. Treatment data. Treatment multiplier
Lithuania						
Luxembourg	2007	7.7	6.5–9.9	2,470	2,089–3,199	Problem drug users. Drug-related deaths, CJS, drug treatment, diseases, methadone progs Multi-methods
Hungary[2]	2005	3.5	2.8–4.2	24,204	19,333–29,075	Problem drug users. Data from drug treatment and police records. Capture-recapture
Malta[1,5]	2006	5.7	5.5–6.0	1,606	1,541–1,685	Problem drug users defined as daily heroin users. Treatment data. Capture-recapture
Netherlands						
Austria[1]	2007	4.1	4.0–4.3	23,178	22,198–24,157	(Poly) drug use including opiates. Treatment and police data. Capture-recapture

Table 3.5 (Continued)

Country	Year	Central rate/1000 Ages 15–64[1]	Lower and upper rates/1000	Estimate no. of users	Lower and upper prevalence estimates[1]	Target group: data sources and estimation methods
Poland[2,6]	2005	4.2	3.7–4.7	112,500	100,000–125,000	Problem drug users. General population survey and treatment data. Benchmark method
Portugal[2*]	2005	n.a.	4.3–7.4	42,037	30,833–53,240	Problem drug users. Treatment and mortality data. Treatment and outreach work teams multiplier
Romania						
Slovenia	2004	7.8	6.6–9.2	10,654	9,078–12,593	Problem opiate and stimulant users. Treatment and police data. Capture–recapture
Slovakia[1]	2008	2.7	2.1–8.5	10,519	8,182–33,489	Problem drug users. Low-threshold agencies. Multiplier method
Finland[1,4]	2005	4.8	4.2–5.5	16,600	14,500–19,100	Problem stimulant and opiate users. Hospital data, CJ, Infectious diseases data. Capture–recapture

	Year	Rate		Number		
Sweden[2]	2007	4.9	n.a.	29,513	n.a.	Problem drug users. In-patient treatment centres (hospitals, emergency services), Swedish prison and probation service. Truncated poisson with Chao's estimator
UK 1	2003–07	10.0	9.8–10.1	400,469	393,247–471,861	Problem drug users. Treatment, population density, prison, drug-related deaths, drug offences, police, probation. Capture–recapture, multivariate indicator method
Croatia						
Turkey	2008	0.5	0.5–1.1	25,853	21,573–51,456	Problem opioid users. Drug-related deaths. Mortality multiplier
Norway						

Notes: n.a. = not available. (1) Interval is a 95 per cent confidence interval. (2) Confidence interval not known. (3) Interval is based on a sensitivity analysis. (4) Finland: the original age range of study was 15–54, the rate was adjusted to ages 15–64. (5) Malta: the original age range of the study is 12–64 years old. (6) Poland: the original age range of the study refers to all ages. (*) The figure shown is based on average between the lower and upper bound of prevalence estimate.
Source: EMCDDA, *Statistical Bulletin 2010.*

Until fairly recently, the EMCDDA has recorded a general state of stability across EU countries with relation to problem drug use. The *Annual Report* from 2002 (EMCDDA, 2002) shows that, in comparison with surveys conducted in 1996, figures have remained roughly the same or have slightly increased, for example, in Belgium, Germany, Italy, Luxembourg, Sweden and the UK. The most recent *Annual Report* (EMCDDA, 2009), however, indicates a slowly mounting increase in opioid users across the past decade. Again, this is an area in which general trends seem to affect countries across the EU rather than individual member states in isolation. While it is difficult to make in-depth comparisons between the levels of problem drug users in different member states due to the methodological problems encountered in this area, what does emerge is evidence that the nature of problem drug use is very similar in different countries.

For example, the different methods of estimating problem drug use are all common to several EU countries. This indicates that problems associated with and arising from problem drug use, such as the need to develop treatment for drug users, the fact that problem drug users often come into conflict with the law and are arrested, the incidence of AIDS in intravenous drug users and the deaths of drug users due to their habits, are universal in their affliction where there is drug use within a country. Although different EU countries may have varying rates of prevalence of drug use within their societies, all have a proportion, albeit relatively small, of drug users who are problematic in their use.

Drug-related infectious diseases

Relatively recently, the EMCDDA has started to collect information on drug-related infectious diseases such as HIV, hepatitis B and hepatitis C. Drug-related infectious diseases can be expensive for a country placing demands on its health and treatment services, but there are harm reduction policies such as needle exchange programmes that can be helpful in reducing levels of these infectious diseases. Data from different countries is obtained from different settings, for example, prisons, needle exchange programmes and/or drug treatment centres, and is therefore difficult to compare. Also there are many EU countries which have only very recently started to collect this data making historical comparisons impossible. The countries that have consistently provided data on the extent of the HIV infection rate among drug users have done so only from 1991 or more recently. In addition to these time-related problems, looking only at the most recent comparisons given in Table 3.6, some countries have submitted national samples while others

Table 3.6 Prevalence of HIV infection among injecting drug users in the EU, 2008 or most recent year available

Country	Year	Number tested	National samples % infected[1]	Subnational samples % infected[1]	Study design[2]	Setting/comments[3-5]
Belgium	2008	528		3.3–6.4	DT; SR	LTS, DTC; serum
Bulgaria	2008	759		2.2	DT	DTC, NSP, LTS, HTC, serum
Czech Rep.	2008	4,420	0.1–0.6		DT; SR	STI, OHC, PRI, HTC, DTC, LTS, NSP, GPS, serum, saliva capillary blood
Denmark	2006	188	2.1		SP (UAT)	ODD, 5 sites; IDUnk
Germany	2007	1,394	3.4		DT	ODD; autopsy rates 62%; drug related deaths through accident, long term effects, suicide. IDUnk
Estonia	2005	449		54.3–89.9	DT	LTS; dried blood spots
Ireland	2003	64		12.5	SP	DTC; serum
Greece	2008	1,563	0.1–0.7	0.0–0.8	DT	DTC, LTS, PHI, OHC, 42 sites; serum
Spain	2007	8,643	34.5		DT	DTC; serum
France	2006	698		5.1–8.0	SP (UAT); SR	NSP, LTS, STR; saliva
Italy	2008	63,989	11.7	2.0–37	DT	DTC, 522 sites; serum
Cyprus	2008	318	0.0–1.6		DT; SP; SR	DTC; serum
Latvia	2007	407		22.6	SP (UAT)	NSP; serum
Lithuania	2006	1,853		0.6–9.7	DT; SP	HTC, NSP, LTS, 22 sites; serum, dried blood spots; IDUnk §
Luxembourg	2008	171	1.8		SR	DTC; register of specialized drugs, 9 sites
Hungary	2008	775	0.0	0	SP	DTC, NSP, STR, OTH; serum, dried blood spots
Malta	2006	175	0		DT	DTC, NSP, 1 site; serum
Netherlands	2008	132		1.7–8.2	DT; SP	DTC; homeless housing projects, 13 sites; serum
Austria	2008	743	1.0–10.7	0.0–1.9	DT	NSP, LTS, ODD, DTC, 46 sites; serum
Poland	2008	1,713	9.2		DT	PHI, HTC; serum
Portugal	2005	7,846	9.2–18.4		DT	DTC, outpatient units, therapeutic communities, public detoxification units; dried blood spots; IDUnk §
Romania	2007–08	607	1.1	0.8–1.6	DT; SR	DTC, NSP, LTS, 66 sites; serum, dried blood spots, urine

Table 3.6 (Continued)

Country	Year	Number tested	National samples % infected[1]	Subnational samples % infected[1]	Study design[2]	Setting/comments[3-5]
Slovenia	2008	442	0.0	0.0	SP (UAT); DT	NSP, DTC, LTS, 21 sites; saliva, serum
Slovakia	2008	97		1.0	DT	DTC, 1 site
Finland	2007	3,645	0.1–1.3	0.6	DT; SP	NSP, PRI, 46 sites; serum, saliva; IDUnk §
Sweden	2007–08	1,206		0.0–8.4	SP; DT	LTS, STR, PRI, OHC, DTC, 218 sites; serum
UK	2008	5,590		0.5–3.9	SP (UAT)	DTC, NSP, LTS, PHL, STR, primary care and outreach, named HIV tests; saliva, serum
Croatia	2007–08	778	0.0	0.0	SP	DTC, NSP, LTS, PHL, HTC, PRI; serum
Turkey	2008	168		0.0	DT	Serum
Norway	2008	4,077	2.8	0.6	SP	NSP, DTC, LTS, 24 sites; serum

Notes: This summary table gives a global overview of HIV prevalence in IDUs in the EU, 2007–08 or most recent year available. Data for more than one year are combined if they clearly improve generalizability (e.g. national data, out-of-treatment data). n.a. = not available. (1) The figures show estimates (or range of estimates) from national and/or subnational level samples. (2) Self reported test results are less reliable than biological test results: DT – diagnostic testing; SP – seroprevalence study; SP(UAT) – seroprevalence study with unlinked anonymous testing; RDS – respondent driven sampling; SR – data (partly) based on self reported test results. (3) Having health problems is one selection criterion for admission to drug treatment in some countries or cities (Greece, Portugal, Rome), due to long waiting lists or special programmes for infected IDUs and this may result in upward bias of prevalence. Prevalence from treatment data should therefore be interpreted in combination with non-treatment data. On the other hand, data from Italy and Portugal include non-IDUs and may thus underestimate prevalence in IDUs. (4) IDUnk = IDU status not known, prevalence in IDUs is likely to be underestimated. (5) ODD = overdose deaths; DEM = drug emergences; DTC = drug treatment centres; NSP = needle exchanges; LTS = low-threshold services; PHL = public health laboratories; STI = STI clinics; ANT = antenatal clinics; OHC = other hospital or clinics; PRI = prisons; ARR = arrests; GPS = general practioners; HTC = HIV testing centres; STR = street; OTH = other. § IDUnk = IDU status not known, prevalence may be too low. Lithuania: one of the six studies available is IDUnk (subnational: *N* = 799; 1.9 per cent infected). Finland: one of the three studies available is IDUnk (national: *N* = 1363; 0.1 per cent infected). Portugal: Two of three studies are IDUnk (all national: *N* = 4436; 13.9 per cent infected and *N* = 2381; 9.2 per cent infected).
Source: EMCDDA, *Statistical Bulletin 2010.*

have only submitted subnational samples and some have tested at only one site (Malta, Slovakia) while others have tested at a great many sites (Greece, Sweden). Furthermore, as note 3 for Table 3.6 indicates, in some countries (Greece, Portugal and Italy), health-related problems can be a condition of entry to popular treatment programmes, making HIV positive people considerably more likely to self-report than in countries where there are no discernable benefits.

Levels of HIV infection amongst injecting drug users vary considerably across countries (and sometimes within them – see Estonia) from about 0 per cent in Hungary and Malta to 34 per cent in Spain. While levels of HIV infection among drug users have not increased by the proportion predicted when the disease first emerged as a widespread problem in the 1980s, levels of hepatitis B and C infection in drug users have been consistently rising across Europe in the last two decades (EMCDDA, 2009). Although levels of HIV and other infectious diseases do vary widely across the individual member states of the EU, all countries have members of the drug using population that are afflicted by some of these infectious diseases. (Although there are some countries that report having no levels of HIV, there are none that report no levels of hepatitis B and C.) There is some evidence that trends that affect the prevalence of infectious diseases among drug dependents are common.

In most countries HIV and AIDS became a problem in the 1980s and, for a few years, there was an explosion in reported numbers. This explosion has levelled off since the 1990s, but levels of hepatitis infection, particularly hepatitis C, have risen dramatically. The exception to this trend is two of the newer Central and Eastern European member states (Latvia and Estonia) where HIV levels are also rising (EMCDDA, 2009). Although general trends seem to be EU-wide, perhaps the difference in prevalence rates between countries indicates that this is an area in which policy implementations can be seen to have had a partial effect on the problem. In many countries, in the 1980s, the threat of an AIDS epidemic drove national governments to implement harm reduction measures aimed principally at the reduction of the possibility of spreading the AIDS virus, such as needle exchange programmes and substitution treatment programmes. While a general trend in the reduction of newly reported HIV cases has been observed across Europe, perhaps this has been accelerated where harm reduction measures, such as those described above, have been employed. Some of the newer EU member states, particularly those from Central and Eastern Europe, have had less time in which to develop their harm reduction responses (Chatwin, 2004) which may explain the rise in levels of HIV reported in countries like Latvia and Estonia.

Drug-related deaths

The EMCDDA (2002, p. 22) defines "acute drug-related death" as being "directly related to drug consumption or overdoses". Once again, however, this definition is open to considerable interpretation in different member states, resulting in some confusion over what actually counts as an "acute drug-related death". Some countries, for example, include accidental poisoning in their estimations, while others do not. Often, the definitions used by countries are vague, stating only that there must be a strong causal relationship between drugs and death. When making comparisons on the data presented in Table 3.7 it is important to be aware that data may have been collected by different methods (police, medical records) and may be based on slightly differing interpretations of what constitutes an "acute drug-related death". Although improvements have been made in this area in recent years, with many countries adopting an EMCDDA standard case definition, important differences relating to the quality of case ascertainment and the quality of reporting to national mortality registries and to the EMCDDA remain. There are also problems with underestimations of the problem as this is an area in which it is notoriously difficult to collect information.

In total, between 6400 and 8500 acute drug-related deaths are reported in Europe each year (EMCDDA, 2009). Although this figure may not seem devastatingly high, the fact that these deaths occur in a group representing less than 1 per cent of all EU adults suggests there is

Table 3.7 Summary of characteristics of the deceased in drug-induced deaths according to national definitions

Country	Year	Definition	No. of DRD	% Male	% Female	Mean age
Belgium						
Bulgaria	2008		74	75.7	24.3	33.6
Czech Republic[1]	2008	D	44	81.8	18.2	31.1
Denmark	2007	B	211	70.1	29.9	42.9
Germany	2008		1,449	84.2	13.2	36.0
Estonia	2008	B	67	89.6	10.4	29.0
Ireland	2007	D	185	79.5	20.5	32.1
Greece	2008	D	110	95.5	4.5	
Spain[2]	2007		519	89.0	11.0	
France	2007	B	333	79.3	20.7	42.4
Italy	2008	D	502	89.6	10.4	35.4
Cyprus	2008	D	11	90.9	9.1	30.1
Latvia	2008	B	24	70.8	29.2	29.5
Lithuania	2008	Approx. B	60	93.3	6.7	31.8

Luxembourg	2008		10	70.0	30.0	33.2
Hungary	2008	D	27	70.4	29.6	30.1
Malta	2006	B	7	71.4	28.6	28.6
Netherlands	2008	B	129	79.8	20.2	40.1
Austria[3]	2008	D	169	79.3	20.7	30.0
Poland	2007		214	64.0	36.0	46.6
Portugal[4]						
Romania[5]	2008	B	33	93.9	6.1	25.2
Slovenia	2008		36	80.6	19.4	34.0
Slovakia	2008	D	25	80.0	20.0	33.2
Finland	2008	B	169	71.0	29.0	36.2
Sweden	2007	B	232	75.9	24.1	40.7
UK (DSD)	2008	B	2,368	78.9	21.1	37.9
Croatia	2008	B	87	91.9	8.1	31.4
Turkey	2008	D	159	95.0	5.0	32.8
Norway	2007	B	275	78.9	21.1	37.6

Notes: The information refers to the last year for which information in the deceased's characteristics was available. Data for Belgium is not included as the most recent year with available
information is 1997. Type of definition refers to the EMCDDA standard definition; if the
national definition matches with the agreed case definition established in the EMCDDA DRD
Protocol: Selection B for general mortality registries and Selection D for Special Registries.
In some countries equivalence is not total but it is, in practice, relatively similar. (1) For the
Czech Republic, EMCDDA Selection D was used instead of the national definition. National
definition includes also poisoning by psychoactive medicines, which accounts for most cases
(194 cases out of 238). (2) From 2008 onwards, the data coverage is national. In previous
years, the information was based on six cities (Madrid, Barcelona, Valencia, Sevilla, Zaragoza
and Bilbao). (3) In the year 2008 the number of cases on which no autopsy has been per-
formed tripled (up to 32 cases) in comparison with previous years. Thus the number reported
for 2008 might be the lower limit, adding up to 201 cases if all 32 suspicious non-confirmed
cases were included. (4) Data has not been included this year due to major discrepancies
existing in previous years between figures from the General Mortality Register and the Special Register (reporting all cases with a positive toxicology, not only Selection D). Ongoing
work is conducted by Portugal to harmonize data reporting with EMCDDA Selection D, and
to make data available in next reporting year. (5) Data refer only to Bucharest and several
counties in the competence area of the Toxicology Laboratory from Bucharest.
Source: EMCDDA, *Statistical Bulletin 2010*.

a high rate of mortality within the group of problem drug users. Indeed,
the EMCDDA (2002, p. 8) states that the "mortality of opiate users, in
particular injectors, is up to 20 times higher than in the general population of the same age". The most recent *Annual Report* records mortality
rates due to drug-related death as varying from 3 to 85 deaths per million population aged 15–64, with rates of over 20 deaths per million in
17 out of 30 EU countries and rates of over 40 deaths per million in six
EU countries (EMCDDA, 2009). Acute drug-related deaths are a problem
in all EU member states. In all countries levels of death in drug using
populations are considerably higher than in equivalent non-drug using
populations and general trends affecting this problem are EU-wide.

Drug-related crime

Drug-related crime covers a large area. According to the EMCDDA (2002a, p. 24) "drug related crime can be considered as covering criminal offences against drug legislation, crimes committed under the influence of illicit drugs, economically driven crimes committed by users to support their drug habit ... and systemic crimes committed as part of the functioning of illicit markets". With such wide-ranging terms of definition, it is obvious that there will be problems collecting statistics of this nature on an EU-wide basis.

These figures do not represent data that is readily available and, again, collection methods are not the same in each country. In contrast to the tables presented thus far, Table 3.8 is a historical breakdown of the numbers of drug-related *offences* reported each year since 1995 in individual member states. (It should be noted here that the EMCDDA also collects data on the numbers of *people* reported for drug-related offences and some of the countries with missing data in Table 8 will have provided data in this format.) The EMCDDA makes historical data of this type available for all the categories in which data is collected and the inclusion of a historical table here serves to further illuminate some of the comparability problems faced. The most obvious point to be noted is that not all countries collect data on the number of drug-related offences reported and, of those that do, some have started only very recently and some have not done so every year. In addition to these problems, some countries have instead collected data on the number of people reported for drug-related offences, rather than the number of drug-related offences. Under the first system if one person committed many offences at the same time only the most major would be reported while under the second system all offences would be reported even if they were committed by the same person on the same occasion. Many countries now collect data in both formats, but some still only do one or the other further clouding the potential for comparability.

Comparability issues are further illuminated by a perusal of Table 3.9 which lists methodological notes for some of the countries which have collected data. The main problem here is that not only do methods of data collection vary between countries, but they also vary within them. In Belgium and Italy, for example, data has varied between being collected on the number of offences or the number of people reported for drug-related crime. In Estonia, Ireland, Latvia and Finland the agency in charge of collating the data before it is passed on to the EMCDDA itself has changed and in Portugal and the UK changes in laws or practices to do with, respectively, the possession of drugs for personal use and

Table 3.8 Drug law offences 1995–2008, part (i) number of reports of offences

Country	1995	1996	1997	1998	1999	2000	2001	2002	2003	2004	2005	2006	2007	2008
Belgium	18,376		215,69	14,328	25,540				23,131	29,385	34,815	35,117	37,867	40,357
Bulgaria														
Czech Rep.														
Denmark			13,454	14,251	12,928	13,178	13,143	13,025	14,316	16,390	19,526	19,900	18,506	18,692
Germany	158,477	187,022	205,099	216,682	226,563	244,336	246,518	250,969	255,575	283,708	276,740	255,019	248,355	239,951
Estonia						3,886	5,458	4,761	6,384	6,970	5,465	5,839	7,039	7,671
Ireland	3,859	2,885	4,156	5,984	7,137	8,395	8,768	7,976	7,150	7,302	13,855	14,380	18,646	
Greece														
Spain		65,705	78,846	81,599	89,994	98,369	129,650	139,264	135,352	164,492	189,395	235,422	278,797	329,396
France	69,432	77,640	89,285	91,048	95,910	100,870	84,533	96,740	108,141	121,256	120,305	110,486	134,320	175,753
Italy														
Cyprus	156	183	245	285	250	292	399	442	475	515	612	654	878	779
Latvia													3,966	5,111
Lithuania		511	630	629	701	926	1,039	937	959	1,392	1,600	1,673	1,734	1,839
Luxembourg													1,372	1,219
Hungary	429	440	943	2,068	2,860	3,445	4,332	4,775	3,378	6,670	7,616	6,734	4,667	5,459
Malta														
Netherlands				12,616	11,675	11,513	13,558	15,848	17,087	22,304	20,548	20,306	19,392	18,785
Austria	13,093	16,196	17,868	17,141	17,597	18,125	21,862	22,422	22,245	25,215	25,892	24,008	24,166	20,043

Table 3.8 (Continued)

Country	1995	1996	1997	1998	1999	2000	2001	2002	2003	2004	2005	2006	2007	2008
Poland	4,284	6,780	7,915	16,432	15,628	19,649	29,230	36,178	47,605	59,356	67,560	70,202	63,007	57,382
Portugal														
Romania								1,291	1,462	2,169	2,305	2,695	2,749	3,727
Slovenia	1,249	1,849	2,737	2,942	3,410	4,803	5,889	5,528	4,843	3,583	3,086	3,912	3,720	5,100
Slovakia														
Finland	9,052	7,868	8,323	9,461	11,647	13,445	14,890	14,634	15,996	15,338	15,334	14,286	16,314	16,539
Sweden												29,972	31,353	34,662
UK										122,459	118,706	124,344	135,655	
Croatia												8,346	7,952	7,882
Turkey											5,515	7,517	10,627	15,433
Norway														

Note: The general term "reports for drug law offence" is used since definitions and study units differ widely between countries.
Source: EMCDDA, *Statistical Bulletin 2010.*

Table 3.9 Drug law offences 1995–2008, part (ii) methodological notes

Country	Methodological notes
Belgium	From 2000 to 2002, data refer to the number of persons and only the main offence is reported, although the same person could be counted several times if arrested several times during the same year. Before 2000 and 2003–05, data refer to the number of offences and each offence is represented as one separate record in the database. Since 2006 data refer to the number of offences and only the main offence and the main substance is mentioned. Offences without a specified substance are included. These changes are likely to affect comparability across time.
Estonia	Since 2007, data are provided by a different source and include both the number of offenders and the number of offences. In addition, the delivery or distribution of narcotic substances in prisons were reported as drug-related crime for the first time. In the past only the number of offences was provided. This change is likely to affect comparability across time.
Ireland	In 2007, responsibility for reporting crime data transferred to a different agency. The new agency reassessed the data for 2005 and 2006 on the basis of information held in a new Garda IT system. This change is likely to affect comparability of the data across time.
Italy	From 1985–94, data include only persons charged with criminal offences held under restriction were reported. From 1995, persons charged with criminal offences but at liberty were included in the submission. Before 1997, only criminal offences were included in the submission. From 1997 onwards, non-criminal offences (sentenced by administrative sanctions) are included in the submission. For the three years 2002, 2003 and 2004, persons for whom the substance is not known were included in the submission. These have been excluded from the table as after 2004 they ceased to be reported. These were respectively 34,282, 34,256 and 32,608. These changes are likely to affect comparability across time.
Latvia	Since 2007, data are provided by a different source, providing number of offenders and number of offences. Previously only data on the number of offenders was reported. 2007 also marks a large increase in the number of offenders reported. Since 2008, data are provided by a different source and include both criminal offences and administrative violation. In addition, different methodology and calculation procedures were applied. This change is likely to affect comparability across time.
Luxembourg	Due to a complete upgrade of the RELIS database, since 2007 data is not comparable with data from previous years.

Table 3.9   (Continued)

Country	Methodological notes
Hungary	In case of number of offenders, statistics refer to the most serious offence committed by an offender and the year of the offence is the year during which criminal investigations were closed rather than the year during which the offences were committed.
Netherlands	Data refer to cases registered by the Public Prosecutor.
Austria	Up to and including 1998, the total number of reports for drug law offences includes reports for drug-related deaths.
Portugal	Since July 2001, drug use and possession for use have been decriminalised and made an administrative offences. Data on such offences, although included in this table, come from a different monitoring system. 2001 data should be treated with caution since this new monitoring system was being tested for the first time.
Slovakia	Up to and including 2005, the unit reported was suspected offenders. No data are available for 2006, during which year a new criminal code was introduced. From 2007 onwards, the unit reported is offenders convicted according to the new criminal code. This change is likely to affect comparability across time.
Finland	Since 2002, data are provided by a different source. This change is likely to affect comparability across time.
UK	Previous data has been on an offender (person basis). Since 2005, data are based on an all drug offence basis, except for Northern Ireland, which continues to be on a principal drug (i.e. person) basis. Since 2004, police have been able to issue cannabis warnings for possession offences of small amounts of cannabis. These are not included in drug law offences data. The increased use of cannabis warnings is likely to affect comparability over time.
Turkey	2002 data refer only to police data, while after 2002 data refer to all data reported by the main prosecuting authorities (police, gendarmerie, customs). This change is likely to affect comparability across time.

Source: EMCDDA, *Statistical Bulletin 2010*.

the possession of small amounts of cannabis, have been made. These are all issues that the EMCDDA has highlighted as having the potential to negatively affect the comparability of data across time.

Any analysis of the figures given in Table 3.8 must therefore be undertaken with extreme caution. However, what can be noted is the steady increase in "reports" for drug law offences within the EU as a whole. The most recent EMCDDA *Annual Report* (EMCDDA, 2009) compares figures between 2002 and 2007 and reports that, during this time period, the number of drug-related crimes has increased by 29 per cent across Europe. Upward trends have been noted in all countries except Bulgaria, the Czech Republic, Greece, Luxembourg, Hungary and Slovenia where figures have remained more stable. The majority of offences are for drug use and possession and cannabis accounts for between 55 and 85 per cent of all drug law offences (EMCDDA, 2009). The number of cocaine-related offences has increased during the same time period by 59 per cent across the EU as a whole (EMCDDA, 2009). Drug-related crime is therefore a considerable problem for all member states of the EU. While the policy implementations directing and governing the criminal outcomes of drug users that commit crimes differ widely between member states, the overwhelming evidence is that no policy has been successful in significantly and consistently lowering the number of drug users coming into contact with criminal justice systems.

Drug markets and availability

The EMCDDA uses data collected on drug seizures to indicate information about the supply and availability of drugs, the theory being that the more drugs that are available within a society, the higher the quantities of illegal drugs that will be seized by the authorities. However, it is important to realize that these figures are not a direct representation of the availability of drugs in society because they are influenced by other factors. These include, for example, the amount of funding allocated to law enforcement, priorities and strategies of law enforcement and vulnerability of drug traffickers. Figures can also be misleading if, for example, a very large drugs haul that is intercepted one year yields a disproportionately large amount of illegal drugs, in turn distorting gross seizure figures. The tables presented here relate to the amounts in kilograms of drugs seized, but data is also collected on the numbers of seizures made. The tables presented here give figures for heroin, cocaine and amphetamines as examples, but the EMCDDA collects data on a much wider variety of drugs. The EMCDDA also collects data in this area on the price and purity of drugs within EU member states, but data is too scarce for any detailed comparison based on this information.

The information presented in Tables 3.10–3.12, as well as the information collected by the EMCDDA on other drugs but not presented here,

Table 3.10 Quantities (kg) of heroin seized, 1995–2008

Country	1995	1996	1997	1998	1999	2000	2001	2002	2003	2004	2005	2006	2007	2008
Belgium	149	133	65	76	74	185		48	51	142	270	176	548	63
Bulgaria[4]						206	1545	1060	831	832	437	726	1300	1227
Czech Rep.[1]								34	9	36	36	28	20	46
Denmark	37	61	38	55	96	32	25	63	16	38	27	29	48	44
Germany	933	898	722	686	796	796	836	520	626	775	787	879	1,074	503
Estonia			0	1	1	0.4	1	4	0.1	0.2	0.4	4	6	0.1
Ireland	6	11	8	38	17	24	30	17	27	27	33	130	147	
Greece[2]	173	190	146	185	97	660	330	324	247	315	331	312	259	448
Spain	546	537	479	418	1,159	484	631	275	242	271	174	472	227	548
France	499	617	415	344	203	444	351	476	545	558	749	1052	1036	1118
Italy	954	1270	477	715	1310	1012	2058	2593	2592	2557	1374	1329	1897	1324
Cyprus[7]					2	5	2	0.3	2	3	0.9	1	1	3
Latvia	0.9	0	0.1		0.8	0.8	0.5	6	0.6	0.5	0.04	0.2	2	2
Lithuania					0.9	1	3	3	0.8	3	2	5	6	14
Luxembourg	13	3	3	4	2	3	1	3	4	6	4	9	9	8
Hungary						670	154	160	256	90	238	131	80	29
Malta							3	1	6	0.8	15	2		
Netherlands[5]	351	516	999	784	770	896	739	1122	417	1200	900	1000	520	
Austria	47	81	102	118	78	230	288	60	43	235	282	34	117	104
Poland[6]						217	389	299	7	255	41	155	124	79
Portugal[3]	66	47	57	97	76	568	316	96	72	99	182	144	62	68
Romania						53	33	20	321	65	285	33	130	385
Slovenia						393	89	69	89	144	134	182	60	136

Slovakia	16	11	90	14	6	99	16	15	7	2	4	2	13
Finland	6	2	2	3	6	8	3	2	0.2	52	0.2	0.4	0.2
Sweden	31	26	12	71	64	30	32	59	13	34	19	103	55
UK[8]	1395	1070	2235	1348	2346	3387	3929	2732	2732	2260	1970	1087	1041
Croatia						20	37	86	114	27	82	74	153
Turkey						3710	2657	4705	8847	8173	10,312	13,228	15,447
Norway	49	74	56	38	46	52	68	59	129	36	93	8	55
Total	5266	5551	5906	4994	7148	10,454	15,606	12,815	13,999	19,040	16,584	18,513	22,056

Notes: (1) Accurate data are not available before 2002 due to double counting of seizure by police and customs reports. (2) All seizures are included (police, coast guard and customs). (3) There were also five doses of liquid heroin seized in 2001. (4) Data refer to seizures made by the Customs and the National Service for Combating Organized Crime (NACOC) from the Ministry of Interior; 5658 doses of heroin were also seized in 2005, 112 in 2006 and 101 in 2007. (5) Both 2004 and 2005 data are based on seizures made only by some police forces: they are not comparable between them, nor with previous years. (6) Up to 2003 the amount of large seizures only is reported; from 2004 all seizures are reported. (7) 1.9 ml of heroin were also seized in 2007. (8) Before 2006 data have been reported on a calendar year basis. Since 2006 seizures data will be published on a financial year basis. (data reported for 2006 is for 2006/07, data reported in 2007 is for 2007/08 and so on). There are no customs data for Scotland and Northern Ireland in 2006/07. In 2007 data are for England, Wales and Northern Ireland only (England and Wales reported both police and customs seizures and Northern Ireland only police seizures); no data for Scotland are available.
Source: EMCDDA, *Statistical Bulletin 2010.*

Table 3.11 Quantities (kg) of cocaine seized, 1995–2008

Country	Crack included	1995	1996	1997	1998	1999	2000	2001	2002	2003	2004	2005	2006	2007	2008
Belgium	Yes until 1999	576	839	3321	2088	1762	1652		3946	644	3522	9228	3946	2,470	3,852
Bulgaria[5]	No						2	9	45	3,107	1	142	144	5	10
Czech Rep.[1]	No								6	3	3	10	5	38	8
Denmark	Yes	110	32	58	44	24	36	26	14	104	32	57	76	88	56
Germany	No	1846	1373	1721	1133	1979	913	1288	2136	1009	969	1079	1717	1,878	1,069
Estonia	No		0	0	3	0	0	0.14	2	31	5	43	1	13	4
Ireland	Yes	22	642	11	333	86	18	5	32	108	167	243	195	1,752	
Greece[2]	No	9	156	17	283	46	156	297	239	201	1152	43	57	255	67
Spain	Yes until 2003	6897	13,742	18,418	11,687	18,110	6165	33,681	17,617	49,279	33,135	48,429	49,650	37,784	27,981
France	No	865	1742	844	1051	3687	1311	2096	3651	4172	4484	5186	10,166	6,579	8,215
Italy	Yes until 2001	2663	2387	1650	2163	2973	2368	1813	4042	3539	3589	4380	4638	3,928	4,110
Cyprus	No	3	0.004	0.02	0.02	5	58	0.1	2	10	1	1	7	2	18
Latvia	No	0.1	0.1	0.2	0.06	2	0.03	1	0.4	0.8	0.7	0.7	1	12	5
Lithuania	No		2	3	10	0.3	2	0.1	0.7	0.2	13	1	3	1	41
Luxembourg	Yes until 2000	0.5	13	9	6	0.3	0.4	8	2	11	4	1	4	3	6
Hungary[8]	Yes						11	6	55	23	94	8	7	15	23
Malta	No							3	5	4	0.15	3	4		
Netherlands[6]	Yes	4851	9222	11495	8998	10361	6472	8389	7968	17,560	12,000	14,600	10,600	10,500	
Austria	No	55	73	87	99	63	20	108	37	58	76	245	62	78	78
Poland[7]	No						81	51	399	801	28	17	22	161	29

Portugal[3]	Yes until 2000	2116	812	3163	625	823	3075	5574	3140	3017	7423	18,083	34,477	7,363
Romania	No						13	3	3	13	25	110	11	47
Slovenia	No						1	1	55	2	107	2	5	42
Slovakia	No			10	10	3	0.2	0.4	0.07	0.9	2	0.4	1	0
Finland	No	0.07	0.07	0	2	2	39	7	0.4	1	2	1	7	4
Sweden[4]	Yes	4	18	34	19	420	50	39	41	42	29	34	1,358	39
UK[9]	No	672	1219	2350	2962	2960	3948	2841	3566	7773	4644	3862	3321	3,457
Croatia	No							1	3	351	18	9	6	105
Turkey	No						12	2	8	3	126	81	78	116
Norway	No	4	24	5	93	60	23	36	31	41	178	41	95	95
Total		20,693	32,296	43,196	31,609	43,367	26,403	56,272	47,052	91,895	71,692	10,6077	120,607	76,828

(Additional right-hand column: Portugal[3] 4,878; Romania 3; Slovenia 91; Slovakia 379; Finland 3; Sweden[4] 49; Croatia 29; Turkey 94; Norway 76)

Notes: (1) Accurate data are not available before 2002 due to double counting of seizures by police and customs reports. (2) All seizures are included (police, coast guard and customs). (3) In 1997 and 1998, coca leaves were also seized. Cocaine liquid was also seized in 1999. Since 2007 quantity of coca leaves seized is included in the total quantity of cocaine seized (17.9 kg in 2007 and 0.28 kg in 2008). (4) Cocaine and crack are reported together (however, there are usually very few, if any, seizures of crack). (5) Data refer to seizures made by the Customs and the National Service for Combating Organized Crime (NACOC) from the Ministry of Interior. 0.947 kg of coca leaves were also seized in 2006 and 0.336 kg in 2007. (6) Both 2004 and 2005 data are based on seizures made only by some police forces: they are not comparable between them, nor with previous years. (7) Up to 2003 the amount of large seizures only is reported; from 2004 all seizures are reported. (8) 0.112 kg of coca leaves were also seized in 2007. (9) Before 2006 data have been reported on a calendar year basis. Since 2006 seizures data will be published on a financial year basis (data reported for 2006 is for 2006/07, data reported in 2007 is for 2007/2008 and so on). There are no customs data for Scotland and Northern Ireland in 2005/2007. In 2007 data are for England, Wales and Northern Ireland only (England and Wales reported both police and customs seizures and Northern Ireland only police seizures); no data for Scotland are available.

Source: EMCDDA, *Statistical Bulletin 2010.*

Table 3.12 Quantities (kg) of amphetamine seized, 1995–2008

Country	1995	1996	1997	1998	1999	2000	2001	2002	2003	2004	2005	2006	2007	2008
Belgium[1]	68	24	77	445	59	75		500	209	2,540	175	119	484	411
Bulgaria[19]						177	65	202	587	957	1,385	657	177	430
Czech Rep.[2]								0.4	0.09	0.05	0.04	6	0.03	0.002
Denmark[3]	40	27	119	25	32	57	161	35	66	63	195	79	69	120
Germany[4]	138	160	234	310	360	271	263	362	484	556	669	713	810	1,279
Estonia[5]	2	1	1	2	11	27	25	34	109	32	13	50	56	23
Ireland[8]	0.1	8	103	45	13	6	18	16	68	92	17	41	58	
Greece[6]	0.1	0.08	0.05	0.003	1	2	0.08	0.5	0.5	0.7	1	0.1	0.1	0.1
Spain[7]	35	53	119	177	49	23	19	56	47	59	34	188	81	56
France	104	128	194	165	233	230	57	152	275	76	111	78	307	109
Italy[9]	1	2	0.4	0.5	5	0.2	0.7	2	1	0.9	7	14	4	1
Cyprus[10]	0.05	0.004	0	0.006	0.012	0.005	0.003	0	0.0005	0.004	0.4	0.01	0.01	0.003
Latvia[11]	0	0	0	0	0.5	0.9	4	5	9	4	4	11	6	5
Lithuania[12]			171	0.01	0.08	20	0.1	3	7	7	8	35	11	8
Luxembourg[13]	0.03	0.02	0.01	0.07	0.02	0.16	0.01	0.006	0.03	0.95	0.8	0.01	2	0.2
Hungary[23]						11	1	4	12	20	28	22	36	62
Malta							0	0.001	0.0005	0.07	1	1		
Netherlands[14]	45	324	815	1450	853	293	579	481	843	500	1600	603	2800	
Austria	2	4	8		63	1	3	9	54	26	9	38	18	13
Poland[22]						1,051	196	129	203	242	345	333	424	356
Portugal[15]			0	0	0	0	0	0.6	0.03	0.5	0.1	34	0.7	0.3
Romania[20]						13	214	0.9	2	0.013	3	2	0.1	0.2
Slovenia[16]						1	0.06	0.03	0	0.2	0.1	3	1	3
Slovakia[17]				10		0.3	0.004	0.006	0.001	0.009	0.01	7	0.004	0.04
Finland	20	22	22	25	71	80	137	129	115	102	115	126	129	130
Sweden[18]	279	127	186	135	124	108	239	330	313	438	417	422	293	361
UK[24]	819	2625	3296	1811	2019	1775	1726	1424	1626	1389	2330	1660	1783	

Croatia	53	30	93	211	52	93	1	28	4	7	14	12	8	15
Turkey[21]											41		233	163
Norway							93	209	215	229	119	318	392	260
Total	1606	3535	5438	4812	3883	4302	3802	4112	5250	7341	7642	5571	8182	

Notes: (1) In 1996, 1998 and 2003 data include both ecstasy and amphetamine seized. 511 amphetamine tablets were also seized in 1997; 22,050 in 1999 and 18,397 in 2000. (2) Accurate data are not available before 2002 due to double counting of seizures by police and customs reports; 56 amphetamine tablets were also seized in 2005. (3) 549 amphetamine tablets were also seized in 2004. (4) In 1995, the number of seizures based on offences; since 1996 the numbers of seizures based on police register. Data include both seizures of amphetamine and methamphetamine. (5) 10 amphetamine tablets were also seized in 2000; 37 in 2001; 1355 in 2002; 1567 in 2003; and 214 in 2005. (6) All seizures are included (police, coast guard and customs). Amphetamine tablets were also seized in 1998, 30,109 in 2000 and 8 in 2001. (7) 2775 amphetamine tablets were also seized in 1996; 13,720 in 1997; 1626 in 1998; 54,215 in 1999; 40,696 in 2000; 11,026 in 2001; 31,427 in 2002; 2726 in 2003; 86,748 in 2004; 8781 units in 2005 and 229,924 units in 2006. (8) 3889 amphetamine tablets were also seized in 1997; 4780 in 1998; 12,015 in 1999; 149 in 2000; 12,728 in 2002; 1019 in 2003; 19,452 in 2005; 7743 in 2006 and 10,471 in 2007. (9) Since 2000 data include seizures of all amphetamine-type products in kg with no differentiation between products. (10) 4 amphetamine tablets were also seized in 1995; 6 in 1996; 1 in 2002; 100 in 2003; 18 in 2005 and 141 in 2006. (11) Before 2004, data include both amphetamines and methamphetamine seizures. 3693 amphetamine tablets were also seized in 2003. (12) 42 amphetamine tablets were also seized in 2000; 229 in 2002; 219 in 2003; 1050 in 2004; 2580 in 2005; 1870 in 2006 and 1000 in 2007. (13) Data include both seizures of amphetamine and methamphetamine. (14)(a) Due to different methods and definitions among agencies and among the years, figures do not permit conclusions about developments and trends. They must be seen as a minimum estimate of seized drugs in the Netherlands. (14)(a) Due to different methods and definitions differ per police region which leads to unreliability in the information and makes it difficult to interpret the figures. Figures and seizures are truncate, less than 10 kg/10 litres are not reported. (c) 850 amphetamine tablets were also seized in 1995; 1025 in 1996; 102,240 in 1997; 242,409 in 1998; 45,847 in 1999; 20,592 in 2001; 1028 in 2002; 14,000 in 2003; 1000 in 2005; 38,100 in 2006 and 1400 in 2007. Both 2004 and 2005 data are based on seizures made only by some police forces; they are not comparable between them, nor with previous years. In 2006 data include 3 kg of amphetamine pasta. 240 l and 40 kg of pasta were also seized in 2007. (15) 26 amphetamine tablets were also seized in 1997; 4 in 1998; 37 in 1999; 18 in 2000; 25 in 2001; 34 in 2002; 125 in 2003; 32 in 2004; 2452 tablets and 35 capsules in 2005; 1535 tablets in 2006; 22,778 tablets in 2007 and 132,078 tablets in 2008. (16) 89 amphetamine tablets were also seized in 2001; 256 in 2002; 218 in 2003 and 1070.5 in 2007. (17) Before 2001, data include both amphetamine and methamphetamine seizures. 5 amphetamine tablets were also seized in 2001; 6 in 2002 and 3 in 2003. (18) Before 2001, data include both amphetamine and methamphetamine seizures. Fenmetrazin is included in amphetamine seizures. 204 amphetamine tablets were also seized in 2000. 782 in 2001; 92 in 2002 and 201 in 2006. (19) Data refer to seizures made by the Customs and the National Service for Combating Organized Crime (NACOC) from the Ministry of the Interior. 8513 amphetamine tablets were also seized in 2000; 660 in 2001; 135,444 in 2002 and 118,201 in 2003. (20) 133,517 amphetamine tablets were also seized in 2002; 93 in 2004; 3701 in 2005 and 250 in 2007. (21) 1089,989 amphetamine (captagon) tablets were seized in 2001; 8,576,884 in 2002; 4,195,481 in 2003; 8,888,752 in 2004; 6,722,032 (6,404,923 captagon) in 2005; 20,003,616 (1,268,873 captagon) in 2006 and 7,768,485 (7,609,327 captagon) in 2007. (22) Up to 2003, the amount of large seizures only is reported; from 2004 all seizures are reported. Police data include both amphetamine and methamphetamine seizures. 1.41 of amphetamine were also seized in 2007. (23) 776 amphetamine tablets were also seized in 2007. (24) Before 2006, data have been reported on a calendar year basis. Since 2006 seizures data will be published on a financial year basis (data reported for 2006 is 2006/07, data reported in 2007 is for 2007/08 and so on). There are no customs data for Scotland and Northern Ireland in 2006/07. In 2007 data are for England, Wales and Northern Ireland only (England and Wales reported both police and customs seizures and Northern Ireland only police seizures): no data for Scotland are available.

Source: EMCDDA, *Statistical Bulletin 2010*.

show that despite considerable national fluctuations in the amounts of individual drugs seized, overall within the EU the number of seizures of illegal drugs is increasing. The same is also broadly true for individual drugs, for example, the amount of heroin, cocaine and amphetamine seized within the EU as a whole is increasing. The only exception to this general trend is ecstasy; countries have reported stabilizing or slightly decreasing numbers of seizures of this drug in the last couple of years (EMCDDA, 2009). Generally speaking, an increase in the number of illegal drugs seized would suggest an increase in the availability of these drugs within the EU. In reality, however, it is impossible to discern whether the increase is due to an actual increase in the availability of the drugs in question or whether it is because of the employment of stronger law enforcement methods against those same drugs.

In addition to the inability to accurately ascertain whether or not the availability of illegal drugs is actually increasing, there are considerable further problems with the comparability of the data collected here. Firstly, the usual problems apply, relating to the fact that not every country has submitted data for every year and that some countries have been submitting data considerably longer than others. Furthermore, the meaningfulness of the totals for amounts of drugs seized in the EU included in the tables here is highly questionable when different numbers of countries have submitted reports year on year. Further problems arise from the fact that some countries use data from the police, some from customs, some from coast guards and some from a mixture of the three. This has also led some countries to declare a double counting issue where some seizures may, for example, be recorded by both the police and customs and may therefore in fact have been submitted twice. Certain drugs, for example, cocaine and amphetamine, present further issues over levels of inclusion. Some countries have included seizures of crack in the data submitted for cocaine and some have not. Similarly, some countries have included seizures of methamphetamine in the data submitted for amphetamine and others have not. Finally, the tables presented here record seizures in terms of kilograms seized; however, this does not always account for different forms of the same drug. Amphetamine, for example, can take a powder, tablet or liquid form which can have significant effect on the results reported. Portugal, for example, reports very low levels of amphetamine seized in terms of kilograms, but the notes accompanying Table 3.12 show that much higher levels of amphetamine tablets were in fact seized. For this reason these tables should be examined in conjunction with EMCDDA tables on the number of seizures made. Nevertheless, the barriers to successful comparison here are substantial.

Conclusions that can be drawn from the EMCDDA statistics

MacCoun and Reuter (2002) describe four analytical challenges for cross-national drug policy analysis: data scarcity, poor data quality and comparability, weak causal inference and unknown generalizability. The EMCDDA data examined above presents all of these challenges. Sometimes data has been scarce, with some EU member states being unable to provide statistics at all, and some EU member states only having recorded statistics in recent years. Often data has been patchy or incomparable due to different collectors of the data itself, different methods of collection and different presentation styles in different member states.

As can be observed from the tables presented earlier in this chapter, to a certain extent, the EMCDDA is working towards overcoming these problems. In the historical tables, as the years go by, greater numbers of member states have consistently provided data. Additionally, the EMCDDA has worked towards instituting standard age categories and standard definitions for terms such as drug-related death. Increasing numbers of countries are adopting these standards, although not all have done so as yet. Over the coming years, practices of data collection should also continue to become even more standardized. However, it will be some years before definite increases in reliability and comparability of data are seen.

Even where suitable data for examination and cross-national evaluation does exist, correlational evidence is weak on the consequences of drug policies. For example, looking at the most recent figures for lifetime prevalence of drug use for all adults, the Netherlands and Sweden, despite having almost diametrically opposed styles of national drug policy, record very similar numbers. In Sweden, with its strongly control-oriented policy, 21.4 per cent of the population report ever having used cannabis, 3.3 per cent cocaine, 5.0 per cent amphetamine and 2.1 per cent ecstasy. In the Netherlands, with arguably the most tolerant European drug policy, the figures are 22.6 per cent for cannabis, 3.4 per cent for cocaine, 2.1 per cent for amphetamine and 4.3 per cent for ecstasy. In terms of problem drug use, both Sweden and France have relatively prohibitive national drug policies, yet France records 6.8 drug-related deaths per 1000 of the general population while Sweden reports only 4.9 per 1000. Furthermore, it is not often possible to make inferences about the reasons behind differences in figures since nations and cultures differ so widely (Desrosieres, 1996).

The evidence overwhelmingly shows that the nature of the data collected by the EMCDDA, and its frequent incomparability, extensively hinders the possibility of drawing conclusions about drug policy in general. The International Coalition of NGOs for Just and Effective Drugs Policy (ICN) (2001, p. 5) has suggested further considerations that any evaluation based on EMCDDA statistics fails to make: "The current evaluation system of drugs policies in Europe does not measure the cost/effectiveness of current policies. It also ignores or minimizes the negative effects on public health and community safety." In order to evaluate drug policy across Europe more effectively, they call for a combination of statistical measures, such as the need to determine the proportion of "problematic use" among the totality of use and the price/quality ratio of substances, with more sociological measures such as the integration of drug users in society and the participation of citizens in the design and implementation of drug policies (ICN, 2001).

Therefore, the overwhelming conclusion to be drawn from the information presented in this chapter is that the statistical information collected by the EMCDDA is not yet, and may never be, of a high enough quality to base scientific comparisons upon. Three minor conclusions, however, may be drawn. Firstly, that the nature of the drug problem is broadly similar across Europe, with all countries experiencing drug use and problem drug use, and with all countries experiencing some kinds of further problems as a result of that drug use, for example, drug-related crime, drug-related death and drug-related disease. Secondly, that broad international trends can be observed across Europe, such as the recent rise in the use of cocaine, or the rise of HIV in the 1980s. Finally, that the statistics pay homage to the universal lack of success of national drug policy across Europe in so far as no country has significantly reduced the number of drug users, the availability of drugs or the problems resultant on drug use. The evidence presented in this chapter therefore suggests that, while it is not possible to judge the success of one national policy over another, there is certainly room for a European level drug policy given the similarity of the problem faced across European member states. The next part of this book will consider the range of national policies in operation across Europe and will further explore the possibilities for harmonization.

Part II

Drug Policy in Individual Member States

The information presented in Part I of this book reveals some desirability of harmonization of illicit drug policy at a European level. The EU itself has long investigated the issue in an attempt to find a solution applicable across European member states. The nature of the illegal drug problem is such that it does not remain contained within national boundaries and therefore demands an international response, at least at the trafficking level. Additionally, all member states experience an illicit drug problem and none have, so far, been successful in significantly reducing the size of their problem. These points therefore suggest that harmonization of policy at the European level would also bring benefits to individual member states. Nevertheless, attempts at harmonization, other than in the area relating to illicit drug trafficking, have been largely unsuccessful. National drug policy is a complex area of social policy where European integration is at its least well-developed and attachment to individual policy options is high. An examination of EMCDDA data collected on the issue throughout Europe is not able to shed any light on the best way forward in an effort to increase harmonization in this area.

This part of the book attempts to further investigate the potential viability of a harmonized European drug policy by offering an in-depth examination of some of the national drug policies currently in operation in Europe. Such an investigation is undertaken, in part, to illuminate the range of policy options in operation in Europe and the extent to which they differ and, in part, to determine the strength of national adherence to the individual policies that have been developed. It should be noted here that all countries in the EU are committed to imposing harsh penalties against drug trafficking and drug traffickers and, while maximum penalties differ slightly, EU-wide minimum penalties have already been successfully imposed. The differentiations between national policies tend to occur in the treatment of drug use and drug users, and it is these areas of policy that will be primarily examined in further detail here.

As observed in Part I of this book, two main paradigms of drug control, with particular reference to drug use and drug users, are currently in operation in Europe. These correspond directly to the division in opinion experienced by both the Stewart-Clark and Cooney commissions, charged by the European Parliament with investigating the illicit drugs issue in the 1980s and 1990s. One set of responses centres around repression and advocates that drug users as well as drug dealers and traffickers must feel the weight of the law if they commit drug-related offences. The other centres around liberalism and typically advocates that drug users and drug use should be afforded some protection from the full weight of the law with reference to minor drug-related offences. In essence, these two differing styles of response to the drug problem can most closely be encapsulated by drug policy in Sweden and the Netherlands, with the former implementing a very restrictive policy and the latter implementing a rather liberal one. This part of the book will provide a case study of both of these countries in an effort to offer an in-depth examination of the differing styles of drug policy and to argue that they do, in fact, represent two entirely different paradigms of drug control.

If Sweden and the Netherlands represent national strategies at either end of the restrictive–liberal spectrum, then the remaining member states lie at different points along the continuum between them. One trend, documented in the previous part of the book, that has recently swept across Europe is the removal of criminal sanctions (decriminalization) for the possession of illicit drugs for personal consumption only. For example, Belgium and Luxembourg have recently effectively removed criminal sanctions for the possession of cannabis for personal use. Germany, Estonia and Lithuania, meanwhile, have written the possibility of waiving prosecution in the case of small amounts for personal use of any drug into their penal codes and Spain, the Czech Republic and Latvia have gone one step further, making administrative sanctions the norm for possession of small amounts of illegal drugs for personal use. Portugal is the most advanced member state in this respect with the possession of small amounts of drugs for personal use now completely removed from the penal code and, instead, deemed a civil offence to be met with administrative sanctions.

Wide-ranging as this trend is across a number of different member states, both Western and Eastern, it is not pervasive. Some EU member states are simply maintaining their already relatively strict national policies and ignoring the trend towards a lighter treatment of drug use and drug users. For example, Hungarian national policy continues to avow that possession of illegal drugs is an offence and that both demand and supply must be reduced in a successful national drug policy. In Greece, national policy continues to dictate that possession of illicit drugs for personal use can be punishable by up to one year's imprisonment and in Cyprus possession, even for personal use, is viewed as a serious criminal offence attracting the same range of penalties as trafficking. Furthermore, some countries have not only maintained a strict national position, but have adopted a more repressive national policy during the same time period.

Bulgaria, for example, removed an exoneration for drug offences relating to personal use in 2004, although this toughening of policy was later softened in 2006 by reducing the penalties for personal use and differentiating between different types of drug. Denmark has recently tightened its laws involving cannabis and has added a codicil to the penal code making a prison sentence mandatory where drugs are being distributed in areas frequented by children. The situation in the UK is also of interest here – in 2004 cannabis was made a Class C drug, attracting significantly lower penalties than other illicit drugs. However, in 2009, this decision was reversed and cannabis users once again became subject to the same penalties as users of drugs such as amphetamines.

The willingness to implement significant changes to national drug policy, in the context of the question of moving to a harmonized drug policy for Europe, is of high importance and worthy of further investigation in the form of in-depth case study similar to those countries offering presentation of policies at either end of the liberal–restrictive spectrum. With many countries displaying changes in style of overall national drug policy, the decision on which countries to choose for in-depth analysis has not been easy. Portugal has been chosen as the country displaying the most radical change towards a more liberal drug policy in recent years and Denmark has been chosen to represent the countries that have moved towards a more restrictive policy. Denmark makes an interesting case as, although it probably does not encompass the most radical changes, it has, arguably, moved from a national policy with extremely liberal aspects to one which is more uniformly restrictive.

National drug policy in Sweden, the Netherlands, Denmark and Portugal will therefore be studied in more detail in this part in an effort to determine the extent of the differences in policy observed in Europe.

Sweden represents the restrictive end of the drug policy continuum and the Netherlands the liberal end. In between these two extreme policies, Denmark represents a country moving from a relatively liberal policy to a relatively restrictive one and Portugal represents a country becoming radically more liberal in its drug policy application. In addition to determining the range of national drug policies in operation in Europe, an attempt will be made to determine the course of development of the individual drug policies since the 1960s, when most countries first began to experience significant problematic drug use, in an effort to understand how different policy styles have arisen and what levels of attachment are given to these national styles. To this end, historical case studies of national drug policy in the four countries in question will be made in this part in an effort to further understand the potential viability of a harmonized European drug policy.

4
Sweden

The case of national drug policy development in Sweden provides an example of the more restrictive paradigm of drug policy in operation within the European Union. The ultimate goal is the attainment of a drug-free society and zero tolerance measures, against drug use and drug users as well as drug trafficking and drug traffickers, are employed to achieve this end. A detailed examination of the historical context of drug policy development in this country charts the increasing commitment to a national war on drugs and deals with the evidence suggesting that, in recent times, Swedish national drug policy may be becoming less restrictive as the principles of harm reduction gain more ground.

Prior to the 1960s

In Sweden, prior to the 1960s, "no clear-cut drug policy existed" (Lenke and Olsson, 1999, p. 136). There had been no major explosion of drug use within society and, as such, the issue did not exist on the political agenda. However, this did not mean that there was no experimentation with drugs within the country. For example, the use of amphetamines in small pockets of society from the 1950s onwards has been well-documented (Lenke and Olsson, 1998). Initially, women trying to control their weight were the main users of amphetamines, but use spread to groups of artists and musicians based in Stockholm. Throughout the 1950s, pockets of young people also began to experiment with cannabis.

The use of amphetamines had already been recognized as a possible danger, and in 1939 their availability by prescription had been limited. In 1945, a further directive was issued by the National Medical Board aiming to inform doctors of the dangers and risks associated with amphetamine use to further discourage their prescription. Nevertheless, use spread, and, more problematically, began to permeate the criminal subculture already existing in Stockholm at that time. The use of morphine also existed, but among much narrower circles within the medical profession and upper middle classes, and its use did not spread onto the streets and into the criminal subculture in the same way that the use of amphetamines did.

Drugs, or more specifically, cannabis, came to the attention of the authorities as a potentially large problem in the 1950s when youth culture began to develop and young people started to smoke cannabis for the first time. When this cannabis smoking among normal youngsters began to be linked to the use of amphetamines within criminal subcultures by the media, the use of drugs became a concern. The first sign of drug use making an impression upon politics came in 1954 when an increasing tendency among young people to smoke cannabis for pleasure was mentioned in parliament by an MP with liberal sympathies (Tops, 2001).

The development of experimentation with cannabis in the 1950s was in line with behaviour across Europe. However, the spread of amphetamine use was relatively unique to Sweden at that time. In most other European countries the problem of drug use started primarily with cannabis and moved on to heroin, without any report of widespread amphetamine use. The period of amphetamine use before 1960 in Sweden is characterized, however, "by a vast and widespread use of stimulant drugs, but relatively few cases of abuse" (Boekhout van Solinge, 1997, p. 38). At this point in the history of Swedish drug policy, drug use was a problem almost entirely contained within the medical profession. Problems were registered on an individual basis rather than being perceived as endangering society as a whole, and drug use was felt to be a matter that should be solved privately between a doctor and their patient.

Alcohol policy, however, was well-developed and strongly orientated towards control within Sweden at this time. At the end of the 1800s, and the beginning of the 1900s, issues relating to alcohol use, such as the wider social problems its use could cause, had begun to be discussed. In the interests of preventing these problems, a temperance culture was championed by both the labour movement and the liberal free church movement (Lenke and Olsson, 2002). The tradition in Sweden at that time, as in other Nordic countries, was to drink heavily (Cisneros Ornberg, 2008). Problems such as violence and poverty due to excessive spending on alcohol were beginning to emerge. In order to combat these problems, a Temperance Committee was initiated in 1911 and most municipalities in Sweden developed a localized Temperance Board of their own. In 1920, the Temperance Committee presented the findings from its investigation into the problems caused by alcohol use and recommended a system of total prohibition. A national referendum was held on instituting a prohibition-based system in 1922, which was only narrowly defeated.

Instead of total prohibition, a very strict rationing system, originally constructed in 1919, was introduced throughout Sweden (the Bratt System). Tops (2001) describes the complicated rule base surrounding this system. Every Swedish citizen above the age of 25 (except in the case of married women), who had passed a suitability check, was allowed to buy a certain quantity of liquor per month from state shops (*Systembolaget*). Every time alcohol was purchased a note would be made in the customer's ration book. In the event of use, the state reserved the right to reduce or withdraw the ration at any time. The use of alcohol was therefore subject to very strict individual control and drinking was minimized until the 1950s.

Generally speaking, this policy of control was regarded as rather successful both in reducing drinking and in minimizing the problems associated with the use of alcohol. Indeed, the introduction of the ration book system was perceived as effective in reducing the criminal subculture existent at the time (Lenke, 1991). In 1955, the system involving the ration book was abolished to make way for an alcohol policy founded on the introduction of extremely high taxes, and limited access to alcohol. This was achieved by establishing state-run shops which were the only outlets licensed to sell alcohol at fixed (and highly expensive) prices. Therefore the alcohol policy in place at the time of the first experiences of drug use in Sweden was not only one of strict control, but also one that had been judged to be highly successful.

1960s

In the 1960s in Sweden, as in most of the rest of the world, drug use and experimentation in particular, began to expand. The problem surrounding the use of amphetamines continued to develop throughout the early to mid-1960s. More visibly, cannabis and LSD came to be associated with the youth culture that was also developing at that time. Initially, the attitude towards the use of illegal drugs by young people was treated liberally – probably due to the fact that it was a new phenomenon. At this time, a distinct difference, in policy terms, was made between drug dealers and drug users. The latter were depicted as victims in need of support and treatment rather than punishment.

The experimental use of cannabis was more or less widely accepted within society at this time. There were few treatment facilities or prevention activities existing in society, and the authorities did not regard it as a major problem. Yates (1996, p. 1) describes the general ambience of Stockholm, with reference to drug policy in the 1960s as: "like one big love-in, beautiful people and good vibes everywhere.... The main park in Stockholm, Kungstradgarden, was full of Hippies and pot was available everywhere. Although cannabis was illegal, the official attitude was one of tolerant acceptance. The atmosphere was cool and the police were friendly." By the mid-1960s, it became obvious that drug use had increased to a stage where there were now thousands rather than hundreds of drug users that had become problematic in their use (CAN, 2009), and, for the first time, the authorities began to encourage law enforcement agencies to apply more pressure to the situation.

The policy focus regarding the problem of drug use was still primarily on treatment and preventive efforts throughout the early 1960s. For example, Lenke and Olsson (1999, p. 138) write, when discussing this time period, "the institutionalization of the drug problem, in terms of specific laws, police forces, treatment facilities, etc., had barely begun". As the problem grew, and the treatment facilities that did exist were increasingly unable to cope, this exclusive focus was questioned. Some measures of control were developed and a national drugs coordinator was appointed. The government recognized the need for information about the extent of drug use and its causes, and, in 1965, the National Board of Health charged a committee with the task of the investigation of the current drug problem. Their report was to include recommendations against the spread of drug use.

Although the committee initially found it very difficult to define the nature of the problem of drug use, one of the consequences of their reports was that the involvement of medical practitioners declined and the field opened up to more control-orientated definitions. At the same time, a National Police Board was created. This centralized the local police forces and their information, and thus allowed the increasingly hard line policy initiatives for dealing with drugs to have considerably more influence. Both of these events helped to create an environment suitable for the reversal of earlier liberal approaches towards the drug problem. However, before the committee produced its report and new initiatives were implemented, another important event in Swedish drugs policy occurred: the legal prescription project.

In 1965, a few doctors were given permission to prescribe narcotics to drug dependents. This mostly involved the prescription of amphetamines (as well as a small amount of heroin), and psychotherapy and social counselling had to be available as part of the prescription programme. The proposal had been drawn up by a users' organization in Sweden, and was launched by the Medical Board (Lenke and Olsson, 1998). The motivation behind the programme was providing aid and relief to drug users to allow them as normal a life as possible.

Unfortunately, the physician in charge of the prescription project and the other doctors involved in prescribing were accused of practising in a rather irregular and uncontrolled manner. Drug users were frequently given responsibility for administering their own prescriptions, and so could go to the pharmacy, pick up a couple of weeks' worth of drugs, and be trusted to self-administer in a sensible manner (UNODC, 2007). It was not a large experiment as it serviced no more than 100 users at a time. However, due to the lack of measures of control practiced by the doctors, and the reliance on the trust and responsibility of the users themselves, when dealing with large amounts of drugs, the police became increasingly curious about the project and the national drugs coordinator made the decision to start an investigation. In 1967, a 17-year-old girl died from an overdose. She was not a part of the prescription programme but had been given her drugs by someone who was, and who had, in turn, received them from medical officials (UNODC, 2007). The media inspired outrage at this, and the project was swiftly closed down. At the time it was evaluated very negatively (Lenke and Olsson, 2002).

The project came to stand for the whole practice of liberal policy regarding the use of illegal drugs. It was tried by the Swedish government, police and media, and found to be guilty of aiding the increase of drug use within Sweden. At the time, and for many years afterwards, the official line towards the project taken by the Swedish National Institute of Public Health was to condemn it and blame it for Sweden's subsequent large increase in numbers of drug users. A survey of pupils in the final grade of compulsory schools in Stockholm conducted in 1967 showed that 17 per cent of girls and 23 per cent of boys had ever used drugs. By far the most common drug used was cannabis. In 1970, even higher figures were reported, with 28 per cent of schoolgirls and 34 per cent of school boys reporting ever having used drugs (Swedish National Institute of Public Health, 1995).

With hindsight, these conclusions have been challenged, predominantly by Lenke and Olsson (1998). They have not only disagreed with the conclusions drawn by officials at the time, arguing that the drug epidemic had clearly started before the experiment was initiated, but also commented that it is unfair to draw such absolute conclusions from a project that was neither soundly designed (UNDOC, 2007) nor properly evaluated. However, at the time, the closure of the project and its subsequent condemnation, combined with the tightening policy measures leading to the initiation of the National Police Board and the first Narcotics Committee, provided the spark for a radical change of direction in Swedish drug policy.

National drug policy swiftly became a hot topic of strong political and public interest with two distinct camps emerging from the debate. Nils Bejerot, a young researcher actively involved in investigating the drugs problem at the time the legal prescription experiment collapsed, gave voice to those who supported a prohibitive drug policy. He defined the drugs problem in moral terms and insisted that national drug policy must include, as its central aim, a desire to completely eradicate drugs from society (Bejerot, 1988). At the same time, the Swedish Organisation for Help and Assistance to Drug Users (RFHL) became a figurehead for those who were sympathetic to the cause of drug users. This organization aimed to give personal assistance to drug users, and to inform and influence the attitudes of the general public in the direction of a more humane and social drug policy.

Initially, much more media attention and public empathy was afforded to RFHL and their liberal ideas. However, with the collapse of the legal prescription project in 1967, the time was ripe for an advocate of a stricter drug policy, and the media embraced Bejerot and his philosophy. Bejerot had started his own lobbying organization – the National Organisation for a drug-free Society (RNS) – which promoted his encouragement of a stricter policy, and, from the late 1960s onwards, his became the dominant voice in debates about Swedish drug policy (Lenke and Olsson, 2002). Not only did he persistently call for a strong and comprehensive moral reaction to the problem of illicit drugs, he even made such far-fetched claims as that Sweden had been the first country in Europe to experience the affliction of drug use and had been responsible for spreading the problem to the continent at large (Bejerot, 1988).

At the time of the legal prescription experiment, Bejerot was completing his PhD. This was a study which he initiated in 1965 and involved inspecting the bodies of recent arrestees for signs of drug use. He started the study to determine whether or not the legal prescription experiment had increased the incidence of intravenous drug use. His results claimed an increase of 20 per cent in the number of intravenous drug users in Stockholm during the time of the project (Bejerot, 1988). Bejerot's conclusions, promoted through the now powerful RNS, ensured the Swedish people did not forget that the legal prescription experiment, and, by association, a liberal attitude towards drug policy, had failed. In the increasingly popular opinion of Bejerot, they had failed because they had not reacted strongly enough against drugs. The moral problem presented to society by drugs could not be met by half measures. Society must be united in its efforts to overcome this problem (Bejerot, 1988). Repressive drug policy now had a powerful range of advocates, and the Swedish government were to turn, ever increasingly, to control measures.

By 1968, drugs were perceived as having permeated the entire country, despite efforts to curb their use. Estimates now put the size of the drug problem at about 10,000 hard core dependents, most of whom were injecting amphetamines (CAN, 2009). The government decided not to wait for its committee to produce a final report, but to move drugs to the foreground of policy immediately. Tops (2001) explains that a nationwide attack on drug dealers by the police was implemented, giving priority to drug offences as well as to the instigation of a massive information campaign aimed at raising public consciousness of the drug problem. In the same year, a new Narcotics Drug Act (1968) was passed setting the maximum penalty for serious drug crime at two years' imprisonment. From now on, Swedish drug policy was set to depend more and more on control and restriction. "At the end of the 1960s Sweden shifted from its socio-medical drug policy to a clear law-enforcement approach, in which repression and formal social control predominated" (Lenke and Olsson, 1996, p. 106). This was a policy trend that would continue and become increasingly well-developed in the 1970s.

1970s

At the beginning of the 1970s, Bejerot, through RNS, had just started to organize his ideas and promote his aims, but the battle was by no means won. In 1972, the Narcotics Act was changed again to considerably increase the maximum penalty for a serious drugs crime from two years' imprisonment to ten years' imprisonment. However, in other ways, the policy at the beginning of the 1970s could still be described as liberal, for example, the practice of allowing those with a small supply of drugs, perhaps for up to one week's consumption and especially of cannabis, to escape prosecution. Tham (1995, p. 113) describes the time as a period when "the debate about drugs and drug policies [was] ... more open and differing views were exchanged and debated".

Treatment facilities were also being tentatively extended at this time, although they still fell far below requirements for the number of drug users. Bejerot and RNS began campaigning, unsuccessfully at this time, for the introduction of laws allowing the compulsory care and treatment of drug users who showed no motivation of their own to give up drug use, in an attempt to reach out and offer treatment to all drug users. Couched in Bejerot's terms, all drug users were at risk of infecting others with their dependency (Bejerot, 1988). Therefore, the only treatment conceivable for implementation by a society that is morally outraged by the illicit drugs problem must be abstention oriented and intended to ultimately "cure" the drug user of their dependency.

Heroin made a significant impact on the Swedish drug scene for the first time in the mid-1970s, although amphetamines were still by far the most common drug to be associated with problematic use in the country. Figures regarding the prevalence of drug use were perceived as having levelled out, but at a relatively high rate. At the beginning of the 1970s, school surveys showed that 13 per cent of school children were reporting they had ever used drugs. In the 1970s, studies relating to drug use were also undertaken on army conscripts determining how many had used drugs in the last month, and data indicated that around 15–18 per cent had (Swedish National Institute of Public Health, 1995).

More importantly, for the first time since the Second World War, in 1976, the Social Democratic government was defeated and replaced by a coalition government dominated by Conservative views. The Social Democrats had been keen to see drugs as a social problem solvable by society, but the new government abandoned these ideas. The fact that the government perceived a strict response to the drug problem to be a vote winner evidences the increasingly negative attitude of the general public towards illicit drugs at this time. This corresponded with an increase in the reliance on the opinions of Bejerot and RNS. The Conservative government was more willing to institute a drug policy strongly founded on principles of control. This policy could be led by the government, but would be supported and enforced by society in general.

In tandem with this emphasis on control and law enforcement, significant developments were also being made in the treatment of illicit drug use in Sweden. At the forefront of this movement was a drug activist, Westerberg, with a theory that young people were turning to drugs because of a bad upbringing, and the solution therefore being to take them away to the country, to re-educate them in society's values and to give them a normal upbringing. He bought a house in Hassela, a village in the North of Sweden, and took young people away for one or two years. He claimed extremely positive results with a near 80 per cent success rate, and the idea caught the Swedish imagination. The general public apparently believed that drug dependency was curable if people could be forced to lead a better life. This reinforced the belief that it was necessary to actively seek out drug users and then treat them to rid them of the affliction of drug use.

Since the late 1960s, Bejerot had developed his ideas relating to the practice of drug policy and government officials and the general public were increasingly listening to him, especially as the estimated number of hard core drug dependents had now risen to 15,000 (CAN, 2009). Essentially, Bejerot's position was that it was useless to continue to pursue the supply of drugs as dealers would always be replaced: instead, Swedish drug policy should focus predominantly on demand, and therefore the police should turn their attention, and their investigative powers, to users on the streets. Indeed, in the perception of drugs as an inherent evil facing society, users should be as much a target as suppliers as they are equally involved in continuing the spread of drug use.

Since its beginning, RNS had adopted as its motto the slogan "a drug-free society". In 1977, this motto was adopted as the official aim of Swedish national policy. From this moment onwards, the focus of drug policy was to rid the country of all use of drugs in all circumstances with equal priority. Experimental or recreational use of any drug would not be tolerated and neither would use of cannabis. Swedish drug policy could now fully be described as a moralistic one. "Within a short space of time in the late 1970s, Swedish drug policy became stricter than in previous years...since the drug abuser was now seen to be a drug-governed creature without a will of his own, he or she had to be prevented from using drugs through penal control and coercive treatment" (Tham, 1998, p. 396). The scene was set for a continuation of strict control policies with relation to drugs. Liberal ideas were increasingly unpopular, and the majority of public and official support was behind Bejerot and RNS.

1980s

By 1980, Bejerot's ideas were generally accepted in Sweden and were representative of the views of most of the general population. Debate within the area of drug policy was abandoned, and the "Swedish Model" of restrictive drug policy, based on control and repression of use, was formed. The government had taken sides and come down heavily on the side of RNS and the goal of a drug-free society, thus turning the problem of drug use into a moral crusade in which the whole of society was encouraged to participate. The zero tolerance policy that thus developed has been described as "a logical consequence of the moralistic approach to drug use" (Hilte, 1999, p. 309). In the early 1980s, the use of waivers of prosecution for possession of minimal amounts of drugs became very restricted. The police were given greatly increased budgets for combating drug use and new research results were released contradicting the generally held opinion that cannabis was relatively harmless (Tops, 2001).

In 1982, the much-talked about coercive treatment laws that Bejerot and RNS had openly been campaigning for, were passed. It became possible to detain by force both youth and adult drug users who were not willing to take part in drug treatment voluntarily. Also in 1982, a new Narcotics Commission was appointed with the task of analysing the drug situation and making proposals about solutions to the problems it posed. The findings of the commission were that Swedish national policy was developing appropriately, but that a statement emphasizing the dangers associated with cannabis use should be released. This evidences the continuing pervasiveness of negative public opinion directed at all drugs: there would be no distinction between drugs based on their perceived level of risk in Sweden.

In 1984, the government presented the drug policy bill "Coordinated and Intensified Drug Policy". Tops (2001) describes this bill as containing reinforced provisions for police, prosecution officers and customs officers involved in policing drugs, extra funding for fighting drug use in general and a reiteration, in the strongest terms, of the goal of a "drug-free society". Social workers were no longer required to help drug users with problems that may have contributed to their dependency, such as unemployment, housing issues and education, until the user had completely given up drugs.

In the 1980s, HIV and AIDS hit Sweden, and were to have a huge influence on Swedish drug policy. In most other European countries it was HIV and AIDS that encouraged the promotion of harm reduction measures such as methadone maintenance treatment and needle exchange programmes. Instead, in Sweden, harm reduction measures were seen as promoting the use of drugs and were therefore judged as incompatible with the national goal of a "drug-free society". To prevent the spread of AIDS and HIV in Sweden, the government developed the idea of tracing every single drug user and offering each one of them treatment. Needle exchange and methadone maintenance were not totally abandoned, but very limited programmes, predominantly in the south of Sweden, were initiated on a trial basis. The vast majority of resources went into drug-free treatment programmes, such as the Hassela movement, which had already attracted support. This strategy of "offensive drug treatment", initiated by the central government and put into practice by local governments, dominated drug policy in Sweden in the 1980s. The amount of money devoted to treatment purposes really was massive in relation to any other country at that time. It provided the justification for the application of such strict control and law enforcement measures to those users who did not take advantage of the many treatment opportunities that would be provided.

With such an effective and all-encompassing treatment policy in place, law enforcement agencies began to lobby for increased penalties for those persisting in remaining outside the treatment system. Throughout the 1980s, the police had campaigned for the criminalization of drug use, and in 1988 their ambition was realized when the consumption of an illicit drug was made a criminal offence. Researchers monitoring statistics reported low or stable figures for drug use in Sweden, and the Swedes claimed a success with their drug policy in comparison with other countries. Levels of ever having used drugs reported among school children had dropped to 8 per cent in 1975 and to 3–5 per cent in 1983. 1988 results showed that the numbers of conscripts reporting drug use in the last month had fallen to 6 per cent (Swedish National Institute of Public Health, 1995). Additional estimates put the number of recorded serious drug dependents at a relatively low 12,000 (Yates, 1998).

These facts and figures helped to create an impression that Swedish drug policy and control measures were working, and causing the lower rates of drug use now reported. In fact, the figures had already begun to fall in the early 1970s before the restrictive policy was fully adopted, and may have been part of a national or international trend that had nothing to do with policy practices within Sweden. However, the government used the figures as a strong indicator of the success of the "Swedish Model". Indeed, the government even "tried to influence other countries' attitudes in drug issues" towards "the Swedish Model" (Tops, 2001, p. 170). The combination of seeming success with curbing drug use, and an aim to promote the "Swedish Model" throughout the world, meant that there was no turning back for Swedish drug policy. The ideas of Bejerot and RNS that had been popularized in the 1970s were now vindicated. The debate on drugs was over and the prohibitionists had won.

1990s

The 1990s in Sweden, with reference to drug policy, were overwhelmingly dominated by the introduction of further control measures and the tightening of restrictive measures in the fight against drugs. "The New Democrats, a newly formed discontent party, entered parliament in 1991 on a platform based on demands for a tougher criminal policy and restricted immigration" (Tham, 1995, p. 122). Since the criminalization of the use of illegal drugs in 1988, the police and RNS had been campaigning for the right to take measures to determine whether or not someone had been using illegal drugs. In 1993, this aim was realized, and the police were allowed to conduct blood and urine tests if they felt someone might be under the influence of illegal drugs. A maximum penalty of six months' imprisonment was set for the violation of this offence.

From here, the catalogue of measures aimed to tighten control continued. Yates (1996) notes the formation of European Cities Against Drugs in 1994, in which Sweden was instrumental. This network of European Cities worked to promote Swedish style aims and objectives in drug policy throughout Europe and was initially entirely funded by the Swedish state. In 1996, police launched a major offensive campaign against Stockholm's notorious drug taking area, *"Platten"*, and introduced a new police rave squad (*Ravekommissionen*) to infiltrate clubs and bars where there may be suspected drug users (Yates, 1998). Finally, in 1998, "the government appointed the Commission on Narcotic Drugs which was given the task of proposing measures for strengthening and streamlining drug policy" (Ministry of Health and Social Affairs, 2002, p. 1).

The 1990s, in Sweden, were also characterized more generally by a period of real economic crisis. The Swedish economy went into steep decline, with unemployment figures drastically rising and government funding being extensively cut. "The Conservative led coalition of 1991–1994 reduced government spending in almost all areas...the current Social Democratic government has not changed the direction of the policies outlined by its predecessor" (Goldberg, 1997, p. 3). For the purposes of drug policy, this meant that funding to the municipalities for the treatment of drug users was drastically reduced.

Many municipalities began to economize as much as possible by cutting back on treatment, particularly of the highly expensive, institutionalized, in-patient kind. Indeed, the changes to the treatment system have been so great that Boekhout van Solinge (1997, p. 121) has suggested "one could even question whether the extensive treatment system as it has existed for a long time [is] relevant to the situation today". These radical changes to the treatment system in Sweden contributed to a situation where treatment for drug offenders was no longer all-encompassing, or necessarily easily obtainable, yet control measures and punishments directed at those same drug offenders were at an all time high.

Added to the treatment crisis, and the introduction of increasingly tighter methods of control, was the fact that, in Sweden, the nature of the drug problem could be seen to have changed during the 1990s. A government report (CAN, 2009) stated that heroin use increased in this decade and claimed that drug seizures were up by 50 per cent and prosecutions by 66 per cent since 1990. Drug-related deaths increased from 50 per year in the 1970s to 250 per year in 2000, and availability of illegal drugs was also judged to be rising at an all time high (Lenke and Olsson, 2002). For the first time since the early 1970s, results from school children reporting ever having used drugs, and from conscripts reporting having used drugs in the last month, began to rise (Swedish National Institute of Public Health, 1995). Also for the first time, a problem with young people using drugs in a recreational manner in discos and bars was noted.

Various reasons have been postulated for this rise in drug use, mostly relating to the economic crisis in this decade. For example, Goldberg (1997, p. 6) cites "the relatively high unemployment rate among teenagers... combined with difficult living conditions for many refugees". These issues contributed to the perception of a "crossroads" being reached in Swedish drug policy and the appointment of a 1998 Narcotics Commission charged with investigating this apparent rise in drug use, and determining the underlying causes and therefore the appropriate solutions (Tham, 2005). It was also necessary to examine the continued justification of a policy that was so restrictive towards drug users in the absence of the provision of sufficient treatment options.

2000s

In 2001, the Narcotics Commission, appointed in 1998, reported back on its findings. Under the title of *The Crossroads: The Drug Policy Challenge*, the commission outlined the renewed need for focus on the issue of illicit drug policy. In terms of policy continuation, this has resulted in the appointment of a new national drugs coordinator and the institution of a series of action plans relating to the drug problem. In January 2002, Bjorn Fries was appointed as the national drugs coordinator. As well as providing a coordinating point for drug policy, he has the additional responsibility of implementing a national action plan drawn up in April 2002. The national drug coordinator is granted overall responsibility for the drugs problem, and is "responsible for implementing and following up the action plan, as well as for coordinating national drug policy in general" (Ministry of Health and Social Affairs, 2002, p. 1).

There is little doubt that the contents of the report overwhelmingly propound a "more of the same" rhetoric with regards to Swedish drug policy; a sentiment that is strongly echoed by the national drugs coordinator and both the 2002 and the 2006 national action plans. In terms of the report itself, it demands stronger leadership in drug policy and a more active role from the government in a new offensive against drug problems. The strict policy of control with regard to drugs is reiterated and enforced. "In its choice of direction, the Drugs Commission has found that Sweden's restrictive policy on drugs must be sustained and reinforced. The Commission finds no arguments or facts to suggest that a policy of lowering society's guard against drug use and drug trafficking would do anything to improve matters for individual users or for society as a whole" (Swedish Commission on Narcotic Drugs, 2000, p. 2). The increase in drug use observed during the 1990s is attributed to the economic crisis and the cutbacks in treatment (Tham, 2005), lending further evidence to suggest that government efforts must once again be raised in this contentious area.

This adherence to control policy is further evidenced in both of the national action plans implemented in 2002 and 2006, which, as they are almost indistinguishable in content, will be discussed together here. The overall objective of a drug-free society is upheld and the latest version states that "long-term preventive work to achieve a drug-free society must continue" (Ministry of Health and Social Affairs, 2008, p. 1). Tham (2005, p. 60) levels the criticism that the government is "pursuing a strategy of denial" and observes that "the crossroads referred to by the Drugs Commission never really existed" (Tham, 2005, p. 70). Looking more closely, however, Goldberg (2005) suggests there may be some signs of a willingness to admit that a more circumspect attitude is needed. Three subgoals have been added to the ultimate quest of a drug-free society: to reduce the number of persons who engage in illicit drug use, to encourage more drug abusers to give up the habit and to reduce the supply of drugs. Goldberg (2005, p. 48) has suggested that these subgoals "reflect a significantly lower level of aspiration" than previously admitted within Swedish drug policy.

Several academics (Goldberg, 2005; Johnson, 2006) have also referred to two further policy initiatives that suggest, despite political rhetoric, that the Swedish government may be loosening its grip on illicit drug control policy. Firstly, the Drugs Commissioner has recommended that the needle exchange programmes in Southern Sweden, which have only been tolerated on a temporary basis, should be made permanent. Secondly, he has recommended that a greater number and a greater variety of substitution treatment programmes should be made available to problem drug users. Taken together, these two policy initiatives represent an important shift towards acceptance of the principles of harm reduction, which do not sit well with the aspiration for a drug-free society. Furthermore, Goldberg (2004, p. 566) notes that "the proposal also speaks of 'improving drug addicts' life situations'... [which] may be an indication of a possible change in treatment goals from 'cure' to 'care'". Hallam (2010, p. 9) interprets these tentative implementations as a sign that "the social foundations on which the strategy of the drug-free society is built are beginning to shift inexorably". Perhaps this may have been the case; however, a recent decrease in the number of recorded Swedish drug users has only served to further cement the implementation of a control-orientated strategy by the Swedish government.

The perceived rise in number of drug users during the 1990s provided the impetus for a re-examination of drug policy, culminating in the 2001 report of the Drugs Commission. Estimates of the number of drug users since a refocusing of state attention on the problem of illicit drugs show a significant decrease (CAN, 2009; Hallam, 2010; Ministry of Health and Social Affairs, 2008). Many have interpreted this decline in numbers of drug users as being directly related to renewed efforts to enforce a control-oriented policy in the field of drugs. The United Nations Office on Drugs and Crime (2007) went so far as to publish a report entitled *Sweden's Successful Drug Policy: A Review of the Evidence* which reports a 35 per cent drop in lifetime prevalence among ninth graders between 2001 and 2006. UNODC (2007, p. 35) have attributed this dramatic decrease to "Sweden's drug policy... [which] seems to have played, once again, a significant role in lowering drug use levels in this country in recent years." Such an analysis may, however, be over-simplistic and, indeed, such a case has been put forward by Swedish academics working in the field.

The Swedish statistics relating to numbers of drug users in Sweden do not give a complete picture. Whilst comparing favourably with other EU member states in this area, as well as showing a national decrease from previous years, Cohen (2006, p. 3) accuses this success as relying on "hand-picked data". In other areas of drug-related statistics, Sweden is reported to have the fastest growing drug-related mortality in the EU (EMCDDA, 2002). Ramstedt (2006) posits that drug-related deaths have increased from 186 to 391 between 1991 and 2002. Furthermore, Hallam (2010) states that problematic drug use is very high in Sweden, taken as a proportion of overall drug use, a point which is recognized by UNODC (2007) itself on page 49.

Nevertheless, the strongest message being signalled from this research, both by the Swedish national government and by international bodies such as United Nations Office on Drugs and Crime, is that Swedish style control-oriented drug policy is a success that should continue to be marketed to other countries. In real terms, this almost certainly means that Swedish drug policy will continue to remain one of strict control that adheres to its goal, in principle at least, of a drug-free society, for the foreseeable future. While some inevitable concessions to the principle of harm reduction have been made, these are unlikely to result in any significant shift towards a more liberal overall policy.

5
The Netherlands

The development of drug policy in the Netherlands has been of a relatively liberal nature with its focus on the normalization of drug users, the separation of the markets for hard and soft drugs and the emphasis on reducing the harm that is a consequence of an illegal drug policy. An exploration of the historical development of drug policy in this country serves as an example of the development of the more liberal paradigm of drug policy in operation in Europe today. The history presented here will illuminate the origins of policies unique to the Netherlands, such as the legal grey area of coffee shops where cannabis may be bought and sold without fear of prosecution, and will examine the evidence that suggests the Netherlands may be moving towards a more restrictive interpretation of its national drug policy than previously seen.

Pre-1960s

Due to its colonial history and early involvement in the trade of both opium and cocaine, the Netherlands was one of the first countries in Europe to have a law relating to illegal drugs with its Opium Act of 1919. Prior to this law, and throughout the 1800s, the Netherlands owned colonies in the East Indies which were major producers of opiates. For the duration of this colonial era, "drugs played a major part both in the Dutch economy and in traditional medicines ... [and] colonial revenues depended for a large part on opium profits" (de Kort and Korf, 1992, p. 124). By the beginning of the twentieth century, it was not just opium that was profitable to the Dutch and an important part of the thriving economy. Trade in cocaine had become equally important, with the Netherlands becoming the largest cocaine producer in the world, sending most of the produce to the Dutch Cocaine Factory in Amsterdam, established in 1900 (de Kort, 1994).

The Dutch were therefore eager to assume a prominent role at the first international conferences on narcotics, given this dependence on cocaine and opiates for economic trade. At the international conference in The Hague in 1912, they provided important counterarguments to the US call for strict regulation of the manufacture of opiates and cocaine, arguing against overly strict regimens, citing an enormous boost to illegal drug trafficking as an undesirable consequence (Korf *et al.*, 1999). Remaining largely opposed to the prohibitive terms of the resulting convention, ratification was a difficult decision for the Dutch, who probably only complied due to pressure from ethical movements within the Netherlands, and from the international community in general. Once the international agreement had been ratified, each country had to develop their own national drug policy. Accordingly, in 1919, the Netherlands passed the Opium Act which made transporting and dealing in drugs illegal. De Kort and Korf (1992, p. 133) explain that Dutch "companies were still able to continue trading under a licensing system but this did not prevent a massive smuggling traffic from developing".

After ratifying The Hague convention, the Dutch became very repressive towards the illicit drug trade. However, control measures were not aimed at users who, in most cases, could obtain their drugs legally (Korf *et al.*, 1999). While the police and justice authorities were keen to treat trade as a legal problem, the Department of Public Health ensured a socio-medical model of treatment was employed regarding users. At this time, it was almost exclusively opiates and amphetamines that were being used, and both medical authorities and the police recognized the need to avoid the criminalization of users to prevent exacerbating the problem of illegal trade (Tops, 2001).

This situation continued until the early 1950s when cannabis began to have an impact on the Dutch drug scene. "The 1950s can be seen as the introductory phase of cannabis in the Netherlands, when marijuana was used by small groups of jazz musicians and other artists who had learned to use it while abroad, as well as foreign seamen and German based US military personnel" (Korf, 2002, p. 853). In 1953, the possession and use of cannabis products was added to the Opium Act, which caused a change in the way users were viewed and treated. Tops (2001) explains that cannabis products lacked any medical usage and therefore control of use was seen as a matter for the law rather than for the medical profession. Rather than being categorized as patients in need of medical help, cannabis users were defined as deviant, and the practice of non-prosecution was abandoned for this drug in favour of an American style line of strict repression.

Prior to this period of illegal drug control, the Netherlands had also developed a strong alcohol policy which is worth exploring briefly to examine its possible influence on drug policy in later years. In the nineteenth century, Dutch society was organized into a system of strong societal blocks or pillars related to different ideologies such as Catholics, Protestants, Jews, socialists, liberals and so on, which later developed into trade unions and temperance movements, and were much stronger in governing the behaviour of the Dutch people belonging to them than the central state was (Levine and Reinarman, 1991). When alcohol was perceived to have caused a problem in the nineteenth century, these societal blocks formed influential anti-alcohol movements, especially against spirits.

The strong involvement of temperance movements in controlling alcohol policy is similar to the situation described in Sweden. However, the main differences were that, in the Netherlands, the state was never fully in control of alcohol, preferring to leave the societal blocks to use persuasion rather than force in preventing the use of alcohol, creating a clear difference in policy relating to "soft" alcohol such as beer, and "hard" alcohol such as spirits. This was achieved by the introduction of special shops where hard liquor could be bought, while allowing only beer and low alcohol drinks to be purchased from supermarkets and ordinary shops.

Between 1890 and 1950, the use of alcohol decreased greatly within the Netherlands – even in comparison with other countries (Levine and Reinarman, 1991). This decrease was perceived as being due to the success, not of laws from the government, but the largely non-coercive measures introduced by societal blocks, and also due to the policy of separating hard and soft forms of alcohol. It is these early features of alcohol policy within the Netherlands with which clear parallels to later policy initiatives regarding the control of the use of illegal drugs can be drawn.

1960s

The 1960s were a time of cultural and societal upheaval and change in the Netherlands, as in most European countries at that time. The strong societal blocks that had been so influential in the implementation of alcohol control policy began to decrease in influence and importance as people rejected being told how to live, think and behave. "During the 'cultural revolution' of the 1960s, patronising control over people's personal lives by religious, political and community leaders was rapidly replaced by self-determination at the family and individual levels" (Kaplan *et al.*, 1994, p. 318). In the absence of a strong central governing state, the 1960s was an era with a lack of guiding influences on behaviour. It was at exactly this time that use of cannabis in Dutch society began to increase markedly.

Occurring simultaneously, the use of cannabis became identified with this move away from societal blocks and with counterculture in general as groups of young people, particularly artists and students, began to regularly hold demonstrations in the centre of Amsterdam at which they frequently smoked cannabis publicly. This use of cannabis rapidly gained in popularity and became associated with "a form of protest against dominant bourgeois culture in general" (Korf, 2002, p. 853). The government in place at the time did not have much experience of influencing people's behaviour, and was unable, at least initially, to provide a comprehensive strategy for dealing with these new problems.

Throughout this period, the police reacted with repressive measures against the use of cannabis. These repressive reactions became more severe as parents, educators and legislators became aware that drug use and counterculture was appealing to young people in general (Leuw, 1994). Penalties for being caught with cannabis at this time were quite severe and could result in imprisonment. In addition to this, the clashes between young people and the police had become increasingly violent, with large numbers of arrests taking place on an almost daily basis.

Towards the end of the 1960s, after a few years of this increasingly untenable situation, it began to be tentatively suggested that perhaps a policy of repression was not having the desired results. Judges and law enforcers realized that normal young people were being increasingly criminalized to no apparent purpose. Reservations about the treatment of drug users, and young cannabis users in particular, quickly became widespread and led to "a growing debate in professional journals and in the daily papers about the merits of the conventional views of drug use" (Cohen, 1994, p. 2). It was clear that the government needed to turn its attention to the formulation of drug policy in order to prevent this undesirable situation in which large numbers of young people were being criminalized because of their drug use.

By 1968, recognition of the need to produce a more effective drug policy, or at least one that was not so damaging to the youth population, was so strong that two commissions were appointed to investigate the parameters of the drug problem and possible solutions to dealing with it. The first commission was set up in 1968 by the National Federation of Mental Health, and was chaired by Louk Hulsman. The commission also included law enforcement officials, alcohol treatment experts, psychiatrists, a drug use researcher and a sociologist, and their broadly defined task was to "clarify factors that are associated with the use of drugs, to give insight into the phenomenon as a whole, and to suggest proposals for a rational policy" (Cohen, 1994, p. 2).

In the same year, a more official commission with a highly similar goal was appointed by the Department of Public Health. It was led by Pieter Baan, and was asked "to investigate causes of increasing drug use, how to confront irresponsible use of drugs, and to propose a treatment system for those who developed dependence of these drugs" (Cohen, 1994, p. 2). It would be several years before either of the commissions would make their final reports, but from the beginning of their investigations the treatment of cannabis users became gradually more tolerant and less repressive. The launch of these commissions marks the beginning of a pragmatic approach to drug policy within the Netherlands. Society had accepted that some young people were going to rebel and use drugs. They were now seeking an alternative to imprisonment and criminal justice sanctions that were so damaging to these young people.

Throughout the whole of the 1960s, it was predominantly cannabis that was treated with repression. The socio-medical model formulated in the 1920s regarding users of opiates and amphetamines was largely upheld throughout this period. Users of these drugs were not prosecuted, and were given access to treatment, either at places traditionally developed to deal with alcoholics or, in the case of heroin users in the late 1960s, being given methadone (Mol and Trautmann, 1992a).

1970s

By 1970, practice regarding the regulation of cannabis use in the Netherlands had effectively evolved into a policy of toleration. Scientific research, and preliminary reports from the two drugs commissions, unanimously rejected the continuation of repression with regard to these drug users (Korf *et al.*, 1999). In 1971, the final report of the Hulsman commission was delivered. Its main recommendations, cited by Cohen (1994), were that the use and possession of small quantities of cannabis should be removed from the criminal law immediately and therefore effectively be legalized. Possession of larger amounts and distribution should remain illegal, but as a misdemeanour rather than as a

serious criminal offence. It also recommended that the use and possession of other drugs should be regarded as misdemeanours for the time
being, and in the long run should also be removed from the criminal
law. Finally, those who did become dependent on drugs should have
adequate treatment institutions at their disposal.

In 1972, the officially recognized Baan commission produced its
report which was very similar in summary to that of the Hulsman commission. In conclusion, however, it recommended the ultimate decriminalization, rather than legalization, of cannabis (Lap and Drucker,
1994), based on the assessment of a relative scale of risk relating to
different illegal drugs (Leuw, 1994). Hard drugs such as heroin and
amphetamine were judged to present an unacceptable level of risk to
society, and therefore should be governed by criminal law. However, the
level of risk cannabis presented to society was minimal and therefore did
not need to be regulated by law, which could cause more damage than
the drug itself. It became a crucial point of policy to avoid marginalizing
and stigmatizing young people experimenting with cannabis, and thus
increasing the risk that they would be drawn towards more dangerous
drugs and criminal subcultures. In short, the risks of drug use for the
individual and society as a whole must be limited as far as possible (de
Kort and Cramer, 1999).

The division of policy between "hard" and "soft", with its similarities
to processes taken in Dutch alcohol policy, represented a further step
towards the adoption of a practical and pragmatic drug policy in the
Netherlands. Since the implementation of the Baan commission's recommendations in 1976, this idea, which came generally to be known
as the "separation of the markets", has been a cornerstone of Dutch
drug policy. An important consideration in the development of this
principle is that these debates and recommendations took place in an
environment in which a heroin epidemic had not yet occurred. Had
such an epidemic already taken place (and drug users not largely been
perceived as highly educated and relatively privileged young people),
the outcomes might have been very different.

In 1976, the government revised the Opium Act, implementing the
recommendations of the Baan commission regarding the use and possession of cannabis which was, from this date, largely decriminalized. The
1976 legislation also laid the foundations of a comprehensive national
drug policy, including education, prevention and treatment, that is still
largely in place today. Boekhaut van Solinge (1999) outlines the major
legal change as creating a distinction between drugs with unacceptable
health risks (for example, cocaine, amphetamine, heroin and LSD) in

schedule I, and cannabis products, which do not present unacceptable health risks, in schedule II. This formal differentiation between the two different kinds of drugs would allow the implementation in the future of different policies regarding the different categories of drugs, thus cementing the idea of "separating the markets" for hard and soft drugs.

Further legislation regarding cannabis products was included in the 1976 amendment of the Opium Act. Possession of 30 grams or more of cannabis was to be maintained as a serious offence. However, possession of smaller amounts was to be regarded as a misdemeanour, and assigned a low priority for prosecution (Boekhout van Solinge, 1999). In order to facilitate this system, the "expediency principle" was introduced to Paragraph 167 of the Dutch Code of Criminal Procedure in 1979. This principle was a tool authorizing non-prosecution for cannabis misdemeanours as not being in the general interest of society and is a watered down version of the Swiss "legality principle" questioning the illegality of a substance where such a position is not in the general interest of society. This position is summarized by Korf (1990, p. 24): "Since the possession of small amounts of hashish or marijuana is only a petty offence, and a repressive policy towards soft drugs would lead to a dangerous overlap with the hard drug market, such a policy would not serve the public interest. So there are no good reasons for a structural, active investigation and prosecution of cannabis offences."

Coffee shops, however, were not officially recognized, nor, at this time, were they a widespread phenomenon. After the publication of the reports of the Hulsman and Baan commissions, the first unofficial coffee shop had been opened but this was by no means a situation that was immediately accepted by the police (Tops, 2001). Instead, Boekhout van Solinge (1999) describes how "house dealers" were tolerated in youth centres from the change to the Opium Act in 1976. House dealers were allowed to sell cannabis products to young people under protection from prosecution in an effort to keep young people who wanted to use cannabis away from harder drugs and the associated criminal subcultures. Towards the end of the 1970s, this practical system of "house dealers" was gradually replaced by the introduction of coffee shops, although it was not until 1980 that they were officially recognized, and some attempt was made to regulate them.

While this intensive debate and policy change regarding cannabis was occurring, a new drug problem had quietly emerged on the Dutch scene. In 1972, heroin arrived in the Netherlands. The introduction of heroin did not have much impact on the change in legislation regarding cannabis, other than to help to persuade police and the medical profession that there was a difference between one drug and the other. Had the heroin epidemic exploded slightly earlier, it may have influenced public opinion against any relaxation in the policy towards drugs and drug users of any kind.

Initially, the people involved with heroin were "white, middle-class young Dutch natives [whose] lifestyle... was counter cultural and critical of society" (de Kort and Cramer, 1999, p. 482). For this reason, policy was initially fairly repressive and any treatment options were strongly focused on abstinence, and were often based on existing alcohol treatment programmes (Wever, 1994). However, this situation was rapidly to change as the underprivileged classes and racial minorities became involved with heroin.

The Surinamese and Chinese, in particular, became heavily involved in heroin dealing and heroin use. This situation directly prompted the authorities to extend methadone services to "hard to reach" dependents by providing bus services as a mobile, low threshold initiative. In Amsterdam, low threshold services designed to reach out to those dependents not attracted to abstinence-based treatment were also developed at this time. For example, an inhabitant of central Amsterdam, Johan Rimans, established the Belangenvereniging Druggebruikers (Amsterdam Users' Association) in 1975. The society received a municipal subsidy in 1977 and was to be highly influential in implementing the extension of methadone services as well as the provision of clean needles. Drug use was beginning to become a semi-accepted part of society and interventions were being designed that would improve the quality of life for drug users and those around them, without necessarily forcing users to become abstinent.

The 1970s therefore marked a major turning point in Dutch drug policy, with the decriminalization of cannabis, the "separation of the markets" policy and the foundations of harm reduction measures in dealing with seriously involved dependents. These practices of harm reduction were to improve and develop into an important strand of national policy in the 1980s.

1980s

The advent of AIDS and HIV in the 1980s also made an impact on Dutch drug policy, in this case leading to the important Dutch concept of "normalization" of the drug user. This concept has become as important a defining strand of Dutch drug policy as the separation of the markets policy implemented at the beginning of the 1970s. It is a further example of the pragmatic nature of Dutch drug policy – drug users are accepted as a normal part of society and drug policy initiatives try to reach out to these people rather than isolating them.

The implementation of this policy strand was brought about by a second boom in the heroin using population that had occurred, comprising mainly of "deprived young people with a low level of education, most of whom came from non-Dutch ethnic groups" (de Kort and Cramer, 1999, p. 482). This situation caused the further expansion and development of harm reduction measures that had been introduced to the Netherlands in the 1970s. Initiatives mainly consisted of risk minimization services, for example, providing accessible methadone services and needle exchange programmes as advocated by the Dutch Medisch-sociale Dienst Heroïne Gebruikers organization for heroin users. A further goal was to reach out to this new group of drug dependents and bring them into contact with treatment services. However, within the concept of normalization exists the idea that if a drug dependent does not wish to seek treatment, harm reduction measures are still more appropriate in dealing with them than law enforcement ones.

The concept of "normalization" can be viewed as the "result of almost twenty years of drug policy making in the Netherlands of social, medical and judicial experience, and of an ongoing public debate about drugs that is rather open and lively" (van Vliet, 1990, p. 468). It encapsulates the idea that a drug dependent person should, as far as possible, be treated as a normal member of society. In 1985, this important concept was formalized in a report by the Interministerial Steering Group on Alcohol and Drug Policy entitled "Drug Policy in Motion: Towards a Normalisation of Drug Problems". Here, the introduction of a distinction between primary and secondary drug problems became the cornerstone of policy (de Kort and Cramer, 1999). Primary problems were designated as those caused directly by the use of drugs, whereas secondary problems refer to those incurred as a negative consequence of the line of policy implemented.

In addition to the ideology of "normalising" drug dependents, important policy measures regarding the regulation of coffee shops and the evaluation and adaptation of treatment services were also implemented in the early 1980s. In 1980, the idea of a coffee shop as a replacement for "house dealers" and a safe environment in which people of all ages could obtain cannabis without coming into contact with hard drugs had been officially recognized, and a set of formal regulations had been imposed. In accordance with these regulations, coffee shops were not permitted to advertise themselves, to cause undue public nuisance, to sell to people under 18 years of age, to sell more than 30 grams to any one customer or to sell or permit the use of hard drugs on the premises.

De Kort and Cramer (1999) have commented that allowing cannabis to be sold in this manner causes a contradiction in terms of drug policy. Coffee shops are legally recognized and the sale of cannabis in them is tolerated, but the supply of cannabis to coffee shops remains illegal. It therefore represents an unusual situation that has occurred as policy has changed over time in reaction to specific aspects of the drug problem in the Netherlands. After the implementation of these regulations, and the legal recognition of the phenomenon of coffee shops, the number of coffee shops boomed throughout the 1980s.

With regard to treatment policy, the suggestion of providing heroin dependents with legal supplies of heroin, allowing them to maintain their habit with minimal cost to society, had been raised in the early 1980s. At this time it had been blocked by The Hague due to commitment to international treaties and regulations, however, in consideration of the new policy initiative to "normalize" dependents as far as possible, an evaluation of drug treatment and assistance policies was commissioned in 1986: "The 1986 Review of Alcohol and Drug Policy". The findings of this report justified the increasing implementation of low threshold harm reduction measures as well as the massive expansion of methadone treatment programmes. The emphasis was firmly removed from abstinence to the maintenance of as normal a life as possible for the drug dependent.

Grapendaal *et al.* (1994) evidence these changes to methadone programmes as being organized on a three-tiered system. At the lowest level, methadone buses provided methadone to heroin dependents on a "no questions asked" basis. They drove around the major cities equipped with methadone to dispense to heroin dependents that turned up to use the service. They also carried clean syringes for drug dependents wishing to inject their own supplies of heroin. Clients could also be administered methadone from community stations, where they had to commit to the cessation of use of other drugs, and were entrusted with supplies to last them over the weekend. Finally, methadone could be dispensed by general practitioners to those dependents deemed responsible enough to have a high degree of control over administering drugs to themselves.

These treatment initiatives, and the policy implementations during the 1970s and 1980s relating to coffee shops, the separation of the markets and normalization were all designed to allow drug users to co-exist with normal members of society as harmoniously as possible. However, one area in which this policy goal was not being achieved was in the perception of public nuisance caused by drug dependents. This issue came to a head in the late 1980s. "Downtown areas of the larger Dutch cities became increasingly dominated by a highly visible drug population, creating feelings of uneasiness and annoyance among the public" (Wever, 1994, p. 61). The policy initiatives outlined above were designed partly in response to this, but it was recognized that they did not go far enough in eliminating the problem. To this end, several law enforcement initiatives designed to curb public nuisance caused by drug dependents were also approved.

These initiatives are encapsulated by the project *straatjunks*: "a package of measures designed to push and force the group of so-called 'extremely problematic drug users' to kick the habit" (Mol and Trautmann, 1992b, p. 4). This project was started in January 1989, and allowed the police special powers of arrest against drug users who repeatedly caused a disturbance in the city centre of Amsterdam. If dependents were found to have committed a minor offence at least four times within one year, they were given the choice of imprisonment or participation in a drug treatment programme. In addition to this specific project, the police were also granted new powers to ban drug users from the city centre for up to a fortnight if they were displaying certain behaviours such as carrying items associated with drug use or displaying behaviour associated with intoxification.

Foreign drug users heading for the Netherlands (in order to obtain drugs and escape more repressive drug regimes) were also attracting international criticism and causing problems for Dutch policy makers. Relations were particularly strained with Germany, as such a high number of German drug dependents were found to reside in the Netherlands. These problems were eventually recognized to be as much a factor of the dearth of care and treatment facilities and the generally repressive climate in Germany with regard to drug users, as to the attractions of the Netherlands (Boekhout van Solinge, 1999). Perceptions of drug-related public nuisance on the national front, however, were harder to dispel, and led to the domination of these issues in drug policy in the 1990s.

1990s

Dutch drug policy throughout the late 1970s, 1980s and early 1990s had remained relatively unchanged since the implementation of the 1976 amendment to the Dutch Opium Act. While changes to drug policy had been made where necessary, the policy had not been evaluated as a whole since 1976. In 1995, the government published a review and evaluation of drug policy since 1976 entitled "Drugs Policy in the Netherlands: Continuity and Change". Boekhout van Solinge (1999) explains that, due to significant changes in the political climate of the time, with a new three-party coalition government excluding the Christian-Democratic party for the first time since the 1920s, expectations surrounding this policy review were that shifts towards more liberal policies would emerge. Indeed, the policy review suggested increasing harm reduction measures appropriate to "new" drugs and new drug populations. However, these increases in harm reduction measures were balanced by recommendations of higher enforcement priority and harsher penalties in some areas.

Synthetic drugs, such as ecstasy and other MDMA-type derivatives, had become popular in the Netherlands in the 1990s and provide an example of the bifurcation of policy during this period. To address this situation, some new harm reduction measures, such as pill testing facilities in nightclubs and guidelines ensuring the provision of free water and "chill out areas" at big nightclubs, were introduced. However, a Unit against Synthetic drugs (USD) was created in 1997 to combat the large factories intended for the production of ecstasy and other synthetic drugs that had sprung up across the country (Collins, 1999). A further example of this bifurcation of policy relating to illicit drugs in the 1990s is provided by the tolerance of safe rooms in which users could take their drugs without risking intervention from the authorities. While outwardly complying with the principles of normalization and harm reduction, seeking to improve the living conditions of users, this measure was as much about ensuring a reduction of drug-related harm to local neighbourhoods. Law enforcement strategies against the production of and trafficking in hard drugs were also increased, and harsher penalties for these offences were introduced at this time.

Some of the most important, as well as the most reported and debated, changes implemented in "Drugs Policy in the Netherlands: Continuity and Change" were related to the policy on coffee shops. Throughout the early 1990s, it had become clear that increasing numbers of coffee shops had led to problematic situations regarding public nuisance and the introduction of restrictive measures in this area was felt to be desirable (de Kort and Cramer, 1999). The maximum amount of cannabis allowed to be sold to one individual customer was lowered from 30 grams to 5 grams, but the amount of cannabis a coffee shop was allowed to hold on its premises at any one point of time was increased from 30 grams to 500 grams.

New regulations governing coffee shops were also introduced, such as not being allowed to operate near a school or to cause public nuisance. Local authorities were also granted more extensive powers to ban or close coffee shops contravening any of the new or old regulations. At the same time, municipal governments were granted the autonomy to decide whether to allow coffee shops within their boundaries at all (Boekhout van Solinge, 1999). These new policy implementations led to a significant reduction in the number of coffee shops from 1179 in 1997 to 813 in 2000 (EMCDDA National Report, 2001a), and were heralded in the international press as a sign that Dutch drug policy was on the way towards becoming more repressive.

The most controversial and dynamic change to Dutch drug policy in the 1990s was the introduction of an experimental programme providing heroin on legal prescription to long-term dependents who had failed to abstain under other treatment programmes. The possibility of such an experiment had first been raised in the 1970s, but had been rejected over and over again in favour of the expansion of methadone programmes and abstention-based treatment programmes. De Kort and Cramer (1999) report, however, that the heroin dependent population had become increasingly medically and socially deprived, and existing treatment programmes and services were no longer judged to be adequate. These perceptions provided the environment in which the question of legally prescribed heroin could again be raised. Under the concept of "normalization", drug dependents could be accepted as such, and, in an attempt to improve their quality of life, the controlled prescription of their drug could be justified.

In the 1995 policy paper, a recommendation regarding the necessity of legally prescribed heroin was included, and in 1996 parliament gave permission for a small number of trials, subject to very strict controls, to be run. The Minister of Health, Welfare and Sport was to have ultimate responsibility for the trials, with an especially created Central Committee on the Treatment of Heroin Addicts to conduct them (Central Committee for the Treatment of Heroin Addicts, 2000). In July 1998, the Netherlands launched the trials which were designed to supply a combination of heroin and methadone to those dependents that could be proved to be chronically addicted. The provision of heroin and methadone would also be accompanied by psychological and social counselling, and the whole programme was introduced on a trial basis in an attempt to determine whether heroin prescription was actually more effective than methadone prescription.

2000s

Since 2000, many researchers (Lemmens, 2003; Uitermark, 2004) have noticed an increasing tendency towards repression in Dutch drug policy. From 1994 to 2002, Dutch politics had been led by political party coalitions that did not include the Christian-Democrats and had introduced relatively liberal legislation in many areas, including illicit drug policy. However, towards the end of this period, Pim Fortuyn's far right political party gained increasing popular support. Despite the assassination of Fortuyn in 2002, one week before elections were due to be held, this new found popularity for the right translated into an election loss for the left and the eventual formation, in 2003, of a centre-right cabinet in which "tolerance has almost become a forbidden word and the new government wants to turn back to 'old norms and values'" (Garretsen, 2003, p. 3). In the following years Dutch politics is best described as having been in a period of considerable turmoil, but the emphasis has consistently been on moving policy practice towards the right end of the political spectrum. While many issues have been affected by this development of events, the impacts for drug policy have been considerable, with many Dutch politicians now wanting to appear tough on drugs (Uitermark, 2004).

Lemmens (2003, p. 247) notes a shift away from "the characteristic Dutch liberal, harm-reduction policy...[towards a] more repressive Swedish-type model aimed at total abstinence". Supporting evidence for such a shift comes from many areas. Several indicators suggest a further tightening up of coffee shop policy, for example. Intraval (2007) figures show that there has been a recent decrease in the overall numbers of coffee shops as well as in the numbers of municipalities with any coffee shops at all. Uitermark (2004, p. 520) states that there has been "talk of a 'die out' policy, since the number of coffee shops can only go down over time under the present arrangement" and suggests that the Conservative government and media would like to go further leading to a ban on coffee shops altogether. There is also evidence of an increasingly law enforcement-based policy towards ecstasy use and users, probably as a result of the rising role of the Netherlands as a producer of this drug (Uitermark and Cohen, 2005). Finally, the alarming rise in prison numbers for drug-related crimes (Goldberg, 2005) is an indication that "power in the drug field is moving from the Ministry of Health to the Ministry of Justice" (Goldberg, 2005, p. 53).

While the influence of a right-wing government on Dutch drug policy should not be underestimated, the importance of national perception of public nuisance as a direct consequence of a liberal drug policy should not be overlooked either. Several researchers have argued that public acceptance of illegal drug use in the Netherlands is declining (Garretsen, 2003; Goldberg, 2005) and that a new drug policy should "pay more attention to the position of the so-called third party, those who suffer most from issues like drug-related nuisance" (Garretsen, 2003, p. 2). While international criticisms of Dutch drug policy have been relatively consistent across the years, it is only relatively recently that similar criticisms have been levelled from within. People living in areas associated with drug use are becoming increasingly irritated by drug-related nuisance and petty crime, and have become a powerful lobbying group for the reform of drug policy along more repressive lines (Goldberg, 2005). It is this decline in public acceptance, in accordance with a political shift to the right, which have caused a recent tendency towards prohibition in Dutch drug policy.

Nevertheless, despite this well-documented repressive turn, many liberal elements of Dutch drug policy remain, suggesting it still has a place at the forefront of European harm reduction and tolerant drug policy practice. The heroin trials that began in 1998 were extended in 2001 after an overwhelmingly positive evaluation claiming a 25 per cent increase in success rate for improving health and criminal behaviour in the users prescribed heroin itself as opposed to those prescribed methadone (van Kolfschooten, 2002). The right-wing government and the public perception of drug-related nuisance were not without influence in this area of policy making: in 2003 the government stated that political support "is limited to continuing... existing treatment capacity" (Bammer *et al.*, 2003, p. 370). By 2004, however, the scheme had again been extended and Goldberg (2005, p. 45) states that the heroin prescription programme "has now become an established part of Dutch drug policy". Additionally, the last decade has seen the Dutch, along with the UK, become increasingly involved in promoting the potential use of cannabis as a medicine in its own right, particularly in treating multiple sclerosis (Sheldon, 2002). At the end of 2007, despite relatively disappointing take-up of this treatment option, the Minister of Health, Welfare and Sport announced that further development of the medicinal use of cannabis would be extended for another five years (de Jong, 2009).

Given the turbulent nature of Dutch politics over the last decade, it is difficult to make concrete predictions about the future nature of drug policy within the Netherlands. On the one hand, the number of coffee shops is declining and law enforcement-based anti-drug measures are on the increase, but, on the other hand, over the same period of time, heroin prescription trials have become an established part of the national policy and the development of the medicinal use of cannabis has enjoyed governmental support. One suggestion raised by both Goldberg (2005) and Uitermark (2004) is that European calls for harmonization in the field of illicit drug policy have made it more difficult for the Dutch to maintain a drug policy that differs so significantly from the norm. Pressures both from within national borders and from without may therefore be bringing the drug policy of the Netherlands "closer to other European countries in some crucial respects" (Uitermark, 2004, p. 526).

6
Denmark

Denmark provides an example of a country which has long occupied a relatively central position on the liberal–restrictive divide of illegal drug policy in Europe, more by dint of constant movement between liberal and restrictive principles than by commitment to a central position *per se*. Certain defining features of Danish drug policy are rather liberal – for example, the development of a free city (Christiania) in part of Copenhagen where the use and sale of cannabis has long been tolerated – and much discussion has been raised over the implementation of some of the more radical harm reduction measures, such as the provision of safe user rooms and the prescription of heroin to addicts who would otherwise be part of a substitution programme. Its proximity to other Nordic states, where the development of drug policy has proceeded along much more restrictive lines, however, has ensured that these second generation harm reduction measures have not in fact been implemented and that law enforcement measures have remained a high priority in dealing with illegal drugs in Denmark.

There are some signs, however, that Denmark is currently undergoing a more decisive shift in national drug policy strategy and that that shift is towards the more repressive end of the scale. The primary evidence cited for this shift is the effective closure of Christiania as a drug market in Copenhagen and a general tightening of policy towards cannabis and cannabis users throughout the country.

Pre-1970s

Unlike Sweden and the Netherlands, drug policy did not emerge as a priority for governmental decision-making in Denmark until the 1970s, and even then there was much less national cohesion on how best to deal with the issue. Of course, drugs had not been entirely absent from Danish society prior to this time; during the 1940s and 1950s "physicians quietly dispensed narcotics and other drugs of abuse to a small group of so called licensed addicts on authorization from the Central Health Authority" (Jepsen, 1989, p. 21). However, these occasional opiate dependents were not a subject of particular political focus and were regarded as a matter for private medical care implemented at the individual level. The first law covering illegal drug supply, production and trafficking (the Act on Euphoriant Drugs) was passed in the 1950s with relatively minor penalties from a fine to a maximum penalty of two years' imprisonment.

Like other European countries, at this stage, Denmark had much more experience in the control of the legal substance alcohol, rather than illegal drugs. However, again, while Denmark had dealt with the problem of controlling the use of alcohol, it had not done so with the zealousness seen in other Scandinavian and Northern European countries (Jepsen, 1992; Laursen, 1996a). Indeed Jepsen (1995, p. 176) commented that "Denmark has always been characterized by a considerably higher level of alcohol consumption than the other Nordic countries, by a higher level of alcohol related problems and by a very liberal attitude to alcohol problems... Danes are anti-control in relation to alcohol." Perhaps the lack of an existing strong controlling policy in the field of alcohol misuse had a part to play in the lack of development of a strong drug policy or prioritization of the problem, at least in these early stages.

The 1960s in Denmark saw the usual growing impact of illegal drugs on society, an impact that was, in comparison with other Nordic countries, relatively prominent. Typically, the first drug to attract attention was cannabis, coinciding with the boom in youth culture and contributing most heavily to official discourse surrounding the issue at this time. The main question arising from the mid- to late 1960s was whether it should be "legalized, decriminalized, or handled from a restrictive attitude" (Laursen and Jepsen, 2002, p. 26). Very little by way of treatment for people using and/or becoming dependent on drugs was available at this time. Mogens Nimb, a prominent Danish psychologist, had briefly experimented with methadone as a substitution treatment for those dependent on opium, but the results were viewed as inconclusive and further experiments were abandoned (Jepsen, 1996a). Towards the end of this decade, the relaxed and tolerant attitude so far afforded to illicit drugs and their users began to wane as the incidence levels of harder drugs such as morphine base and amphetamine began to rise. In reflection of this, a new paragraph was added to the penal law Act on Euphoriant Drugs increasing the maximum penalties for dealers in illegal drugs. For the first time a connection between illegal drugs and international drug crime and the importance of the role of the penal system in their control were recognized.

Although developments within Danish national drug policy were being made at this time, they were not as significant as in other countries. While the correct approach to dealing with cannabis users or drug traffickers was discussed, there was no underlying attempt to define the terms and nature of the "illicit drug problem". In Sweden, as we have seen, drug policy was beginning to take on a moral dimension by the end of the 1960s. The end of the 1960s was also to be an important time for the Netherlands in their more pragmatic definition of the "illicit drug problem". No such clear aims or objectives were foreseen by Danish national drug policy at this time. Nor was the problem clearly founded in either moralistic or pragmatic terms.

1970s

The 1970s brought the first serious discussion on how to responsibly deal with the problems the use of illegal drugs caused to Danish society. Again, the issue of cannabis use formed a cornerstone of these discussions, particularly as an unusual situation had developed in a corner of Copenhagen known as the Free City of Christiania. Jepsen (1996b) describes how a group of intellectuals and academics had taken over an abandoned military barracks in the city creating a shared commune that had been allowed to develop by the government of the time as a social experiment. Some of those attracted to the Christiania lifestyle were drug users and dealers, and a thriving drug culture was rapidly established. Initially the drug scene revolved around cannabis and a limited use of harder drugs, but, in 1976, as a condition of its continued existence, Christiania outlawed the use of drugs other than cannabis.

Echoing practices in Christiania, Denmark as a whole was struggling to reconcile the use of cannabis among young people, perceived as being relatively harmless, with the increase in the use of drugs such as morphine, heroin and LSD. In an effort to resolve this contradiction, another change to the Act on Euphoriant Drugs was implemented in 1975. The penal law paragraph was changed so that the new maximum penalty for contravening the Act was ten years' imprisonment, with a possible maximum of 15 years in aggravating circumstances. However, in recognition of the fact that cannabis represented a lesser danger than other drugs, the maximum penalty for cannabis was retained at six years' imprisonment. At the same time, the attorney general issued a circular which made the distinction between cannabis and hard drugs, encouraging the police to be more lenient in pursuing cases of cannabis as opposed to harder drugs. The decision to implement a policy recognizing a difference in seriousness between the use of cannabis and other drugs was very important in Denmark. It marked the beginning of a rift between Denmark and the other Nordic countries which, until then, had tried to keep together on policy regarding drugs (Laursen, 1996b). This differentiation between cannabis and other drugs had put Denmark out on a limb.

In addition to the distinction made between cannabis and other drugs in Danish policy, the 1970s also saw considerable extension of the drug treatment system. Similar to the Hassela movement developed in Sweden, and at about the same time, a form of detoxification treatment was initiated where young social workers and young drug users would go away together to small houses in the countryside in search of a drug-free environment. By the end of the 1970s, small methadone programmes had also been established and the practice "of methadone prescribed by GPs for long term maintenance gradually spread" (Jepsen, 1996a, p. 2). The extension of these small-scale methadone programmes into a large-scale, national policy regarding substitution treatment was discussed at this time, but such a system was turned down. Laursen and Jepsen (2002) ascribe this general attitude against the distribution of methadone on a national basis to an unwillingness to surrender to the widespread acceptance of drugs, primarily championed by social–psychological treatment ideologists.

1980s

The 1980s signified a time of turbulence and debate in relation to the issue of drug use with nine parliamentary debates being held between 1980 and 1982. These debates centred on the fact that Denmark had recognized the dominant role of marginalization and social exclusion in relation to the use of illicit drugs, but was also under considerable pressure from the Nordic Council to bring drug policy in line with the rest of Scandinavia by raising penalties for contravening the Act on Euphoriant Drugs and by criminalizing the use of drugs *per se*. This decade saw the beginnings of a Danish drug policy awkwardly caught between toleration of drug users and understanding of the societal problems they faced, and greater efforts to control their activities through the penal system. A middle road was steered between the conflicting principles with some intensification of police control measures but a reluctance to pursue a typically Scandinavian line overall.

In the early 1980s, the recognition of the link between problematic heroin use and social and/or ethnic marginalization, coupled with official statistics showing a dramatic increase in the number of drug-related deaths (Laursen and Jepsen, 2002), contributed to the perception of the drug problem as being strongly related to social factors such as poor housing or health care and suggested that a treatment-oriented response was the most appropriate. On the other hand, new legislation was being enacted to penalize those who profited from drug trafficking and police powers in general were being intensified. Denmark, however, was not wholly persuaded to pursue a typically Scandinavian line with regards to the drug problem. For example, proposals such as the termination of the situation in Christiania and the tightening up of minimum and maximum penalties outlined in the Act on Euphoriant Drugs were rejected.

Developments in the treatment field in the 1980s also differed considerably from those in other Scandinavian countries. Expensive programmes involving trips away to stay in the countryside were judged as unsustainable, but, with the introduction of AIDS and the understanding of the social problems facing some drug users, a treatment solution needed to be found. In 1984, the Official Council on Alcohol and Drugs issued a report calling for the re-evaluation of the treatment goal of abstention. Its results paved the way for the widespread use of methadone maintenance treatment (Jepsen, 1996a).

1990s

Drug policy in the 1990s in Denmark continued along the lines originated in the 1980s and was thus characterized by expansion on both control and harm reduction fronts. In terms of expansion of control measures, in 1990 the Copenhagen police announced its *Narkostrategi 90* which sought to reinforce preventative methods of drug control, increase drug-related education and increase cooperation with other agencies in an effort to clean up the open drug scene that had emerged in the Vesterbro district of the city (Jepsen, 1996b). At the same time, control measures surrounding the policing of Christiania were increased, leading to raids and riots throughout the early 1990s and culminating in 1994 in a, largely ignored, government directive to bring Christiania's drug policy in line with the rest of Denmark.

A further area of police influence was connected to the idea of enforced treatment. The Danish police advocated the idea of implementing more restrictive measures within the treatment system, both to keep people within that system and to prevent them from causing more trouble for the police. Largely due to police influence, the Danish government passed a bill on the detention of drug dependents in treatment centres in 1992 (Laursen, 1999). Rather than being coercive treatment *per se*, this bill allowed a drug dependent and a treatment centre to enter into a contract allowing the centre to forcibly return an absconding drug dependent to treatment.

Despite these considerable increases in police power to combat the illicit drug problem, very little impact was actually made on either the drug market in general or the open drug scenes in Vesterbro and Christiania in particular (Jepsen, 1996b), leading to a prevailing attitude of disappointment in the failure of restrictive policy. This cleared the way for an expansion of harm reduction measures and other liberal practices in the second half of the decade. In 1994, the attorney general issued a reminder that police should deal with first-time cannabis offences by issuing a warning, as laid out in the 1969 directive (Jepsen, 1996b). In addition to this, the government published a White Paper in 1994 which "put Danish drug policy back into an old track in which drug addicts should be treated and not policed" (Laursen and Jepsen, 2002, p. 28). Control measures were not abandoned as such, but the emphasis was placed on treatment services, and the introduction of low threshold facilities designed to help drug dependents and reduce the levels of harm to which they were exposed. For the rest of the decade, most of the policy changes and rhetoric surrounding the problem of illegal drugs centred on the treatment system and social services in general.

The 1990s were very much a decade of mixed messages regarding drug policy. Debate surrounding the failure of the restrictive model was rife and supported to some extent by the government. However, few changes were made to control policy. The issue was sidestepped by improving the treatment system and introducing a new series of harm reduction measures without attempting to address the underlying issues which had led to the failure of more restrictive measures, or to make any underlying change to control measures.

2000s

Over the last years of the 1990s and the very first years of the 2000s, the implementation of some of the more radical harm reduction measures was much debated in Denmark. While many harm reduction measures, such as drop-in centres, street-level nursing and expansion of the methadone system had been implemented in the 1990s, interventions in this area had stopped short of offering either heroin on prescription or safe user rooms. At the end of the 1990s, optimism for the eventual adoption of these measures was fairly high but, in the early 2000s, this optimism was not borne out. Laursen and Jepsen (2002, p. 21) record that, on the recommendation of the International Narcotics Control Board, safe user rooms were "turned down by the Ministry of Health in a secret process of negotiation with Nordic colleagues but without an open debate in parliament". The implementation of prescription heroin trials was more publically debated but was formally turned down at a parliamentary referendum in 2002. Since then, overall national drug policy in Denmark has taken an increasingly repressive turn.

In 2001, a new liberal–conservative government came into power in Denmark with a much more law enforcement-orientated approach to drug policy encapsulated in their 2003 document *The Fight Against Drugs: Action Plan Against Drug Misuse*. Anker *et al.* (2008, p. 17) comment that the very language used in this document "resembles the American drug rhetoric of 'war on drugs' " and Laursen Storgaard (2005, p. 36) designates the resultant changes "some of the most significant...in Danish drug policy over the last 40 years". Under the terms of this document, any distinction between the sale and purchase of drugs has been removed, as has the differentiation between types of drugs that may be involved in offences. Sentences relating to drug offences have also risen substantially and are now comparable for those administered in cases of manslaughter and murder (Asmussen, 2008). The overall tone of the policy is one of zero tolerance with increasing recourse to law enforcement measures to be practiced against dependent drug users to the point where "no amount of drugs is too small for confiscation, even if they are single doses of drugs that a user in withdrawal desperately needs" (Frantszen, 2003, p. 50).

The regulation of cannabis, in particular, has become increasingly tough in recent years. As previously described, Denmark has always practiced a particularly liberal national drug policy with respect to cannabis, most obviously observed in its free trade within the walls of the free city of Christiania. At the end of the 1990s, a situation had arisen involving the unofficial implementation of "hash clubs" along the lines of the Dutch coffee shop policy. Hash clubs had sprung up across Denmark, providing a safe place for cannabis to be purchased and used by young people without risk of coming into contact with harder drugs. There was a push to officially recognize the existence of these clubs which Asmussen and Moesby-Johansen (2004) blame for the sudden governmental tightening of cannabis controls at this time. Instead of allowing the semi-legal situation to continue, a law outlawing hash clubs was implemented in 2001 and the distinction between cannabis and other drugs was removed in 2004, thus criminalizing cannabis possession for personal use. The new laws also stipulate that small-scale dealing of cannabis should attract a penalty of imprisonment and that there should be no right of waiver for first-time offences (Laursen Storgaard, 2005). Once these initial laws against cannabis had been implemented, the next area relating to drug policy to attract attention was Christiania itself.

Up until the 2000s, Christiania had been left to pursue its singular practice of permitting the trade in cannabis within its confines by successive Danish national governments. There had been occasional threats to bring an end to the situation resulting in clashes between the occupants of Christiania and the Danish police force. These, however, had eventually come to nothing and trade in cannabis had continued more or less unchecked. Asmussen (2007, p. 15) describes Pusher Street, the centre of cannabis trade in Christiania, in 2003 as consisting "of about 40 decorated stalls where different kinds of cannabis were sold". Yet, one year later, in 2004, Pusher Street was closed and the police presence in this area vastly increased in what Asmussen (2008, p. 165) deems "a 'show of strength', as seen in...the use of undercover agents, the simultaneous arrest of so many dealers and security guards [and] the involvement of detectives from Norway and Sweden". Since this crackdown, there have been several clashes between the police and potential cannabis traders in the Christiania area, but Pusher Street has remained closed. Asmussen (2007) reports that cannabis use and dealing continues in Christiania but that it is now a hidden activity and that it has also been dispersed to other parts of the city.

It is important to document here that, although Denmark has always reported relatively high levels of cannabis use in European terms, there is no indication that cannabis dealing had changed or increased in the years leading up to the wider cannabis changes recorded here (Asmussen, 2008). If the new laws and policy initiatives had come in response to a worsening illegal drug problem, they may have been seen less as a clear step towards a repressive policy and more as a legitimate response to an increasing problem. As it is, it is very difficult to argue that anything other than a serious tightening of national policy has occurred, with ever-increasing recourse to law enforcement and zero tolerance methods, despite the fact that such a move may appear to buck European trends. To this end, Laursen and Jepsen (2002, p. 21) argue that Danish drug policy has "in recent years approached the restrictiveness of hardliners of Sweden and the United States" and Laursen Storgaard (2005, p. 45) cautions that "Denmark has clearly moved back to a more restrictive and prohibitionist stance since 2001".

7
Portugal

Portugal provides a strong example of a country that has, in terms of illegal drug policy, relatively recently made a bold move from a fairly central position along the liberal–repressive continuum to a much more liberal one. In 2001, radical new laws were introduced, greatly increasing the influence of harm reduction principles in general and removing criminal sanctions from the personal possession and use of all illegal drugs in particular. Initially surrounded by doubt and uncertainty, the implementation of these new laws has now been extensively evaluated, on both a national and an international basis, and the result has been overwhelmingly positive. A historical exploration of the development of drug policy in Portugal highlights the factors that have resulted in this fundamental change to national drug strategy.

In comparison to the other countries discussed here in detail, much less information is generally available about the illicit drug problem in Portugal and the specific national drug strategy that has been implemented. Much has been written for an international audience about the radical change to Portuguese drug law that took place in 2001, but little is known about the historical context of national drug policy development outside of Portugal itself. The first national survey of drug use was not implemented until 2001 (Balsa *et al.*, 2002) and research into the prevalence of drug use or the wider nature of the drug problem was not initiated until the 1980s (Hughes, 2006). As van het Loo *et al.* (2002, p. 53) remark, data on drug use in Portugal is therefore "scant and not reliable". For these reasons, drug policy in Portugal will here be examined in only three sections: prior to 1990, the 1990s and the 2000s.

Prior to 1990

The first drug law was developed in Portugal in 1926 and was directed at drug traffickers rather than drug users; in fact, the consumption of drugs was not even mentioned in this document. This is perhaps unsurprising, considering Portugal's location at the South Westerly tip of Europe, making it an ideal gateway for drug trafficking from countries outside of Europe to countries within Europe. Hughes and Stevens (2010) state that the three main drugs trafficked through Portugal are cocaine from Brazil and Mexico, heroin from Spain and cannabis from Morocco and Southern Africa. It is important to note, however, that the vast majority of drugs that are trafficked into Portugal are destined for other countries in Europe and that Portugal is therefore more of a trafficking route than a destination country. Consumption of drugs in Portugal did not become widespread until the 1970s and 1980s. Prior to this, drugs were consumed by a small number of well-off members of society and use was mainly restricted to cannabis (Hughes, 2006). Drug use therefore did not attract significant attention or sanction from the authorities.

The use of drugs themselves did not become a criminal offence, written into the Portuguese penal code, until 1970 when teenagers and less well-off members of society began to be involved, still on a very small scale, in the phenomenon, but, even at this time, sanctions were regarded as symbolic and were not heavily enforced (Hughes, 2006). A Portuguese expert on drugs, Candido Agra (summarized from the Portuguese in Hughes, 2006), has written an extensive history of the development of Portuguese drug policy and describes the mid- to late 1970s as a time during which an interdisciplinary approach to illicit drugs was implemented, encompassing not just the criminal justice field but also psycho-social and medical practitioners. In 1974, the dictatorship governing Portugal ended and the new laws that were developed put considerable emphasis on human rights and proportionality in punishment (Hughes, 2006) which may have contributed to the beginnings of a movement to view illicit drugs as more than a criminal justice-related issue.

In 1983, a new drug law was implemented in Portugal incorporating elements of UN drug policy conventions and updating Portuguese national drug policy. Agra (cited in Hughes, 2006) notes that, for the first time, a distinction was drawn between drug traffickers, who were viewed primarily as delinquents, and drug users, who were viewed primarily as patients in need of treatment and cure. This change in the law coincided with a relatively rapid increase in the use of drugs in Portugal as well as a move from cannabis as the most popular drug of choice towards cocaine and heroin (Mendes, 2000). Perhaps because of this increase, Almeida (cited in Hughes, 2006) documents that, despite the supposedly symbolic nature of punishment for drug users, in practice penalties for drug use began to increase at this time. Illegal drugs were no longer the pastime of the elite few or of rebellious youth but had entered into society as a whole.

As a direct result of this rise in drug use amongst the general population, a National Drug Abuse Prevention Programme, *Projecto Vida* (Project Life), was initiated in 1987. Hughes (2006, p. 51) describes how the first stage of this programme, which continued into the 1990s, used "shock tactics" to try to prevent people and, in particular young people, from consuming drugs. Hughes (2006) further suggests that one of the over-arching objectives of Projecto Vida was to develop a national drug policy that addressed drug use as well as drug trafficking, through the medium of education and the development of treatment options. As Projecto Vida developed in the late 1980s and early 1990s the focus shifted from shock tactics to treatment services and addicts were increasingly afforded non-criminal sanctions (Allen *et al.*, 2004).

During most of the time period covered here, illegal drugs were an issue ascribed relatively low political importance in Portugal. Hughes (2006, p. 52) suggests that the key influences on Portuguese national drug policy were "international pressure to criminalize drug use and trafficking and the ideological objective of a drug-free lifestyle". These influences contributed to the initial development of criminal justice sanctions and inhibited the development of harm reduction measures such as needle exchange and substitution treatment that were gaining popularity elsewhere in Europe. Throughout the 1970s and 1980s, neither the Ministry of Justice nor the Ministry of Health took ultimate control of the problem and the issue bounced back and forth between them (Hughes, 2006) making it difficult for a coherent national strategy to be developed. In the 1990s, this was to change as Portuguese drug policy matured and gained a distinctive flavour of its own.

1990s

The 1990s was a decade of turbulence and change for Portuguese drug policy. Over this time period an issue that had previously been ascribed only low importance and that had been dominated by increasingly severe laws and poor harm reduction development was to be prioritized and drug users themselves were to be placed firmly at the centre of policy making. The beginnings of this process were, however, relatively slow. The first needle exchange programmes were implemented, as part of Projecto Vida, in 1993, but, in the same year, a new law was introduced increasing maximum penalties for drug users to three months' imprisonment for possession of small amounts and one year's imprisonment for larger amounts (Allen *et al.*, 2004). The maximum penalty for the trafficking of drugs was 12 years' imprisonment, but, in practice, the penalty was reduced for users who sold drugs to finance their own consumption (ELDD, 2010). The further development of harm reduction measures at this time was hampered by a continued commitment to abstinence and a drug-free ideology. For example: "the head of the Drug Addiction Treatment and Prevention Service (SPTT) Dr Jose Castanheira who was appointed in 1994 was openly anti-methadone. As he summed up, harm reduction would encourage drug use" (Hughes, 2006, p. 99).

As the 1990s progressed, however, the number of drug users and, perhaps more importantly, the number of dependent drug users, increased dramatically, forcing the Portuguese government to place more emphasis on the illicit drug problem and to develop appropriate strategies. Mendes (2000) reported that in the mid-1990s there were an estimated 25,000–100,000 drug users out of a population of ten million. Portugal developed a significant population of heroin users with six to ten cases per 1000 adults being reported in the 1990s (Allen *et al.*, 2004). Rates of drug-related infectious diseases such as HIV, AIDS and hepatitis B and C increased dramatically from 47 in 1990 to 590 in 1997 (Hughes and Stevens, 2010), while arrests for drug-related offences increased from 4667 in 1991 to 6380 in 1995 and 11,395 in 1998 (van het Loo *et al.*, 2002). A significant proportion of heroin users were injecting drug users which Allen *et al.* (2004) have attributed as contributing to the rises in infectious diseases and arrests reported above as well as a threefold increase in drug-related deaths during this decade. At the end of the 1980s, Portugal had joined the EU and, as encouraged by the EMCDDA, had begun research and data collection regarding the illegal drug problem. International comparisons provided by the EMCDDA helped to highlight the significance of Portugal's drug problem as Portugal compared unfavourably with other European countries in terms of drug-related deaths, drug-related infectious diseases and drug-related arrests (Allen *et al.*, 2004; Hughes, 2006).

One particular aspect of the rising drug problem in Portugal deserves further mention here: the development of one of the largest and most notorious open drug scenes in Europe – Casal Ventoso. Located on the outskirts of Lisbon, Casal Ventoso was "a slum, characterized by extreme poverty and social exclusion amongst a predominantly migrant population" (Hughes, 2006, p. 85). In the late 1980s and early 1990s, Casal Ventoso became a drug mecca for Portuguese heroin addicts, with up to 5000 visiting each day and with problems such as HIV and homelessness being pervasive (Hughes, 2006). Dr Jackob Hartman, a Dutch psychiatrist, noted its unique position amongst open drug scenes in Europe: "It can only be compared with what I have seen in The Bronx, in the City of New York, many years ago" (cited in Hughes, 2006, p. 36). Casal Ventoso served as a highly visible indicator of the rising drug problem in Portugal, particularly as it attracted increasing media coverage in the late 1990s (Hughes, 2006), and impacted upon both the Portuguese government and the general population in terms of increasing the importance attributed to the drug problem at this time.

In 1995, a Socialist government was elected in Portugal and an increased emphasis was placed on solving the drug problem. In response to highly visible rising levels of drug use and dependent drug use, as well as increasing recognition of their consequences for wider society, harm reduction measures began to be implemented in Portugal at an increased rate, and the need for drug policy reform was recognized. Hughes (2006) documents the provision of mobile needle exchange programmes from 1996, outreach work from 1997 and methadone treatment programmes from 1998. At the same time, an influential group of health professionals and politicians, including the President of Portugal, Jorge Sampaio, began to advocate strongly for a change in the national drug policy strategy (Hughes, 2006). It is important to note here that the over arching impetus behind the appeal for reform was not that illegal drugs were an insignificant problem that should therefore avoid criminal sanction, but that they were "a highly significant problem [and] that criminalization was *exacerbating* the problem" (Greenwald, 2009, p. 6).

In the late 1990s, steps towards drug policy reform in Portugal gathered pace. In January 1997, drug abuse was declared the public enemy number one and in 1998, a Commission for a National Drug Strategy (CNDS) was appointed. Allen *et al.* (2004, p. 2) describe how the commission comprised "a panel of experts, including leading academics and medical professionals" who would work towards producing a proposal for a national drugs strategy that would be based on the best of scientific knowledge and evidence (Council of Ministers, 1999). The overwhelming conclusion reached by the commission was that the last 20 years of drug policy in Portugal had been a failure (Hughes, 2006) and detailed recommendations for the development of future strategy in this area were given. By far the most famous of these was to decriminalize the personal use of all drugs so that drug users would not be criminalized or stigmatized because of their drug use, but would instead be drawn to the attention of the authorities and, where appropriate, offered treatment. The recommendations, however, encompassed far more than a call for decriminalization and, in fact, amounted to a comprehensive move towards a national drug strategy based firmly on harm reduction principles. In further recommendations, treatment was to be ensured for all who sought it, harm reduction programmes such as needle exchanges and substitution treatment were to be extended, effort was to be expended to ensure the reintegration of drug addicts into wider society, harm reduction measures were to be extended to prisoners and, where possible, drug addicts were to be given treatment rather than imprisonment (van het Loo *et al.*, 2002). All in all, a much more humanistic and pragmatic policy (Council of Ministers, 1999) was proposed.

While the appointment of a commission to examine the national drug problem and make recommendations about future strategy is by no means unusual in terms of European experience, it is extremely rare for recommendations, especially where they are rather radical as in the case of Portugal, to be adopted wholeheartedly. Nevertheless, this is more or less what happened in Portugal. The commission's report was completed by October 1998 and debates into the results were opened in November of the same year. The future of national drug policy became a cross-party issue with both left- and right-wing parties entering fully into discussions. Hughes (2006) and Moreira *et al.* (2007, p. 24) postulate that this "national, participative and transparent approach" was instrumental to the positive reception of the CNDS proposals. International actors had been watching Portuguese developments with interest and, at this stage, were broadly complimentary of the direction developments were taking (Portuguese National Institute of Public Administration, 2005).

In 1999, the Socialist Party was re-elected and began to adopt the commission's recommendations into national strategy representing a "significant achievement" (Hughes, 2006, p. 119) for the CNDS, although the most controversial aspects such as the proposed decriminalization had yet to be passed into law. Treatment facilities also began to be expanded at this time in order to meet the new demands that would be placed on them in relation to the revised drugs strategy. From this point onwards, however, criticism began to be levied at the new policy, and particularly the outlined decriminalization, by the Conservative Party who urged the government to call a referendum on the issue

(Allen *et al.*, 2004). Nevertheless, a drugs strategy coordinator, Vitalino Canas, was appointed and the Portuguese Institute for Drugs and Drug Addiction was created, both of which may have "helped to raise public awareness of the benefits of the policy" (Allen *et al.*, 2004, p. 2). The support of the general public would be needed if Portuguese authorities were to take the next step and decriminalize the possession and use of small quantities of all drugs, as outlined in their national drug strategy of 1999.

2000s

As outlined in the previous section, by the early 2000s, support for the new drugs strategy had waned within Portugal with criticism being centred around the proposal to decriminalize the use and possession of small amounts of all drugs. Decriminalization was fully debated by the Portuguese Parliament in June 2000 leading to an appeal for a referendum on the issue which was later denied by the president. Despite this increasing internal pressure, from 2001, the use and possession of up to ten days' supply of all drugs (Vastag, 2009) was formally decriminalized in a move unique in Europe. While other countries, such as the Netherlands, have implemented policies whereby criminal prosecution for the use and possession of small amounts of all drugs is deemed not to be in the public interest, Portugal went one step further making it an administrative rather than a criminal offence (Hughes and Stevens, 2010). It is important to note that, despite these drastic changes to the treatment of drug users in Portugal, hefty sanctions remained in place against drug dealers and traffickers.

In order to effectively implement the new law, administrative strategies to deal with drug offenders naturally had to be put in place. Each of the 18 Portuguese administrative districts was tasked with implementing one or more "Dissuasion Committees" comprised of three people – two from a medical background and one from a legal background (van het Loo *et al.*, 2002). Those discovered using drugs, or with drugs in their possession, are referred to the Dissuasion Committees, who then have the ability to impose a fine of between 25 and 150 euros, or various other sanctions such as a driving ban or a travel ban (van het Loo *et al.*, 2002). In practice, however, fines are used as a last resort (Greenwald, 2009) and "where the offender is deemed to be a nonaddicted consumer of drugs and has no prior offenses, the commissions are *mandated* by Article 11(1) of the decriminalization law to 'provisionally suspend proceedings', whereby no sanction is imposed" (Greenwald, 2009, p. 2).

In the case of addicts, sanctions are commonly applied, but are suspended on the condition that treatment is sought. In this way, the new law effectively distinguishes between recreational users and problem drug users and treats them accordingly. Indeed, it is a specific aim of the new policy that Dissuasion Committees try to take into account the individual circumstances of those brought before them and that their ultimate goal should be to reintegrate them back into society as far as possible (Portuguese Institute for Drugs and Drug Addiction, 2005). Vitalino Canas, the Portuguese drug strategy coordinator, summarizes: "the new framework, born of humanist principles, rests on the cornerstone of treatment, prevention and the attempt to dissuade new consumers rather than on punishment" (Canas, 2002, p. 18).

While the new decriminalization law attracted the most attention at this time, many more changes, mainly concerned with solidifying the objectives of the 1999 national drug strategy, were also being implemented. In 2001, two important new documents were drawn up: *30 Objectives in the Fight Against Drugs* and a *National Action Plan on Drugs* covering the period until 2004. One important aspect of the new action plan was that the drug strategy would be evaluated at the end of this period before deciding whether to continue with the new approach. In 2002, the Socialist Party was defeated and the Social Democrats came into power. Despite some "threats to re-criminalise consumption, acquisition and possession [of drugs] for personal use" (Felner and Gomes, cited in Hughes, 2006, p. 176), the existing strategy and action plan were adhered to, notwithstanding the change in government.

In 2004, the effects of the new policy thus far were externally and independently evaluated as stipulated in the first action plan. The overall result was a declaration that the new strategy had "had a positive overall contribution" (Portuguese National Institute of Public Administration, 2005, p. 7) and that, of the 30 main objectives outlined in 2001, only five had not been attained (Moreira *et al.*, 2007). The main benefits of the new strategy were summarized by the Portuguese National Institute of Public Administration (2005) as an expansion of the treatment system and outreach workers, fewer drug-related deaths and fewer drug-related HIV cases. The evaluation was not, however, overwhelmingly positive – important failings were also highlighted. A greater increase in drug use, especially amongst young people, had been noticed, fewer individuals had been charged with trafficking and a lack of information sharing and coordination between sectors had been observed (Portuguese National Institute of Public Administration, 2005). With the inclusion of an attempt to address these issues, the decriminaliza-tion and overall strategy were extended until 2012. A new action plan was also drawn up and set to run until 2008 when another evaluation would take place.

In fact, prior to this designated point of evaluation, an interim eval-uation took place in 2006, resulting in the publication of further data by the Portuguese Institute of Drugs and Drug Addiction (2007). Vastag (2009, p. 1) reports that "the number of deaths from street drug over-doses dropped from around 400 to 290 annually, and the number of new HIV cases caused by using dirty needles to inject heroin, cocaine and other illegal substances plummeted from nearly 1,400 in 2000 to about 400 in 2006". Furthermore, and perhaps more importantly, the prevalence of drug use in Portugal was deemed to be well below the European average (Portuguese Institute of Drugs and Drug Addiction, 2007). These preliminary findings are echoed in the official evaluation conducted in 2008, which is summarized in the Portuguese national report to the EMCDDA. A leading objective of the recent Portuguese drug strategy had been to lower the incidence and related harms of dependent drug use. Judged on these terms, it seems to have been a resounding success. In addition to the results reported above, relating to drug-related deaths and drug-related diseases, the national report docu-ments a continued decrease in the number of individuals imprisoned for drug law offences and a decrease in the number of offenders arrested for contraventions of the drug law (Institute on Drugs and Drug Addiction, 2008). Furthermore, the number of drug users in treatment expanded from 23,654 in 1998 to 38,532 in 2008 (Hughes and Stevens, 2010) and Portuguese figures continued to compare favourably with the rest of Europe and America (Szalavitz, 2009).

In relation to statistical data, the main area of contention contin-ued to be the slight increase observed in prevalence of overall drug use. Hughes and Stevens (2010, p. 9) report that "key stakeholders in Portugal were in general agreement that there has been small to mod-erate increases in overall reported drug use among adults". The authors, however, make the important observation that this may well to do with an increase in reporting of drug use, rather than an increase in actual drug use itself, due to a reduction in the stigma associated with this activity following the decriminalization law. An outreach worker (cited in Easton, 2009, p. 1) appears to confirm this hypothesis: "When drug use was a crime, people were afraid to engage with the teams. But since decriminalization, they know the police won't be involved and they come forward. It has been a great improvement."

A further issue that has been flagged as one of continuing concern in Portugal is the issue of drugs in prisons. In European terms, Portugal has one of the highest recorded levels of drug use in prisons (do Carmo Gomes, 2007), including a relatively high proportion of female drug offenders (da Cunha, 2005). The European Committee for the Prevention of Torture (2008, p. 26) further reports that "a significant number of prisoners had become addicted to drugs only after they had entered the prison system" and recommends that harm reduction and treatment measures be made available to prisoners as well as members of the general population. This criticism comes despite treatment in prisons being mentioned as a specific issue in the 2004–08 action plan and the Institute on Drug use and Drug Addiction (2007, p. 8) stating that: "Responses in the criminal justice system continue to be developed to ensure treatment availability to drug users in prison, specific training for prison staff and the prevention of infectious diseases." There is evidence, however, that Portuguese authorities continue to work towards combating this problem as needle exchange programmes have recently been introduced to several prisons on a trial basis (European Committee for the Prevention of Torture, 2008).

Over and above the specific problems outlined here, there have been a number of general criticisms levelled at the implementation of Portuguese national drug policy since 2001. These, however, are largely rather vague and are not generally supported by strong evidence. Luis Patricio, director of a rehabilitation centre in Lisbon (cited in Roberts, 2004) has alluded to the lack of rationalization or medical basis for the figure of ten medical doses that has been evoked in relation to the application of the 2001 decriminalization law and has questioned the consistency of the application of the law in this respect. Van het Loo *et al.* (2002) have also referred to the vagueness and lack of clarity in general of the law and its application. It is notable, however, that these criticisms, and others like them, were levied in the earlier part of the decade suggesting a growing confidence in relation to the national strategy. External criticism has come from UN bodies who have expressed concern over decriminalization approaches, branding them likely to encourage drug use amongst the general population (Ferreira, 2010).

In light of the implementation of such a controversial policy, it is perhaps surprising that Portugal has not attracted more criticism for its national drug strategy and decriminalization law. Hughes (2006) attributes this to the fact that decriminalization was framed as a process designed to increase the number of addicts interfacing with the system, thereby increasing the likelihood of achieving a drug-free society, rather than as a radical shift towards the legalization of drug use, as it might have been. Greenwald (2009, p. 10) concurs with this viewpoint: "Portuguese decriminalization was never seen as a concession to the inevitability of drug abuse. To the contrary, it was, and is, seen as the most effective government policy for reducing addiction and its accompanying harms." Furthermore, Portuguese authorities have maintained a dedication to increased preventive activities in order to counteract the potential negative connotations of the 2001 decriminalization. The Portuguese National Drug Strategy, for example, states that it is "important to advocate specific and appropriate drug prevention policies, that are able to mobilise the different institutions representing civil society and, above all, young people" (Council of Ministers, 2006). These factors may well have been instrumental in deflecting much of the international criticism that countries like the Netherlands have seen.

Indeed, rather than being plagued by criticism, Portuguese national strategy has, of late, been held up as an example to the rest of the world in terms of its success in dealing with the illicit drug problem. Perhaps the most famous external evaluation of policy to date is that by Glenn Greenwald, conducted in 2009 for the Cato Institute. Its title – *Drug Decriminalization in Portugal: Lessons for Creating a Fair and Successful Policy* – speaks volumes. In the introduction to his paper, Greenwald summarizes his analysis of the data thus: "Although postdecriminalization usage rates have remained roughly the same or even decreased slightly when compared with other EU states, drug-related pathologies – such as sexually transmitted diseases and deaths due to drug usage – have decreased dramatically" (Greenwald, 2009, p. 10). He further stipulates that levels of drug use in Portugal are now amongst the lowest in the EU and that 95 per cent of drug cases in Portugal involve Portuguese citizens. He concludes with a statement that "the Portuguese model ought to be carefully considered by policymakers around the world" (Greenwald, 2009, p. 28).

This appeal to Portuguese drug policy to provide an example to the rest of the world is becoming more common. Ferreira (2010) describes how Norway's government sent a committee to Portugal to learn from their experiences with decriminalization and Beaumont *et al.* (2010) report that even more recently Britain has done the same. Easton (2009, p. 3) goes further and suggests that Portugal has already been instrumental in effecting change in drug policy across Europe: "In the eight years since Portugal shocked the world with its drug policy, the idea that users need care not punishment has swept across Europe. In 10 EU countries, possession of some, if not all illegal substances is not generally pursued as a crime." Others, however, have recommended more caution in designating the policy such a resounding success. Hughes and Stevens (2010) observe that it is impossible to definitively state that any of the positive (or indeed negative) changes in the Portuguese drug problem are a direct result of the decriminalization policy. Peter Reuter, a professor of criminology and public policy and drug policy expert (cited in Szalavitz, 2009), has further suggested that changes in the Portuguese drug problem may be more to do with cyclical trends in drug epidemics than the national strategy *per se*. Nevertheless, Portugal provides an excellent example of a country that has recently undergone a liberalization of its drug laws and that has done so in a way that has generally been regarded as successful.

Part III

Multi-level Governance and the Way Forward for European Drug Policy

The case studies of Sweden and the Netherlands, undertaken in the previous part of this book, reveal a deep divide between national styles of drug control currently in operation within the EU. In Sweden, drug policy is based on the fundamental goal of a drug-free society, which has led to policies that target users as heavily as dealers, allow police to administer on the spot drug tests and primarily invest in abstention-based or coercive treatment programmes. Conversely, in the Netherlands, a strategy of normalization of the drug user has been pursued, resulting in policies that focus on the minimization of the harm and nuisance associated with drug use, without marginalizing or alienating drug users themselves. These overall national strategy differences have translated into the emergence of two distinct paradigms of drug control that are in operation in Europe at the same time. While Sweden and the Netherlands represent the prototypes of, respectively, a repressive or moralistic drug policy and a liberal or pragmatic one, depth of commitment to one or the other of these drug policy paradigms varies amongst other member states.

The development of these two paradigms has serious implications for the creation of a unified European drug policy. Whether the illicit drug problem is defined in moralistic or pragmatic terms has led to different approaches to the issue, the involvement of different actors that influence the issue and the development of different terms of reference in discussing it. Attitudes towards illicit drugs in Sweden and the Netherlands, for example, are so different that many policies that have gained acceptance in the Netherlands could not even be suggested in Sweden and vice versa. Furthermore, the historical exploration of drug policy conducted in the previous part reveals a deep-seated and enduring sense of pride in national drug policy, at least in the cases of Sweden and the Netherlands, making it unlikely that either country would be willing to compromise on this issue or engage in a major change in policy direction in this area.

Comparing policy development in Sweden and the Netherlands in a historical context, it quickly becomes apparent that, although they have been subjected to similar trends regarding the use of drugs and the numbers of users of drugs since the 1960s, the way they have reacted to these trends has been radically different and has heavily contributed to the development of such different national policies. Even before the illicit drug problem emerged as a significant issue, important differences were to be seen in the alcohol control polices of these two countries, a policy area that may have been drawn heavily on in the development of national drug policy. In Sweden, from the outset, the problem of drinking to intoxication and, in particular, the problematic use of spirits and hard liquor, was greeted with measures of strict control and repressive policy initiatives (Swedish National Institute of Public Health, 1995). In the Netherlands, meanwhile, although anti-alcohol movements were vigorous in extolling the dangers of excessive drinking and the virtues of sobriety, the state itself did not adopt a central role in this issue and, · furthermore, a very early distinction was made between hard liquor and beer and other low alcohol drinks (Steffen, 1994).

Prior to the 1960s, before illicit drugs became a significant societal problem, the medical profession represented the frontline in dealing with drug users in both Sweden and the Netherlands (Lindberg and Haynes, 2000). In the 1960s, this was a situation that was to dramatically change: for the first time, young people of all classes and cultures were becoming involved with drugs and, more seriously, drug use was perceived as having permeated criminal subcultures. Governments throughout Europe, including in Sweden and the Netherlands, realized the need to define the nature of the problem and propose appropriate solutions. It was at this point that Swedish and Dutch national drug strategies began to diverge. In Sweden, the explosion in cannabis use by young people was initially responded to with an extension of the medical model which had previously been used to control the dependent users of amphetamines and heroin. Criminal justice sanctions were not deemed to be appropriate. In the Netherlands, conversely, cannabis users were generally regarded as significantly different to dependent users of other drugs. Instead, they were classified as highly deviant and their drug use was perceived as a rebellion against societal norms. Cannabis users in the Netherlands were thus, initially, dealt with by the criminal justice system resulting in many arrests and the frequent application of penal sanctions.

During the 1970s, however, the numbers of drug users rose rapidly in both Sweden and the Netherlands, resulting in both countries initiating a re-evaluation of national drug policy. Both countries blamed existing illicit drug policies for the epidemic levels of drug use that they were now facing. In Sweden, the brief period of toleration towards drug users described above was condemned and practices turned instead to the increasing use of penal sanctions against drug users and the adoption by parliament of the national motto of "a drug-free society" in 1977. Conversely, in the Netherlands, relatively harsh responses enforced against young cannabis users came to be viewed as counterproductive and were deemed to be a fruitless line of policy to continue to pursue. Instead, tolerance towards the use of cannabis was adopted in a policy move that came to be known as "separation of the markets" intended to enable users of cannabis to be kept free from penal sanctions and sheltered from situations in which they would have to come into contact with other, more dangerous, drugs. Thus the beginnings of Sweden's moralistic policy and the Netherlands' pragmatic one were founded.

In the 1980s, the advent of HIV and AIDS in Europe affected drug policy across the continent. Intravenous drug users, as well as drug users who turned to prostitution to fund their habits, were regarded as a high risk in the potential spread of the disease to epidemic proportions. Individual countries developed their own strategies to deal with the prevention of such an epidemic, largely resorting to harm reduction strategies to contain the problem, but this was not always the case. Re-evaluations of drug policy were made but, this time, rather than seeking radically new solutions, more of the same was prescribed. In Sweden, in line with the strictly defined and nationally maintained goal of "a drug-free society", harm reduction measures were, unsurprisingly, not considered appropriate. Instead, an all-encompassing treatment policy was developed based on the principle of abstention from drug use. In the Netherlands, harm reduction principles were given more weight and the concept of "normalization", the second defining strand of Dutch drug policy, was introduced. Considerable effort was made to ensure that drug users did not become marginalized members of society unknown to the treatment system and practical measures such as needle exchange services and methadone maintenance programmes were implemented on a national scale.

Towards the end of the 1980s and into the 1990s, levels of drug use across Europe began to level off. Both Sweden and the Netherlands, as well as many other countries, interpreted this as a sign that their respective drug policies were having the desired effect and even engaged in promotion of their drug control strategies on an international basis. As levels of drug use once again began to rise, however, in the 1990s, countries like Sweden and the Netherlands, operating at the extremes of drug policy, attracted external criticism and re-evaluations of national drug policy in both countries were once again conducted. These re-evaluations, however, continued to recommend more of the same, albeit with minor concessions to their critics. Sweden has now accepted the necessity of basic harm reduction measures as part of an overall national drug policy and the Netherlands has enforced some tightening of drug policy in response to a decrease in toleration of drug-related nuisance. In the main, however, both countries continue to operate their radically different strategies of drug control.

A historical exploration of drug policy development in Sweden and the Netherlands thus reveals not only the differing central ideologies at the heart of their respective drug policies, but also a strong tie between drug policy and national identity that has become highly resistant to pressure to change. Given this entrenchment of national policy observed in Sweden and the Netherlands, future aims to effect a harmonization of European drug policy appear unlikely to be successful. The development of policy in Sweden and the Netherlands, however, does not tell the whole story. The previous part also included case studies of the situation in Denmark and Portugal, countries which indicate that movement of national drug policy is possible – albeit that that movement has been observed in both directions.

Drug policy development in Denmark had been fairly standard up until the 2000s. National strategy had not been as polarized as in either Sweden or the Netherlands and there had been less overall cohesion of ideologies or unison in dictating overall policy direction. Nevertheless, up until 2001, there had been several rather liberal aspects to Danish drug policy. The most obvious of these is the situation that was allowed to develop in the part of Copenhagen known as the Free City of Christiania in the 1970s whereby the sale and purchase of cannabis was allowed to flourish without intervention from the state. Unsurprisingly, such a practice was not without influence on overall national policy which has always afforded a relatively liberal outlook towards cannabis, even at times when the focus elsewhere has been on increasing law enforcement. Additionally, liberal drug-related interventions such as heroin on prescription and the implementation of drug user rooms have long been freely debated within Denmark, even if this debate has not given rise to any concrete policy decisions.

However, since 2001 drug policy development in Denmark has taken a much more decisively repressive turn, with much of the tightening of policy taking place with reference to cannabis and cannabis users. The long-standing situation in Christiania has been brought to an end, the development of hash clubs have been legislated against and the penalties faced by cannabis users are now much tougher. Although the changes to national policy have arguably been centred around cannabis, they have not been limited to it with a new action plan on drugs that references the "war on drugs" and tougher law enforcement measures and sentencing practices in general. Denmark has always been near the top of EMCDDA tables of cannabis use in Europe, but figures have not risen over the time period in question. It is therefore difficult to attribute the changes to anything but a new government more aligned to the right of the political spectrum coinciding with a re-evaluation of national drug policy strategy. In terms of the harmonization of drug policy at a European level, it suggests that, within some countries at least, the willingness to change national policy, in this case from relatively liberal to more repressive, exists.

In contrast to the situation that has recently occurred in Denmark with reference to a general tightening of national drug policy, Portugal has undergone a considerable liberalization of drug policy during the same time period. Similarly to the Danish situation, drug policy was not a priority in Portugal for many years and, reflecting this, national policy was not as comprehensive, well-developed or entrenched as in Sweden or the Netherlands. The issue did not become significant until the 1980s and 1990s when EMCDDA statistics revealed that Portugal was at the high end of the European scale in terms of drug-related deaths and infectious diseases. This statistical information was compounded by the development of a particularly visible open drug scene in Lisbon which helped to bring the matter to the attention of the general public as well as the national policy makers. Although changes did not begin to be made to Portuguese national strategy until the 2000s, the foundations for these changes were laid in the 1990s with the development of a new national drug strategy and action plan based on the principles of harm reduction.

The changes that were implemented in 2001, the most dramatic of which was the decriminalization of all drugs for personal use, have brought Portugal to the forefront of international drug policy making. Portugal is now the European country most committed to the decriminalization of drug use and drug users, ahead even of the Netherlands with its policy that is based on the "expediency principle", a much discussed legal grey area. While Portuguese authorities cannot make possession of drugs for personal use a criminal matter, Dutch authorities have merely deemed it not to be in the public interest to prosecute in these cases. The difference may seem subtle, but is important nonetheless. The example that Portugal provides therefore suggests that movement in national drug policy direction towards policies that are more liberal is also possible within the EU.

An in-depth examination of the four countries provided in the previous part of this book raises many interesting questions for the possibilities of drug policy harmonization at a European level. In countries such as Sweden and the Netherlands, the implementation of a harmonized European drug policy seems a remote possibility. Other countries, such as Denmark and Portugal, have been much more receptive to changes in overall national drug policy strategies, however, these changes have occurred both in favour of increased liberalization and increased restrictiveness in different countries at the same time. The overall prognosis for harmonization does not, therefore, look good. The final chapter of this book will summarize the situation with respect to both the desirability and the viability of a European drug policy and will further seek to outline a potential solution to the *impasse* that has developed in this area: a European drug policy based on the principles of multi-level governance as discussed in the first chapter of this book.

8
Multi-level Governance and the Way Forward for European Drug Policy

To date, the prognosis for harmonization of drug policy within the EU is not particularly positive. Two main obstacles to achieving this goal remain: the inability of the EU to decide in favour of either a liberal or a restrictive drug policy and the development of very varied styles of drug policy at the national level, in combination with a high degree of national attachment to individual policy practices. This final chapter seeks to summarize the arguments presented thus far on both the desirability and the viability of a harmonized European drug policy, to examine the various forms that such a policy could take and, finally, to propose a system of harmonization based on the principles of subsidiarity and multi-level governance which were outlined in the first chapter of this book.

The desirability of a European drug policy

In Chapter 1, the dependence of successful harmonization on the perceived benefits of integration for individual national governments was discussed. Areas where perceived benefits are high, such as economic policy, have experienced considerable integrative success, while areas where perceived benefits are negligible, such as social policy, have experienced much less integrative success. Drug policy is a complicated area, much of which, particularly in the contentious area of dealing with drug use and drug users, falls under the category of social policy. It is perhaps not surprising, therefore, that harmonization in this area has not been extensive thus far. Nevertheless, there are important benefits in harmonization to both member states and the EU itself which should not be overlooked and which have led to a continual presence of this issue on the integration agenda. This first section of this final chapter will examine the arguments for the overall desirability of a European drug policy.

Thinking first in terms of perceived benefits of an integrated or harmonized drug policy to the national governments of individual member states, these do exist, but are mainly associated with the control of drug trafficking and drug dealing. It is fairly easy to infer that all EU member states will recognize the need for cooperation in fighting international organized crime and drug trafficking, and be able to work towards common goals. The disruption of criminal gangs operating outside national and international legal frameworks is an aim all member states can relate to and its result would prove an invaluable benefit to the heads of national governments. Therefore, harmonization, in this strand of drug policy at least, is desirable, not only within the confines of the EU, but also to the heads of individual member states.

Not only are national governments eager to reap the benefits of unity in the area of controlling organized crime and the illegal trafficking of drugs, but they also welcome harmonization efforts in this area as an opportunity to prove their continuing commitment to world-wide aims of drug prevention. All European countries are committed to practicing a drug policy that is broadly prohibitive in nature. Individual countries may be moving away from policy interventions that are exclusively prohibitive in their treatment of drug use and drug users. However, by unifying harmonization on the control of traffickers they can assert their fundamental support of a prohibitive policy. Countries like the Netherlands and Portugal may have liberal attitudes towards drug users and drug use, but they can show their commitment to the prohibition of drugs by implementing strict coercive measures against traffickers. By cooperating in this area they can also show that, despite the divergence of certain aspects of their national policies from generally held norms, they are, at heart, in full subscription to the prohibitive aims all drug policies are ultimately based upon.

The evidence presented suggests that in the fight against international drug trafficking, harmonization of national drug policies is promoted by both the EU and individual member states. Indeed, drug policy in this area is continually moving towards increased cooperation between member states as well as increased powers for EU institutions. However, spillover of cooperation to areas other than control and prevention has not been as extensive. Trends towards the implementation of harm reduction initiatives and the decriminalization of the drug user can be observed across Europe, with notable exception, but unity of policy in this area does not enjoy the same degree of official encouragement. The same benefits for national governments and thus individual member states are not present.

In fact, treatment of drug use and drug users is one area in which countries can acceptably defer from following traditionally prohibitive strategies and develop an individual, and highly nationalized, drug policy. Governments have proved incredibly reluctant to give up this right. Hamaide (1995, p. 147) has noted this: "prohibition is the fundamental principle that inspires all policies towards illicit drugs, whether concerning their cultivation, manufacture, distribution or possession. Only the approach to the drug user in person escapes this absolute rule, and may display differences between European countries."

While the harmonization of policy towards drug traffickers is welcomed by national governments, any intrusion into national policy towards drug users and drug use is not. Harmonization in policy towards drug traffickers is beneficial and therefore desirable to both the EU and its individual member states. However, the same cannot be said of policy towards drug use and drug users. On balance, many individual member states appear to have decided that the negative loss of national sovereignty outweighs any positives that may be gained from increased unity against international drug traffickers. It is therefore difficult to argue that a European drug policy based on the imposition of top-down European control, encompassing both drug users and drug traffickers, would be desirable, at least outside of EU power structures.

Given this unwillingness to compromise on national strategies towards drug use and drug users that is so evident within the member states of Europe, what is perhaps surprising is that the goal of harmonization in this area has been so long-lived. If individual member states remain so attached to their national policies and perceive so few benefits in harmonization, why is this an area that persists in featuring on the integration agenda? The first reason is that the statistics collected by the EMCDDA highlight the commonality of the problems facing each member state in the illicit drug field and therefore lend support to the idea that a harmonized policy ought to be an attainable goal. If the phenomenon of illicit drugs was a new problem only just emerging in Europe at this time, instead of one to which national responses had been developed in isolation over time, there is no doubt that it would be earmarked for EU intervention and control from the outset and that a fully harmonized policy would be implemented. The second is that considerable desirability in harmonization of illicit drug policy exists at the EU level and that the EU itself has been a significant driving force in keeping the issue on the integration agenda. On one level, the EU has stated its intention to remain neutral on this issue, content to gather and present statistics without passing judgement on the degree of success enjoyed by certain countries or policies. There is, however, compelling evidence of a continued EU desire to work towards eventual harmonization in this area which will now be examined.

The information presented in Chapter 2, for example, demonstrates an EU preoccupation with and continual prioritization of the issue of illicit drugs. Since the creation of the Comite Europeen de la Lutte Anti-Drogue (CELAD) in 1989 and the recognition of the illicit drug problem as an area relevant for EU-level intervention, a wealth of EU working bodies and groups have been created to monitor developments in this area. Additionally, the issue of illicit drugs has been raised by the European Parliament, the European Commission and the Council of Europe, at different times. Aspects of the problem are referred to under all three pillars of EU governance and several Articles from the Amsterdam Treaty also relate directly to this area. Indeed, EU intervention in this area has been so great that Boekhout van Solinge (2002, p. 121) has commented that "politicians have spoken so much about it, and the question has generated so much media attention, that some EU citizens are under the impression that the decision to harmonise has already been made". It has not, but this abundance of activity within the EU is indicative of the fact that the aim of harmonization is far from having been abandoned.

While harmonization in the field of illicit drug policy has been ruled out for the moment, the sheer number of EU bodies developed in this field strongly suggests that it has not been ruled out forever. In fact, many policy makers within the EU have openly referred to this possibility. The head of the EMCDDA in 1995, Georges Estievenart (1995, p. 93), commented that the foundations for an EU drug policy have been laid by the creation and development of drug policy as a priority within the EU and that these foundations will wait until "the member states, the Commission, the European Parliament, and also society at large and the professional world, evince the good sense and the good will needed to arbitrate – or reconcile – their aims". Doherty (1995, p. 324) also discusses the drug problem as "an issue on which we must all cooperate together effectively or face up to the consequences". Such information sends a clear message that international cooperation in the field of illicit drugs is highly desirable within the EU. Member states and EU bodies themselves are urged towards it and, in the meantime, policy structures are set up as foundations for the day when differences in national drug policies lessen and a truly European drug policy can be built.

An examination of one of the more successful areas of drug policy-related integration goes some way towards revealing why such an EU-level effort has been made and maintained in this area. The problem of drug trafficking and organized crime has already been highlighted as an area in which member states share goals and aspirations and, as such, has enjoyed the most comprehensive harmonization of policy at the European level. Indeed, integrated policy in this area is so advanced that van Outrive (cited in Dorn, 1996a, p. 155) reports that "some observers feel that the way Europe is going with trafficking law the European authorities will see the need to have a European Criminal law to oversee it". Perhaps this is indicative of some of the aims behind an EU prioritization of drug policy.

If harmonized EU law on drug trafficking continues to develop, then the need for increased powers, at the EU level, in criminal law may be realized. Once powers like these are granted to the EU, they cannot be taken away again and new control may spill over into other policy areas boosting its supranational power status and further eroding national sovereignty. The spillover of authority created by increased criminal justice powers at an international level would drastically further the functionalist cause and would be a considerable step towards the development of a federal EU. Dorn (1996a) postulates that the more cooperation is called for in the area of drug trafficking and the more the threat posed by organized international crime of this type is emphasized, the more powers the EU will gain for itself. Illicit drugs are a phenomenon that can be depended on for a strong emotional response throughout the EU. This response is amplified because all member states can agree that drug trafficking and international criminal organizations must be prevented, and can therefore work together to impose similar penalties. It is therefore possible that the continual prioritization of this issue by the EU is as much an attempt to increase its own powers as to prevent organized crime and drug trafficking.

Further evidence, both for the continued desire for harmonization of illicit drug policy by the EU itself and for the gradual working towards this goal, can be found in an examination of EU policy related to the acceptance of new member states. Before any applicant country can become a member of the EU, it must first demonstrate that it is ready and willing to accept the existing body of European law which is collectively known as the "Acquis Communautaire". Part of this important body of law refers to EU drug law and policy practice and evidence suggests that this is an area on which considerable emphasis is placed when preparing candidate countries for entry into the EU. Prior to the largest EU enlargement to date in 2004, a project known as the Phare Programme was sent up "to help applicant countries in their economic and political transition to EU membership" (Boekhout van Solinge, 2002, p. 136). Indicative of the importance of the illegal drugs issue, a subgroup of the Phare Project, the Multibeneficiary Drugs Programme, was set up specifically to deal with policy alignment in this area.

The Multibeneficiary Drugs Programme was created to manage the difficult task of ensuring that anti-drug measures already existing in EU member states were adopted by candidate countries and encompassed "greater co-operation between national and international drug law enforcement agencies, drug detection, disrupting drug supply channels, dismantling drug trafficking organizations and placing drug traffickers under arrest" (Phare Multibeneficiary Drugs Programme, 2002, pp. 1–2). Furthermore, Boekhout van Solinge (2002, p. 135) has reported that "taking drug-related measures is presented to third countries as one of the main conditions for cooperation". That the EU have made combating international drug trafficking and organized crime in general such a key issue for its candidate countries is indicative of the importance this issue holds within the EU. Even before they have joined the EU, candidate countries must not only agree to accept existing EU law in this area but must "continue to reinforce their policies, institutions and co-ordination mechanisms and allocate the necessary resources" (EMCDDA, 2001b, p. 4) in this field.

A final piece of evidence relating to the continued desire for harmonization in the illicit drugs field, within the power structures of the EU, is clearly documented in the most recent European Action Plan on Drugs and European Anti-Drugs Strategy. Both of these documents identify one of the five over arching themes of European-level drug policy making as "improving international cooperation" and the latest European Action Plan on drugs furthermore states: "we are ready to intensify our commitment in the field of international cooperation" (*Official Journal of the European Union*, 2008, p. 3). The importance of this is increased by the fact that, as mentioned above, the EU makes many stipulations on new member states in the area of drug policy and one of these is that they must develop a national action plan on drugs. For ease of implementation, one presumes, many member states have chosen to stylize their national action plans on the European Action Plan on Drugs and have therefore identified the deepening of international cooperation in this area as one of the central aims of their national policies.

While the benefits of harmonization of illicit drug policy to the heads of member states may be negligible, the evidence presented here suggests that, to the internal power structures of the EU, they may be considerable. Furthermore, while individual member states are strongly protective of the more unique aspects of their national policies, the EU is quietly putting into place all the processes needed to eventually institute a fully harmonized European drug policy. Yet, the problem remains, that, thus far, no one has been able to satisfactorily suggest what this European drug policy would look like and its viability is therefore very much in question. The next section of this chapter will examine some of the potential models of a European drug policy and will determine their viability.

The viability of a European drug policy

As argued above, the desirability, or attendant benefits, of a unified European drug policy are by no means proven, however, the viability of such a policy is also an important consideration. Were a truly harmonized European drug policy to be developed, harmonization of policy towards drug dealers and traffickers would clearly be based around measures of control and criminal justice sanctions. Difficulties would surround fixing exact penalties and amounts of drugs attracting different penalties but, ultimately, a unified policy in this area would be possible. It would certainly be no more complicated than measures required to introduce a free market within the EU or to adopt the single currency. However, in order to also harmonize policy towards drug use and drug users, the EU would face the difficult task of choosing between the promotion of either a policy that fundamentally prioritized control in dealing with use and users (as in Sweden) or one that fundamentally prioritized harm reduction and the consequent suspension of some control measures against use and users (as in the Netherlands). Alternatively, a united European drug policy could attempt to enforce a position someway between the two described above, combining elements of control and toleration in response to drug users and drug use.

Laying the considerable problems discussed previously aside for a moment, even were the EU to be able to achieve this monumental task of persuasion, none of the three options described above would be without further problems. For example, looking first at a unified European drug policy based around the principle of toleration towards drug use and drug users, even were all EU member states persuaded of the appropriateness of such a response, attitudes outside of Europe would also have to be considered. All EU member states are signatories of several international conventions committing themselves to the prohibition and prevention of the spread of drug use. While individual member states may be able to argue cultural anomalies allowing them to interpret these commitments in ways that are compatible with national policy, it is difficult to imagine this being acceptable at an EU wide level.

For example, while the Netherlands may be able to argue that its coffee shop policy remains within the confines of international treaties, as its implementation was designed to prevent the spread of use of hard drugs (Korf, 2002), it would be a far more serious matter if the EU was to argue for this policy to be adopted on a European scale. In implementing its coffee shop policy the Netherlands can argue that it is a country that culturally allows people a high degree of autonomy, relies on a low level of intervention from the state in practicing its policies in general and has specifically adopted a drug policy that is pragmatic and tolerant of drug users in the recent past (Korf, 1990). For the EU as an institution, and considerably powerful international structure, to consider adopting such a policy would signify a major shift in terms of world-wide drug policy. The EU as a whole has no such cultural history and catalogue of recent practice. Indeed, such an intervention would involve major changes in philosophy of drug policy for many EU member states. The adoption of such a policy intervention at an EU-wide level would also have serious implications for the continuing relevance of international treaties such as the 1961 UN single convention.

Furthermore, as one of, if not the, most important world power(s), American attitudes towards drug policy are highly relevant to the development of a united European drug policy. While there is increasing evidence of American-based criticism towards a zero tolerance approach towards the control of drugs (Beyers *et al.*, 2004; Greene 1999; Rhodes *et al.*, 2005; Shiner, 2003; Small *et al.*, 2005) and Obama has famously abandoned the term "war on drugs", America remains fundamentally prohibition based and control orientated in its responses both to drug traffickers and drug users. MacCoun and Reuter's suggestion that despite an investment of resources in developing alternatives to current drug policy and a stimulation of public debate in this area, the liberalization movement is "falling largely on deaf ears" (2001, p. 51) seems pertinent here. Any change, at a European level, that jeopardized the continual international focus on control in relation to all aspects of illicit drugs would be challenged by America. America already levels constant and severe criticism at Dutch practices in relation to drug policy (Collins, 1999; Lemmens and Garretsen, 1998; Reinarman, 1998; Reinarman and

Cohen, 1999). As a single, and relatively small country, the Netherlands can conceivably ignore these criticisms and be allowed to develop its own drug policy without more serious intervention. These criticisms, however, would considerably escalate in relation to EU-wide adoption and America would, in all probability, be in a position to prevent them from occurring.

Neither would a European drug policy based on control towards both traffickers and users be likely to succeed. All EU member states have now adopted basic harm reduction measures, such as needle exchange and methadone maintenance treatment, and the vast majority have embraced the principle of minimizing the harm drug users do to their own health and the well-being of society in general (Chatwin, 2004; EMCDDA, 2001a, 2005). Many countries are now taking this principle to the next level and are either relaxing current drug laws or introducing the next generation of harm reduction measures (Flynn, 2001). For example, Portugal has recently decriminalized the possession of all drugs for personal use, the Netherlands and Germany have developed safe user rooms for dependent drug users (de Jong and Weber, 1999) and Germany, Spain, the UK, Belgium and the Netherlands have experimented with offering heroin on prescription for the most dependent users (Small and Drucker, 2006).

This European shift towards increased harm reduction has been accompanied and underpinned by an increasing volume of literature criticizing American style drug policy and research linking a zero tolerance approach with an increasingly bleak drug problem. In 1993, Elliott Currie commented on the depressing failure of American drug policy: "Twenty years of the 'war' on drugs have jammed our jails and prisons, immobilized the criminal justice system in many cities, swollen the ranks of the criminalized and unemployable minority poor, and diverted desperately needed resources from other social needs. Yet the drug crisis is still very much with us" (p. 3). More recent drug policy research indicates that little has changed: Shiner (2003) and Small *et al.* (2005) link repressive drug policy with burgeoning imprisonment rates, Beyers *et al.* (2004) associate abstinence-based policies with higher levels of drug use and MacCoun and Reuter (2001) brand the American drug problem as "worse than that of any other wealthy nation" (p. 1). Furthermore, a raft of current research has warned of the adverse effect of intolerant drug policy towards injecting drug users on the levels of HIV and AIDS (Bastos and Strathdee, 2000; Burris and Strathdee, 2006; Maher and Dixon, 1999; Moore and Dietze, 2005). Indeed, in a recent evaluation of UN and national responses to the illicit drug problem, Wolfe and

Malinowska-Sempruch (2004) have called for a greater focus on harm reduction and HIV prevention and less on the war on drugs. While the results of this have yet to be convincingly evidenced in American drug policy, the continuing progression of harm reduction within Europe, coupled with the increasing mound of evidence against the worth of pursuing a zero tolerance approach, means that it would be difficult to entirely base a European drug policy on control towards drug use and drug users.

Based on either of these top-down models of European governance, it would therefore appear that a harmonized European drug policy would not be viable. Either strategy would be desirable for the EU itself in terms of increased supranational power and the common sense of developing an international policy to face an international problem. It would also be desirable in relation to preventing drug trafficking and organized crime for the national governments of individual member states. In practice, however, the problems involved in implementing either policy across Europe would be too great. The decision to make European drug policy either broadly liberal or broadly restrictive in its totality cannot be made, leaving the future of drug policy precariously balanced between these two approaches and the prospect of further cooperation in this area of policy making redundant (Chatwin, 2003).

One possible way round this *impasse* would be the development of a unified EU drug policy containing elements of both control and toleration in its attitude towards drug use and drug users: such an approach would, however, be equally unworkable. Adopting control measures and harm reduction measures against drug users would be both confusing and counterproductive. Perhaps cannabis users could be treated leniently while users of drugs perceived to be more dangerous could face criminal justice sanctions. However, many would argue that this would be grossly unfair as it is users of drugs such as heroin and crack cocaine that stand to benefit most from harm reduction measures. Conversely, however, if users of the most dangerous and problematic drugs were treated leniently while cannabis users were to face criminal justice sanctions, policy could also be criticized for unjustly criminalizing those who are involved with drugs that are reported, by an ever-increasing minority, to be no more harmful than alcohol and nicotine.

Arguably, Denmark, up to the 2000s, practiced a policy that contained both elements of toleration and control in relation to drug use. Criminal justice sanctions were routinely tightened while cannabis use was simultaneously tolerated in Christiania. This led to a situation where both a move towards toleration, with the introduction of heroin on prescription and safe injecting rooms, and a move towards control, by closing down Christiania, were hotly debated. These debates, however, were not fruitful in terms of leading to concrete policy changes. Instead policy became stagnated and politicians were unable to move on from the debating stage, until, that is, a decision was made to prioritize restrictive practices over liberal ones which has been implemented over the last decade. It is highly likely that a Europe-wide drug policy based on the same principles would face the same problems and, ultimately, would be forced into making the same choice between liberal and restrictive.

On the whole it would seem, therefore, that a harmonized European drug policy would not be viable. Such a policy would be desirable for the EU itself in terms of increased supranational power and the common sense of developing an international policy to face an international problem. It would also be desirable in relation to preventing drug trafficking and organized crime for the national governments of individual member states. However, in practice, the implementation of a European drug policy based on any of the three models described above would not be viable. The problems faced at a national and international level regarding making some changes to the basic perception of the problem of illicit drugs would be too great.

Multi-level governance: the way forward?

The theory of multi-level governance, however, outlined in Chapter 1, provides a lifeline for harmonization in the field of European illicit drug policy. Unlike intergovernmentalism and neo-functionalism, multi-level governance does not see the development of integration as a two-way fight for control between European government and national heads of state. Instead, complex issues are decided with input from the European level, the national level and, crucially, the local level. Marks *et al.* (1996), who have been instrumental in promoting the concept of multi-level governance at the European level, have conceptualized the EU as a "single, multi-level polity ... [with] multiple levels of governments and the interaction of political actors across those levels". Under this style of European governance, collective directives and framework agreements are made at the European level, but room is made for member states, together with their social partners, to fill in the details (Barnard, 2002). Integration of national policy under this system would defy traditional notions of convergence of policy: "instead of harmonizing national-level social policy regimes, EU social policy may actually encourage them to diversify" (Geyer, 2000, p. 212).

Dorn (1996a, 1996b) has elaborated on this point, with reference to international drug policy. He postulates that if drug policy remains ultimately in the hands of individual countries, it will converge more because decisions will continue to be made by those in power for each country (Dorn, 1996a). If, however, European harmonization of drug policy were to be achieved, Dorn (1996b) argues that, in the absence of an ultimate judgement between liberal and restrictive styles, decision-making would be encouraged at local, regional and city levels, allowing citizens a higher involvement in drug policy. European harmonization would result in more diversity because, rather than being able to impose top-down drug policy decisions on countries, European institutions would have to listen to individual ideas and strategies and incorporate them into an overall framework. The working of this system of harmonization as described by Dorn is, basically, a European drug policy conceptualized in accordance with the principles behind European multi-level governance.

A harmonized European drug policy, based on the principles of multi-level governance, and encouraging a diversification of policy response, would bring many benefits and possibilities in this area. Such a strategy would avoid the futile attempt to choose between a broadly liberal or broadly restrictive pathway, particularly in relation to drug use and drug users, and would, arguably, be desirable both to member states and to the EU itself. The EU would achieve its desire to harmonize and, for the first time, would be able to present a truly international response to an international problem, while member states would be able to maintain the national flavour of their individual drug policies, where they were particularly wedded to them. The application of multi-level governance to the illicit drug problem, however, has greater benefits than this cosmetic realigning of the conceptualizing of integration. The data examined in Chapter 3 of this book strongly suggests that no drug policy has so far been successful, at least in terms of consistently and significantly reducing the amount of drug use and number of drug users in society or eradicating the many harms associated with drug use. While success on these terms remains an elusive goal, surely it is sensible to seek to increase the range of options that are developed to deal with this issue, rather than to narrow them.

In practice, rather than enforcing a predominantly liberal or predominantly restrictive approach to drug policy, guidance from the EU would impose international standards against drug traffickers and an international flavour to response directed at drug use and drug users. As confidence and experience in organizing drug policy around this system grew, so would local authorities' practice of adopting interventions that have been developed in response to problems that are similar to their own. While drug policy would not be unified in the nature of its response, member states would be working together in response to the illicit drug problem, despite their individual strategies, rather than against each other. The situation with respect to drug policy anomalies may not be that different from today, if anything they may be more likely. However, working within a general system headed by the EU, these anomalies would no longer be sources of contention but would be respected as a signal of a new era in European drug policy, in which individual policy measures were judged on their effectiveness, rather than their ability to fit within a national paradigm of policy making.

While the development of a harmonized European drug policy as outlined above might seem like a distant aim, there is some evidence to suggest that it, to some extent, describes what is already occurring. The multi-level governance approach to European integration theorizing is not a prediction of the way that integration could develop in the future, but is rather a lens for viewing the way that integration is developing now and offers "the best single description and explanation of how the EU actually functions" (Piattoni, 2010, p. 255). While it would be very difficult to suggest that increasing cohesion of European drug policy is occurring along either intergovernmentalist or neo-functionalist lines, there are several facets that suggest that it may be occurring in a way that is compatible with a multi-level governance approach to European integration.

So far, this discussion has focused on the development of drug policy at the national and supranational level, and the interaction between these levels. If the theory of multi-level governance were to be relevant to the development of European drug policy, there must be evidence of involvement at the local level as well. EU bodies and institutions would play a guiding role in providing a framework for drug policy, but practical decisions would be made at the increasingly local level, including the greater involvement of citizens and local residents in the formulation of policy. Citizen participation, in particular, would further benefit drug policy as important EU-wide objectives in this area are to reduce drug-related public nuisance and drug-related harm to society (Council of the European Union, 2004). If citizens were involved in the formulation of drug policy for their areas of residence, effective interventions most suited to culture, history and public attitude of a geographical area could be chosen.

There is considerable evidence for the promotion of citizen partici-pation in policy making across the EU. Citizen participation in policy has been a guiding principle in governance of the EU since the Treaty of Maastricht and has been inextricably linked to effective govern-ment in the White Paper on European Governance (Commission of the European Union, 2001). "Participation is one of the keywords of the White paper on European governance. It is defined as one of the five major principles of 'good governance', and appears in the argu-ments of the White Paper and its preparatory documents as one of its most important principles" (Garcia, 2006, p. 1). In relation specifically to European drug policy, the idea of greater involvement at the level of the citizen has recently been championed by the ENCOD, a non-governmental organization campaigning for a more humane European drug policy and the authors of the "Catania Report" which demands attention for "the impact of drug policies at the level of citizens" (ENCOD, 2004, p. 1).

Furthermore, there is some evidence to suggest that, subnational, city level authorities have also already participated in the development of European drug policy. Le Gayles (2002, p. 75) has commented that "European cities are not organised solely by the state but, increas-ingly, in relation to cities and regions in other countries – the hori-zontal dimension of European institutionalisation." Evidence for this, in the form of the city networks (ECAD and ECDP), discussed in Chapter 2, exists in the drug policy sphere. The emergence of city networks in dealing with the response to illicit drugs is a sign that situational factors have become increasingly important in determining drug policy responses. These city networks have been formed by cities from different member states that perceive the illicit drug problem in the same terms and have pledged to act together in conquering the problem.

Generally speaking, large cities are hit the hardest by the illicit drug problem in member states and countries across the globe (Bless *et al.*, 1995; Kaplan and Leuw, 1996). Large cities tend to be a focal point, both for those wishing to sell and distribute drugs and for those drug users who have become dependent and problematic in their use. This has led to the development of both problems and responses that are similar across European cities. While ECAD and ECDP have broadly different ideologies, the important factor here is that some cities throughout Europe are finding it makes sense to adhere to similar principles in responding to and dealing with the specific city-level illicit drug problem, despite vastly different traditional national philosophies of drug policy.

So, the operation of multi-levels of governance in the issue of drug policy formation at the European level is evidenced. At the European level, minimum penalties have been adopted in the area of drug trafficking and the development of the European Action Plan on Drugs and the European Anti-Drugs Strategy has gone some way towards implementing a set of guidelines or a framework for national drug policy to work within, particularly since these documents have been so influential in the development of national drug policy in the newer member states. At the national level, governments have remained free to implement strategies that are either broadly liberal or restrictive in their treatment of drug use and drug users. At the local level, the moderate success of the "Catania Report" documents an increasing commitment to citizen participation and the development of city networks provides a working example of policy development at the subnational rather than national level.

A further principle of multi-level governance is the development of cooperation in the form of exchange of best practice rather than in the convergence of policy *per se* (Roberts and Springer, 2001). Again, evidence exists that best practice is an important emerging principle in the development of European drug policy. For many years, the role of the EMCDDA has been to collect and disseminate information on the illicit drug problem in Europe. While these statistics are not reliable enough to determine overall policy strategies at the European level, as outlined in Chapter 3, in more recent years the EMCDDA has expanded its role to deal not just with statistics, but also with the collation of instances of "best practice" in relation to drug policy. In practice, in the areas of prevention, treatment, harm reduction, prevention of drug-related crime, drug supply reduction and data collection tools, the EMCDDA now collects information on individual strategies that have been positively evaluated and makes this information available to interested parties. Furthermore, it uses this information to develop guidelines and frameworks within which EU member states are encouraged to construct their drug policies. Nor is this a practice that is confined to the institutions of the EU itself. As documented in Chapter 7, the radical new policy adopted in Portugal has been the focus of much international attention and has attracted visits from the governments of both Norway and Britain in the search for answers as to which direction the future drug policies of their own countries should take.

It is important, however, not to overstate the status of multi-level governance within the EU, either in general or in relation to drug policy. As a guiding principle in government, its reach is, so far, virtually confined to the areas of environment and welfare (Garcia, 2006) and, while the White Paper on European Governance (Commission of the European Union, 2001) provides official support for the concept, Armstrong (2002) has questioned how far the EU is really willing to accept this distribution of power. Furthermore, Bache (1998, p. 155) has suggested that "national governments operate as gatekeepers at various stages of the policy process to put a brake on the emergence of a truly multi-level system of governance" and that, rather than multi-level governance, it has more akin to multi-level participation: "actors from sub-national and supranational levels participate, but do not significantly influence decision-making outcomes" (Bache, 1998, p. 155). More recently, Getimis *et al.* (2006, p. 265) have commented that the "gatekeeping role of the central state has remained unchallenged and prominent in almost all of the cases". These are certainly issues that can be applied to the field of illicit drug policy where attachment to national control in some member states remains high. The continuing, and potentially deepening, commitment to national ideals of drug policy, as evidenced by the case studies of Sweden and the Netherlands, casts a shadow over the potential success of the application of multi-level governance to the issue of illicit drugs.

Nevertheless, if the continued convergence of illicit drug policy remains as a European goal, as is suggested by a review of activity in this area, then the full application of a system of multi-level governance could provide the way forward. There is some evidence that tentative steps are being taken towards such an outcome but the path ahead will be tricky, obscured as it is by commitment to national ideals. In comparison to the possibilities for a harmonized European drug policy outlined earlier in this chapter and based around either a liberal or a restrictive overall ethos, a drug policy based on the principles of multi-level governance would at least be viable. Furthermore, if principles of sharing incidences of "best practice" are adhered to, it may yet be possible to develop a drug policy underpinned by scientific evidence and rational argument, which would be an achievement to be proud of. If the harmonization of drug policy in Europe has a future, it is in accordance with the principle of multi-level governance.

References

Albrecht, H. and van Kalmthout, A. (1989) "European perspectives on drug policies", in H. Albrecht and A. van Kalmthout (eds) *Drug Policies in Western Europe*. Criminological Research Reports by the Max Planck Institute for Foreign and International Penal Law, Freiburg, Vol. 41.

Allen, L., Trace, M. and Klein, A. (2004) *Decriminalisation of Drugs in Portugal: A Current Overview*, London: DrugScope and the Beckley Foundation.

Anker, J., Asmussen, V., Kouvonen, P. and Tops, D. (2008) "Drug users and spaces for legitimate action", in G. Broring and E. Schatz (eds) *Empowerment and Self-organisations of Drug Users: Experiences and Lessons Learnt*, Correlation, http://www.correlation-net.org (accessed 01 September 2010).

Armstrong, K. (2002) "Rediscovering civil society: the European Union and the White Paper on governance", *European Law Journal*, 8, 102–132.

Asmussen, V. (2007) "Danish cannabis policy in practice: the closing of Pusher Street and the cannabis market in Copenhagen", in J. Fountain and D. Korf (eds) *Drugs in Society: European Perspectives*, Abingdon: Radcliffe Publishing.

Asmussen, V. (2008) "Cannabis policy: tightening the ties in Denmark", in S. Rodner Sznitman, B. Olsson and R. Room (eds) *A Cannabis Reader: Global Issues and Local Experiences*, EMCDDA monograph, http://www.emcdda.europa.eu (accessed 01 September 2010).

Asmussen, V. and Moesby-Johansen, C. (2004) "The legal response to illegal 'hash clubs' in Denmark", in T. Decorte and D. Korf (eds) *European Studies on Drugs and Drug Policy*, Brussels: VUB Press.

Bache, I. (1998) *The Politics of European Union Regional Policy: Multi-level Governance or Flexible Gatekeeping?* Sheffield: Sheffield Academic Press.

Balsa, C., Farinha, T., Nunes, J.P. and Chaves, M. (2002) "Inquerito nacional ao consumo de substancias psico-activas na populacao portuguesa, CEOS, FCSH-UNL, Lisboa", http://www.annualreport.emcdda.eu.int (accessed 01 September 2010).

Bammer, G., van den Brink, W., Gschwend, P., Hendriks, V. and Rgen Rehm, J. (2003) "What can the Swiss and Dutch trials tell us about the potential risks associated with heroin prescribing?", *Drug and Alcohol Review*, 22, 363–371.

Barnard, C. (2002) "The social partners and the governance agenda", *European Law Journal*, 8, 80–101.

Bastos, F. and Strathdee, S. (2000) "Evaluating effectiveness of syringe exchange programmes: current issues and future projects", *Social Science and Medicine*, 51, 1771–1782.

Beach, D. (2005) *The Dynamics of European Integration: Why and When EU Institutions Matter*, Houndmills, Basingstoke: Palgrave Macmillan.

Beaumont, P., Townsend, M. and Helm, T. (2010) "Britain looks at Portugal's success story over decriminalising personal drug use", *Observer*, Sunday 5th September, 2010 http://www.guardian.co.uk (accessed 01 September 2010).

Bejerot, N. (1988) *The Swedish Addiction Epidemic in Global Perspective*, Stockholm: The Swedish Carnegie Institute.

Beyers, J., Toumbourou, J., Catalano, R., Arthur, M. and Hawkins, J. (2004) "A cross-national comparison of risk and protective factors for adolescent substance use: the United States and Australia", *Journal of Adolescent Health*, **35**, 3–16.

Bless, R., Korf, D. and Freeman, M. (1995) "Open drug scenes: a cross-national comparison of concepts and urban strategies", *European Addiction Research*, **1**, 128–138.

Blom, T. and van Mastright, H. (1994) "The future of the Dutch model in the context of the war on drugs", in E. Leuw and I. Haen Marshall (eds) *Between Prohibition and Legalisation: The Dutch Experiment*, Amsterdam and New York: Kugler Publications.

Boekhout van Solinge, T. (1997) *The Swedish Drug Control System: An In-depth Review and Analysis*, Amsterdam: Uitgevenj Jan Mets, Cedro.

Boekhout van Solinge, T. (1999) "Dutch drug policy in a European context", *Journal of Drug Issues*, **29**, 511–528.

Boekhout van Solinge, T. (2002) *Drugs and Decision-making in the European Union*, Amsterdam: CEDRO/Mets en Schilt.

Bongers, P. and Chatfield, J. (1993) "Regions and local authorities in the governance of Europe", in A. Duff (ed.) *Subsidiarity Within the European Community*, London: Federal Trust for Education and Research.

Branegan, J. (1996) "Desperately seeking Mr. Europe", *TIME International*, **147**, 8 April, http://www.time.com (accessed 01 September 2010).

Bruun, K., Pan, L. and Rexed, I. (1975) *The Gentleman's Club*, Chicago and London: University of Chicago Press.

Burris, S. and Strathdee, S. (2006) "To serve and protect? Toward a better relationship between drug control policy and public health", *AIDS*, **20**, 117–118.

CAN (2009) *Drug Trends in Sweden in 2009*, http://www.can.se (accessed 01 September 2010).

Canas, V. (2002) "The policy for the fight against drugs and drug addiction in Portugal: recent developments", Speech given to DrugScope, London.

do Carmo Gomes (2007) "Perceptions of drug use and drug users in Portugal", in J. Fountain and D. Korf (eds) *Drugs in Society: European Perspectives*, Oxon: Radcliffe Publishing.

Carter, C. and Scott, A. (1998) "Legitimacy and governance beyond the European nation state: conceptualising governance in the European Union", *European Law Journal*, **4**, 429–445.

Cary, A. (1993) "Subsidiarity – essence or antidote to European union?", in A. Duff (ed.) *Subsidiarity Within the European Community*, London: Federal Trust for Education and Research.

Central Committee for the Treatment of Heroin Addicts (2000) *Clinical Trials in the Netherlands*, http://www.minjust.nl (accessed 01 September 2010).

Chatwin, C. (2003) "Drug policy developments within the European Union: the destabilizing effects of Dutch and Swedish drug policies", *British Journal of Criminology*, **43**, 567–582.

Chatwin, C. (2004) "The effects of new member states of the European Union on drug policy", *Drugs: Education, Prevention and Policy*, **11**, 437–448.

Churchill, W. (1998) "The tragedy of Europe", in B. Nelson and A. Stubb (eds) *The European Union: Readings on the Theory and Practice of European Integration*, Second edition, London: Lynne Reinner Publishers.

Cisneros Ornberg, J. (2008) "The Europeanization of Swedish alcohol policy: the case of ECAS", *Journal of European Social Policy*, **18**, 380–392.

Cohen, P. (1994) 'The case of the two Dutch drug policy commissions. An exercise in harm reduction 1968–1976', Paper presented at the 5th International Conference on the Reduction of Drug Related Harm, 7–11 March, Addiction Research Foundation, Toronto.

Cohen, P. (2006) *Looking at the UN, Smelling a Rat. A Comment on "Sweden's Successful Drug Policy": A Review of the Evidence, UNODC, September 2006*, Amsterdam: CEDRO.

Collins, L. (1999) "Holland's half-baked drug experiment", *Foreign Affairs*, **78**, 82–98.

Commission of the European Communities (1999) *Communication from the Commission to the Council, the European Parliament, the Economic and Social Committee and the Committee of the Regions on a European Union Action Plan to Combat Drugs (2000–2004)*, Luxemboug: Office for Official Publications of the European Communities, L-2985.

Commission of the European Communities (2001a) *Proposal for a Council Framework Decision Laying Down Minimum Provisions on the Constituent Elements of Criminal Acts and Penalties in the Field of Illicit Drug Trafficking (Presented by the Commission)*, Luxembourg: Office for Official Publications of the European Communities, L-2985.

Commission of the European Communities (2001b) *Proposal for a Council Framework Decision on Combating Terrorism (Presented by the Commission)*, Luxembourg: Office for Official Publications of the European Communities, L-2985.

Commission of the European Communities (2003) *Communication from the Commission to the European Parliament and the Council on Coordination on Drugs in the European Union*, http://eur-lex.europa.eu (accessed 01 September 2010).

Commission of the European Communities (2004) *Communication from the Commission to the Council and the European Parliament on the Results of the Final EU Drugs Strategy and Action Plan on Drugs (2000–2004)*, http://www.emcdda.europa.eu (accessed 01 September 2010).

Commission of the European Union (2001) *European Governance: A White Paper*, COM2001(428), http://www.emcdda.europa.eu (accessed 01 September 2010).

Council of Ministers (1999) *National Drug Strategy*, Resolution of the Council of Ministers No. 46/99, http://www.drugtext.org (accessed 01 September 2010).

Council of Ministers (2006) *Action Plan Against Drugs and Drug Addictions Horizon 2008*, http://www.idt.pt (accessed 01 September 2010).

Council of the European Union (2004) *EU Drugs Strategy (2005–2012) 15/074/04*, http://register.consilium.europa.eu (accessed 01 September 2010).

Currie, E. (1993) *Reckoning: Drugs, the Cities and the American Future*, New York: Hill and Wang.

da Cunha, M. (2005) "From neighbourhood to prison: women and the war on drugs in Portugal", in J. Sudbury (ed.) *Global Lockdown: Race, Gender and the Prison-Industrial Complex*, London: Routledge.

Delors, J. (1998) "A necessary union" "The uniting of Europe", in B. Nelson and A. Stubb (eds) *The European Union: Readings on the Theory and Practice of European Integrationi*, Second edition, London: Lynne Reinner Publishers.

Desrosieres, A. (1996) "Statistical traditions: an obstacle to international comparisons?", in L. Hantrais and S. Mangen (eds) *Cross-national Research Methods in the Social Sciences*, London and New York: Pinter.

Dinan, D. (1994) *Ever Closer Union: An Introduction to European Integration*, Second edition, Houndmills, Basingstoke and New York: Palgrave Macmillan.

Dinan, D. (2006) *Origins and Evolution of the European Union*, Oxford: Oxford University Press.

Doherty, E. (1995) "Possible guidelines for a European Union Global Action Plan on Drugs", in G. Estievenart's (ed.) *Policies and Strategies to Combat Drugs in Europe. The Treaty on European Union: Framework for a New European Strategy to Combat Drugs*, Dordrecht: Martinus Nijhof Publishers.

Dorn, N. (1996a) "The EU, home affairs and 1996: intergovernmental convergence or confederal diversity", in N. Dorn, J. Jepsen and E. Savona (eds) *European Drug Policies and Enforcement*, Houndmills, Basingstoke: Palgrave Macmillan.

Dorn, N. (1996b) "Borderline criminology: external drug policies of the EU", in N. Dorn, J. Jepsen and E. Savona (eds) *European Drug Policies and Enforcement*, Houndmill, Basingstoke: Palgrave Macmillan.

Dorn, N. and Jamieson, A. (2000) *Room for Manoeuvre: Overview of Comparative Legal Research into National Drug Laws of France, Germany, Italy, Spain, the Netherlands and Sweden and their Relation to Three International Drugs Conventions*. A study of DrugScope for the Independent Inquiry on The Misuse of Drugs Act 1971, London.

Duff, A. (1993) "Towards a definition of subsidiarity", in A. Duff (ed.) *Subsidiarity Within the European Community*, London: Federal Trust for Education and Research.

Easton, M. (2009) "How Portugal treats drug addicts", BBC News, http://news.bbc.co.uk (accessed 01 September 2010).

ELDD (2001) *Main Trends in National Drug Laws*, http://www.eldd.emcdda.org/trends (accessed 01 September 2010).

ELDD (2010) *Country Profiles*, http://eldd.emcdda.europa.eu (accessed 01 September 2010).

EMCDDA (1998) "EMCDDA in brief", http://www.emcdda.org (accessed 01 September 2010).

EMCDDA (2001a) "Decriminalisation in Europe? Recent developments in legal approaches to drug use. ELDD comparative analysis", November, http://www.emcdda.org/databases/eldd (accessed 01 September 2010).

EMCDDA (2001b) *News Release: Annual Report on EU Drugs Problem: Special Focus on CEECs*, 15/2001, Lisbon.

EMCDDA (2002) *2002 Annual Report on the State of the Drugs Problem in the European Union and Norway*, Luxembourg: Office for Official Publications of the European Communities.

EMCDDA (2005) *Statistical Bulletin 2005*, http://www.emcdda.europa.eu (accessed 01 September 2010).

EMCDDA (2010) *Statistical Bulletin 2010*, http://www.emcdda.europa.eu (accessed 01 September 2010).

ENCOD (2004) *Catania Report: European Parliament Recommendation to the Council and the European Council on the Drugs Strategy 2005–2012*, http://www.action.encod.org (accessed 01 September 2010).

ENCOD (2005) *On Democracy and Drug Policy in the EU*, http://www.encod.org (accessed 01 September 2010).

ENCOD (2007) 'Common Press Release of Giusto Catania MP and ENCOD', http://www.encod.org (accessed 01 September 2010).

Estievenart, G. (1995) "The European Community and the global drug phenomenon. Current situation and outlook", in G. Estievenart (ed.) *Policies and Strategies to Combat Drugs in Europe. The Treaty on European Union: Framework for a New European Strategy to Combat Drugs*, Dordrecht: Martinus Nijhof Publishers.

EUROPA (1998) *The Amsterdam Treaty: A Comprehensive Guide*, http://www.europa.eu.lnt/scadplus (accessed 01 September 2010).

EUROPA (1999) *The European Union Action Plan to Combat Drugs (2000–2004)*, www.europa.eu.int

EUROPA (2001) *Europol Convention: European Police Office*, http://www.europa.eu.int/scadplus (accessed 01 September 2010).

EUROPA (2002) *The Schengen Acquis and Its Integration into the Union*, http://www.europa.eu.int (accessed 01 September 2010).

European Committee for the Prevention of Torture (2008) *Report to the Portuguese Government on the Visit to Portugal Carried Out by the European Committee for the Prevention of Torture and Inhuman or Degrading Punishment from 14th to 25th January 2008*, http://www.cpt.coe.in (accessed 01 September 2010).

European Parliament (1996) *The Fight Against Drugs*, http://www.europarl.eu.int/topics/drugs (accessed 01 September 2010).

European Parliament (2004) *European Parliament Recommendation to the Council and the European Council on the EU Drugs Strategy (2005–2012) 2004/2221/INI*, http://www.europarl.europa.eu (accessed 01 September 2010).

Ferreira, S. (2010) "Portugal's drug laws draw new scrutiny", *Wall Street Journal*, European Coalition for Just and Effective Drug Policies, http://www.encod.org (accessed 01 September 2010).

Flynn, P. (2001) *Social Consequences of and Responses to Drug Misuse in Member States*. Social, Health and Family Affairs Committee, Parliamentary Assembly, Luxembourg: Office for Official Publications of the European Communities, L-2985.

Frantszen, E. (2003) "Drug enforcement in Copenhagen: negotiating space", in E. Houbourg Pedersen and C. Tigerstedt (eds) *Regulating Drugs – Between Users, the Police and Social Workers*, NAD Publication 43, Nordic Alcohol and Drug research Council, Helsinki.

Galtung, J. (1990) "Theory formation in social research: a plea for pluralism", in E. Oyen (ed.) *Comparative Methodology*, London: Sage.

Garcia, M. (2006) "Citizen practices and urban governance in European cities", *Urban Studies*, **43**, 745–765.

Garretsen, H. (2003) "Guest editorial: the decline of Dutch drug policy?", *Journal of Substance Use*, **8**, 2–4. European Community, Federal Trust for Education and Research, London.

Gasoliba i Bohm, C. (1993) "The application of subsidiarity", in A. Duff (ed.) *Subsidiarity Within the European Community*, London: Federal Trust for Education and Research.

de Gaulle, C. (1998) "A concert of European states", in B. Nelson and A. Stubb (eds) *The European Union: Readings on the Theory and Practice of European Integration*, Second edition, London: Lynne Reinner Publishers.

le Gayles, P. (2002) *European Cities: Social Conflict and Governance*, Oxford: Oxford University Press.

George, S. (1996) *Politics and Policy in the European Union*, Third edition, Oxford: Oxford University Press.

George, S. (2004) "Multi-level Governance and the European Union", in I. Bache and M. Flinders (eds) *Multi-level Governance*, Oxford: Oxford University Press.

Getimis, P., Parakevopouos, C. and Rees, N. (2006) "Domestic governance structures and policy learning East and West: the limits of Europeanization", in C. Paraskevopoulos, P. Getimis and N. Rees (eds) *Adapting to EU Multi-level Governance: Regional and Environmental Policies in Cohesion and CEE countries*, Hampshire: Ashgate.

Geyer, R. (2000) *Exploring European Social Policy*, Cambridge: Polity Press.

Goldberg, T. (1997) "The Swedish narcotics control private model – a critical assessment", *International Journal of Drug Policy*, 8, 82–92.

Goldberg, T. (2004) "The evolution of Swedish drug policy", *Journal of Drug Issues*, 34, 551–576.

Goldberg, T. (2005) "Will Swedish and Dutch drug policy converge? The role of theory", *International Journal of Social Welfare*, 14, 44–54.

Grapendaal, M., Leuw, Ed and Nelen, H. (1994) "Legalization, decriminalization and the reduction of crime", in Ed Leuw and I. Haen Marshall (eds) *Between Prohibition and Legalization: The Dutch Experiment in Drug Policy*, Amsterdam and New York: Kugler Publications.

Greene, J. (1999) "Zero tolerance: a case study of policies and practices in New York City", *Crime and Delinquency*, 45, 171–187.

Greenwald, G. (2009) *Drug Decriminalization in Portugal: Lessons for Creating Fair and Successful Drug Policies*, The Cato Institute, http://www.cato.org (accessed 01 September 2010).

Haas, E. (1998) "The uniting of Europe", in B. Nelson and A. Stubb (eds) *The European Union: Readings on the Theory and Practice of European Integration*, Second edition, London: Lynne Reinner Publishers.

Hakim, C. (2000) *Research Design: Successful Designs for Social and Economic Research*, Second edition, London: Routledge.

Hallam, C. (2010) "What can we learn from Sweden's drug policy experience?", The Beckley Foundation Drug Policy Programme, Briefing paper 20, January.

Hamaide, J. (1995) "Repression of illicit drugs in Western Europe: aspects of legal practice", in G. Estievenart (ed.) *Policies and Strategies to Combat Drugs in Europe. The Treaty on European Union: Framework for a New European Strategy to Combat Drugs*, Dordrecht: Martinus Nijhof Publishers.

Hansch, K. (1995) *Preface to "The Fight Against Drugs"*, Report on behalf of the Civil Liberties and Internal Affairs Committee on the communication from the Commission to the Council and the European Parliament on a European Union action plan to combat drugs (1995–1999), Brussels: European Parliament.

Hantrais, L. (2007) *Social Policy in the European Union*, Third edition, Houndmills, Basingstoke: Palgrave Macmillan.

Hellenic Presidency of the European Union (2003) *"Towards an Effective Policy on Drugs: Scientific Evidence, Day-to-Day Practice and Policy Choices". Overcoming Obstacles to the Implementation of Evidence-based Drug Policies and Interventions*, Report of the Greek Presidency of the European Union on the High Level Conference on Drugs, Athens, 8 March.

Hill, C. and Smith, M. (2005) *International Relations and the European Union*, Oxford: Oxford University Press.

Hilte, M. (1999) "The social construction of drug control: the case of Sweden and the Netherlands", *International Journal of Social Welfare*, 8, 308–314.

Hix, S. (1998) "The study of the European Union II: the 'New Governance' agenda and its rival", *Journal of European Public Policy*, 5, 38–65.

Hix, S. (2005) *The Political System of the European Union*, Second edition, Houndmills, Basingstoke: Palgrave Macmillan.

Hoffman, S. (1966) "Obstinate or obsolete?", *Daedalus, Journal of the American Academy of Arts and Sciences*, 95, 862–915.

Hooghe, L. and Marks, G. (2001) *Multi-level Governance and European Integration*, Oxford: Rowman & Littlefield Publishers.

Horizontal Working Party on Drugs (2005) *EU Drugs Action Plan (2005–2008) 8652/1/05*, http://register.consilium.eu.int (accessed 01 September 2010).

Hughes, C. (2006) "Overcoming obstacles to reform?: making and shaping drug policy in contemporary Portugal and Australia", PhD Thesis, Department of Criminology, University of Melbourne.

Hughes, C. and Stevens, A. (2010) "What can we learn from the Portuguese decriminalisation of illicit drugs?", *British Journal of Criminology*, 50, 999–1022.

International Coalition of NGOs for Just and Effective Drug Policy (2001) *Guidelines for Just and Effective Drug Policies*, ENCOD, http://www.drugpolicy.org (accessed 01 September 2010).

Intraval (2007) *Coffeeshops in Nederland* (English summary), http://www.wodc.nl (accessed 01 September 2010).

Jepsen, J. (1989) "Drug policies in Denmark", in H. Albrecht and A. Van Kalmthout (eds) *Drug Policies in Western Europe*, Criminological Research Reports by the Max Planck Institute for Foreign and International Penal Law, Freiburg, Vol. 41.

Jepsen, J. (1992) "Drugs and social control in Scandinavia: a case study in international moral entrepreneurship", in H. Traver and M. Gaylord (eds) *Drugs,Law and the State*, Hong Kong: Hong Kong University Press.

Jepsen, J. (1995) "Implementation of national drug legislation", in G. Estievenart (ed.) *Policies and Strategies to Combat Drugs in Europe: Framework for a New European Strategy to Combat Drugs*, Dordrecht: Martinus Nijhofft.

Jepsen, J. (1996a) "Methadone as substitution for treatment? A history of Danish methadone policy", Paper presented at the 7th International Conference on Harm Reduction, Hobart, Tasmania, 3–7 March.

Jepsen, J. (1996b) "Copenhagen: a war on socially marginal people", in N. Dorn, J. Jepsen and E. Savona (eds) *European Drug Policies and Enforcement*, Houndmills, Basingstoke: Palgrave Macmillan .

Johnson, B. (2006) "The development of user influence on Swedish drug policy, 1965–2004", in J. Anker, V. Asmussen, P. Kouvonen and D. Tops (eds) *Drug Users and Spaces for Legitimate Action*, NAD Monograph No. 49, Helsinki: Nordic Alcohol and Drug Council.

de Jong, F.A. (*2009*) *Medicinal Use of Cannabis in the Netherlands: Towards a Responsible Pattern of Use* (English abstract), http://www.ncbi.nlm.nih.gov/pubmed (accessed 01 September 2010).

de Jong, W. and Weber, U. (1999) "The professional acceptance of drug use: a closer look at consumption rooms in the Netherlands, Germany, and Switzerland", *International Journal of Drug Policy*, **10**, 99–108.

Kaplan, C. and Leuw, E. (1996) "A tale of two cities: drug policy instruments and city networks in the European Union", *European Journal on Criminal Policy and Research*, **4**, 74–89.

Kaplan, C., Haanraadts, D., van Vliet, H. and Grund, J. (1994) "Is Dutch drug policy an example to the world", in Ed Leuw and I. Haen Marshall (eds) *Between Prohibition and Legalizaiton: The Dutch Experiment in Drug Policy*, Amsterdam and New York: Kugler Publications.

Kleinman, M. (2002) *A European Welfare State?: European Union Social Policy in Context*, Houndmills, Basingstoke: Palgrave Macmillan.

van Kolfschooten, F. (2002) "Dutch investigators recommend prescription of heroin to addicts", *The Lancet*, **359**, 590.

Korf, D. (1990) "Cannabis retail markets in Amsterdam", *International Journal of Drug Policy*, **2**, 23–27.

Korf, D. (2002) "Dutch coffee shops and trends in cannabis use", *Addictive Behaviors*, **27**, 851–866.

Korf, D., Riper, H. and Bullington, B. (1999) "Windmills in their minds? Drug policy and drug research in the Netherlands", *Journal of Drug Issues*, **29**, 451–472.

de Kort, M. (1994) "A short history of drugs in the Netherlands", in Ed Leuw and I. Haen Marshall (eds) *Between Prohibition and Legalization: The Dutch Experiment in Drug Policy*, Amsterdam and New York: Kugler Publications.

de Kort, M. and Cramer, T. (1999) "Pragmatism versus ideology: Dutch drug policy continued", *Journal of Drug Issues*, **29**, 473–492.

de Kort, M. and Korf, D. (1992) "The development of drug trade and drug control in the Netherlands: a historical perspective", *Crime, Law and Social Change*, **17**, 123–144.

Lap, M. and Drucker, E. (1994) "Recent changes in the Dutch cannabis trade: the case for regulated domestic production", http://www.drugtext.org (accessed 01 September 2010).

Laursen, L. (1996a) "Denmark and the Nordic Union: regional pressures in policy development", in N. Dorn, J. Jepsen and E. Savona (eds) *European Drug Policies and Enforcement*, Houndmills, Basingstoke: Palgrave Macmillan.

Laursen, L. (1996b) "Scandinavia's tug of war on drugs", in P. Hakkarainen, L. Laursen and C. Tigerstedt (eds) *Discussing Drugs and Control Policy. Comparative Studies on Four Nordic Countries*, NAD Publication 31, Helsingfors: Nordic Council for Alcohol and Drug Research.

Laursen, L. (1999) "The case of compulsory drug treatment – construction on drug policy in Denmark", in J. Derks, A. van Kalmthout and H.-J. Albrecht (eds) *Current and Future Drug Policy Studies in Europe*, Freiburg: Max-Planck-Institut fur auslandisches und internationals strafrecht.

Laursen, L. and Jepsen, J. (2002) "Danish drug policy – an ambivalent balance between repression and welfare", *Annals of the American Academy of Political and Social Sciences*, **582**, 20–36.

Laursen Storgaard, L. (2005) "Trends in cannabis use and changes in cannabis policy in Denmark", in L. Kraus and D.J. Korf (eds) *Research on Drugs and Drug Policy From a European Perspective*, Lengerich: Pabst Science Publishers.

Lemmens, P.H. (2003) "Dutch government backs down on heroin prescription, despite successful trial", *Addiction*, **98**, 247–249.

Lemmens, P. and Garretsen, H. (1998) "Unstable pragmatism: Dutch drug policy under national and international pressure", *Addiction*, **93**, 157–162.

Lenke, L. (1991) "The significance of distilled beverages. Reflections on the formation of drinking cultures and anti-drug movements", Paper presented at a meeting of The Kettil Bruun Society for Social and Epidemiological Research on Alcohol, Sigtuna, Sweden, June.

Lenke, L. and Olsson, B. (1996) "Sweden: zero tolerance wins the argument", in N. Dorn, J. Jepsen and E. Savona (eds) *European Drug Policies and Enforcement*, Houndmills, Basingstoke: Palgrave Macmillan.

Lenke, L. and Olsson, B. (1998) "Drugs on prescription – the Swedish experiment of 1965–67 in retrospect", *European Addiction Research*, **4**, 183–189.

Lenke, L. and Olsson, B. (1999) "Swedish drug policy in perspective", in J. Derks, A. van Kalmthout and H-J. Albrecht (eds) *Current and Future Drug Policy Studies in Europe: Problems, Prospects and Research Methods*, Freiburg: Max-Planck-Institut.

Lenke, L. and Olsson, B. (2002) "Swedish drug policy in the twenty-first century: a policy model going astray", *Annals of the American Academy of Political and Social Science*, **582**, P64–P79.

Leroy, B. (1995) "Assessing the legalization debate", in G. Estievenart (ed.) *Policies and Strategies to Combat Drugs in Europe: Framework for a New European Strategy to Combat Drugs*, Dordrecht: Martinus Nijhoff Publishers.

Leuw, Ed (1994) "Initial construction and development of the official Dutch drug policy", in Ed Leuw and I. Haen Marshall (eds) *Between Prohibition and Legalization: The Dutch Experiment in Drug Policy*, Amsterdam and New York: Kugler Publications.

Levine, H. and Reinarman, C. (1991) "From prohibition to regulation: lessons from alcohol policy to drug policy", *Millbank Quarterly*, **69**, 461–494.

Lindberg, L. (1963) *The Political Dynamics of European Integration*, Stanford: Stanford University Press.

Lindberg, O. and Haynes, P. (2000) *A Comparison of Drug Treatment Policy in Britain and Sweden: Politics, Culture and Elite Interest Groups*, Sweden: Orebro University.

van het Loo, M., van Beusekom, I. and Kahan, J. (2002) "Decriminalisation of drug use in Portugal: the development of a policy", *Annals of the American Academy of Policitical and Social Science*, **582**, 49–63.

MacCoun, R. and Reuter, P. (2001) *Drug War Heresies*, Cambridge: Cambridge University Press.

MacCoun, R. and Reuter, P. (2002) "The varieties of drug control at the dawn of the twenty-first century", *Annals of the American Academy of Political and Social Science*, **582**, 7–19.

MacGregor, S. and Whiting, M. (2010) "The development of European drug policy and the place of harm reduction within this", in T. Rhodes and D. Hedrich (eds) *EMCDDA Monographs. Harm Reduction: Evidence, Impacts and Challenges*, http://www.emcdda.europa.eu (accessed 01 September 2010).

Maher, L. and Dixon, D. (1999) "Policing and public health: law enforcement and harm minimization in a street-level drug market", *British Journal of Criminology*, **39**, 488–512.

Marks, G. (1992) "Structural policy in the European Community", in A. Sbragia (ed.) *Europolitics: Institutions and Policymaking in the "New" European Community*, Washington: The Brookings Institute.

Marks, G. and Hooghe, L. (2004) "Contrasting visions of multi-level governance", in I. Bache and M. Flinders (eds) *Multi-level Governance*, Oxford: Oxford University Press.

Marks, G., Nielsen, F., Ray, L. and Salk, J. (1996) "Competencies, cracks and conflicts: regional mobilization in the European Union", in G. Marks, F. Scharpf, P. Schmitter and W. Streeck (eds) *Governance in the European Union*, London: Sage Publications.

McCormick, J. (1999) *Understanding the European Union: A Concise Introduction*, Houndmills, Basingstoke: Palgrave Macmillan.

McCormick, J. (2008) *Understanding the European Union: A Concise Introduction*, Fourth edition, Houndmills, Basingstoke: Palgrave Macmillan.

Mendes, S. (2000) "Property crime and drug enforcement in Portugal", *Criminal Justice Policy Review*, **11**, 195–216.

de Menil, G. (2007) "Economic implications of the social provisions of the stalled EU constitution", in A. Aslund and M. Dabrowski (eds) *Europe After Enlargement*, New York: Cambridge University Press.

Ministry of Health and Social Affairs (2002) *National Action Plan on Narcotic Drugs*, Sweden, February.

Ministry of Health and Social Affairs (2008) *The Swedish Action Plan on Narcotic Drugs 2006–2010*, http://www.sweden.gov.se (accessed 01 September 2010).

Mitrany, D. (1998) "A working peace system", in B. Nelson and A. Stubb (eds) *The European Union: Readings on the Theory and Practice of European Integration*, Second edition, London: Lynne Reinner Publishers.

Mol, R. and Trautmann, F. (1992a) "The official methadone circuit in Amsterdam: in the interests of the users?", in R. Mol, E. Otter and A. van der Meer (eds) *Drugs and Aids in the Netherlands – The Interests of Drug Users*, Amsterdam: Interest Group for Drug Users MDHG.

Mol, R. and Trautmann, F. (1992b) "The liberal image of the Dutch drug policy – Amsterdam is singing a different tune", in R. Mol, E. Otter and A. van der Meer (eds) *Drugs and Aids in the Netherlands – The Interests of Drug Users*, Amsterdam: Interest Group for Drug Users MDHG.

Monnet, J. (1998) "A ferment of change", in B. Nelson and A. Stubb (eds) *The European Union: Readings on the Theory and Practice of European Integration*, Second edition, London: Lynne Reinner Publishers.

Moore, D. and Dietze, P. (2005) "Enabling environments and the reduction of drug-related harm: re-framing Australian policy and practice", *Drug and Alcohol Review*, **24**, 275–284.

Moravcsik, A. (1994) "Why the European Community strengthens the state: domestic politics and international cooperation", Paper presented at the Annual Meeting of the American Political Science Association, New York, 1–4 September.

Moreira, M., Trigueiros, F. and Antunes, C. (2007) "The evaluation of the Portuguese drug policy 1999–2004: the process and the impact on the new policy", *Drug and Alcohol Today*, **7**, 14–25.

Nugent, N. (2003) *The Government and Politics of the European Union*, Fifth edition, Houndmills, Basingstoke: Palgrave Macmillan.

Official Journal of the European Union (2004) *Council Framework Decision 2004/757/JHA of 25 October 2004 Laying Down Minimum Provisions on the Constituent Elements of Criminal Acts and Penalties in the Field of Illicit Drug Trafficking*, http://eur-lex.europa.eu (accessed 01 September 2010).

Official Journal of the European Union (2007) *Decision Number 1150/2007/EC of the European Parliament and of the Council of 25th September 2007 Establishing for the Period 2007–2013 the Specific Programme "Drug Prevention and Information" as Part of the General Programme "Fundamental Rights and Justice"*, http://eur-lex.europa.eu (accessed 01 September 2010).

Official Journal of the European Union (2008) *Notices from European Institutions and Bodies. Council: EU Action Plan for Drugs (2009–2012)*, http://eur-lex.europa.eu (accessed 01 September 2010).

Oostlander, A.M. (2001) *Report on the Commission Proposal with a View to the Adoption of a Council Framework Decision Laying Down Minimum Provisions on the Constituent Elements of Criminal Acts and Penalties in the Field of Illicit Drug Trafficking*, Committee on Citizens' Freedoms and Rights, Justice and Home Affairs, COM (2001)259 – C5 – 0359/2001 – 2001/0114(CNS).

Peterson, J. and Bomberg, E. (1999) *Decision-making in the European Union*, London: Palgrave Macmillan .

Phare Multibeneficiary Drugs Programme (2002) "Phare Regional Drug Project press release", European Commission, Vilneus, Lithuania.

Piattoni, S. (2010) *The Theory of Multi-level Governance: Conceptual, Empirical and Normative Challenges*, Oxford: Oxford University Press.

Pierson, P. and Leibfried, S. (1995) "The dynamics of social policy integration", in S. Leibfried and P. Pierson (eds) *European Social Policy: Between Fragmentation and Integration*, Washington: The Brookings Institution.

Portuguese Institute for Drugs and Drug Addiction (2005) *National Plan Against Drugs and Drug Addiction 2005–2012: Executive Summary*, http://www.idt.pt (accessed 01 September 2010).

Portuguese Institute for Drugs and Drug Addiction (2007) *Drugs in Portugal: Situations and Responses 2006 Data*, http://www.idt.pt (accessed 01 September 2010).

Portuguese Institute for Drugs and Drug Addiction (2008) *"Portugal" New Development, Trends and In-depth Information on Selected Issues. 2008 National Report (2007 Data) to the EMCDDA by the Reitox Focal Point*, http://idt.pt (accessed 01 September 2010).

Portuguese National Institute of Public Administration (2005) *External and Independent Evaluation of the "National Strategy for the Fight Against Drugs" and of the "National Action Plan for the Fight Against Drugs and Drug Addiction – Horizon 2004"*, Portuguese Institute of Drugs and Drug Addiction, http://www.idt.pt (accessed 01 September 2010).

Ramstedt, M. (2006) "What drug policies cost. Estimating drug policy expenditures in Sweden, 2002: work in progress", *Addiction*, **101**, 330–338.

Reinarman, C. (1998) *Why Dutch Drug Policy Threatens the US*, Centre for Drug Research, University of Amsterdam http://www.cedro-uva.org (accessed 01 September 2010).

Reinarman, C. and Cohen, P. (1999) *Is Dutch Drug Policy the Devil?* Amsterdam: Centre for Drug Research, University of Amsterdam.

Reuter, P. (2009) "Ten years after the United Nations General Assembly Special Session (UNGASS): assessing drug problems, policies and reform proposals", *Addiction*, **104**, 510–517.

Rhodes, T. and Hedrich, D. (eds) (2010) *EMCDDA Monographs. Harm Reduction: Evidence, Impacts and Challenges*, http://www.emcdda.europa.eu (accessed 01 September 2010).

Rhodes, T., Singer, M., Bourgois, P., Friedman, S. and Strathdee, A. (2005) "The social production of HIV risk among injecting drug users", *Social Science and Medicine*, **61**, 1026–1044.

Roberts, A. (2004) "How Portugal dealt with drug reform", BBC News, http://news.bbc.co.uk (accessed 01 September 2010).

Roberts, I. and Springer, B. (2001) *Social Policy in the European Union: Between Harmonization & National Autonomy*, London: Lynne Rienner Publishers.

Ross, G. (1995) "Assessing the Delors era and social policy", in S. Liebfried and P. Pierson (eds) *European Social Policy: Between Fragmentation and Integration*, Washington: The Brookings Institution.

Sandholtz, W. and Zysman, J. (1992) "Recasting the European Bargain", *World Politics*, **42**, 95–128.

Sassoon, D. (1996) *Social Democracy at the Heart of Europe*, London: Institute for Public Policy Research (IPPR).

Schuman, R. (1998) "The Schuman Declaration", in B. Nelson and A. Stubb (eds) *The European Union: Readings on the Theory and Practice of European Integration*, Second edition, London: Lynne Reinner Publishers.

Scott, J. and Trubek, M. (2002) "Mind the gap: law and new approaches to governance in the European Union", *European Law Journal*, **8**, 1–18.

Sheldon, T. (2002) "Netherlands to run trials of marijuana in patients with multiple sclerosis", *British Medical Journal*, **324**, 504.

Shiner, M. (2003) "Out of harm's way? Illicit drug use, medicalization and the law", *British Journal of Criminology*, **43**, 772–796.

Small, D. and Drucker, E. (2006) "Policy makers ignoring science and scientists ignoring policy: the medical ethical challenges of heroin treatment", *Harm Reduction Journal*, **3**, 16.

Small, W., Wood, E., Jurgens, R. and Kerr, T. (2005) "Injection drug use HIV/AIDS and incarceration: evidence from the Vancouver injection drug users study", *HIV AIDS Policy Law Review*, **10**, 5–10.

Smith, M. (1986) "The United States, the European Community and Japan: trade policies and the world cconomy", Paper presented at a conference held at St George's Hall, University of Reading, 22–23 September, organized by the University Association of Contemporary European Studies.

Springer, B. (1992) *The Social Dimension of 1992: Europe Faces a New EC*, London: Praeger Publishers.

Steffen, V. (1994) "Individualism and welfare. Alcoholics anonymous and the Minnesota model in Denmark", *Nordic Alcohol Studies*, English Supplement, **11**, 13–20.

Streek, W. (1995) "From market making to state building? Reflections on the political economy of European social policy", in S. Liebfried and P. Pierson (eds) *European Social Policy: Between Fragmentation and Integration*, Washington: The Brookings Institution.

Swedish Commission on Narcotic Drugs (2000) *Summary of the Report "The Crossroads" from the Swedish Commission on Narcotic Drugs*, SOU 2000: 126.

Swedish National Institute of Public Health (1995) *Swedish Alcohol Policy. Background and Present Situation*, Stockholm: Sweden.

Szalavitz, M. (2009) "Drugs in Portugal: did decriminalization work?", *Time*, http://www.time.com (accessed 01 September 2010).

Tham, H. (1995) "Drug control as a national project: the case of Sweden", *Journal of Drug Issues*, **25**, 113–128.

Tham, H. (1998) "Swedish drug policy: a successful model?", *European Journal on Criminal Policy and Research*, **6**, 395–414.

Tham, H. (2005) "Swedish drug policy and the vision of the good society", *Journal of Scandinavian Studies in Criminology and Crime Prevention*, **6**, 57–73.

Tops, D. (2001) *A Society With or Without Drugs? Continuity and Change in Drug Policies in Sweden and the Netherlands*, Lunds Dissertations in Social Work 5, Lund University, Lund.

Uitermark, J. (2004) "The origins and future of the Dutch approach towards drugs", *Journal of Drug Issues*, **34**, 511–532.

Uitermark, J. and Cohen P. (2005) "A clash of policy approaches: the rise (and fall?) of Dutch harm reduction policies towards ecstasy consumption", *International Journal of drug policy*, **16**, 65–72.

United Nations (1961) *Single Convention on Narcotic Drugs, 1961*, http://www.druglibrary.org/schaffer/legal (accessed 01 September 2010).

United Nations Office on Drugs and Crime (2007) *Sweden's Successful Drug Policy: A Review of the Evidence*, http://www.ecad.net (accessed 01 September 2010).

Vastag, B. (2009) "5 year's after: Portugal's decriminalization policy shows positive results", *Scientific American*, 7 April 2009, http://www.scientificamerican.com (accessed 01 September 2010).

van der Veen, A.M. (2005) "The purpose of the European Union: framing European integration", in E. Jones and A. Verdun (eds) *The Political Economy of European Integration: Theory and Analysis*, Abingdon: Routledge.

van Vliet, H-J. (1990) "Separation of drug markets and the normalization of drug problems in the Netherlands: an example for other nations?", *Journal of Drug Issues*, **20**, 463–471.

Wever, L. (1994) "Drugs as a public health problem", in Ed Leuw and I. Haen Marshall (eds) *Between Prohibition and Legalization: The Dutch Experiment in Drug Policy*, Amsterdam and New York: Kugler Publications.

Wolfe, D. and Malinowska-Sempruch, K. (2004) *Illicit Drug Policies and the Global HIV Epidemic: Effects of UN and National Government Approaches*, New York: Open Society Institute, International Harm Reduction Development.

Wyplosz, C. (2007) "Has Europe lost its heart?", in A. Aslund and M. Dabrowski (eds) *Europe After Enlargement*, New York: Cambridge University Press.

Yates, J. (1996) "*The Situation in Sweden*", http://www.drugtext.org (accessed 01 September 2010).

Yates, J. (1998) *Sweden: A Totalitarian Threat to Europe*, http://www.drugtext.org (accessed 01 September 2010).

Index

Acquis Communautaire, 153
America, influence on European drug
    policy by, 28–9, 32, 127, 156–9

Bejerot, Nils, 94–7, 98, 99–100
Belgium, drug policy in, 86, 157
Best practice in drug policy, sharing
    incidences of, 46, 163, 164
Bulgaria, drug policy in, 87

Catania report, 42, 162–3
Christiania, free city of, 121, 123,
    125–6, 127–8, 146, 158–9
Churchill, Winston, 3
Citizen participation, 13–14, 16, 26,
    33, 162
    in drug policy, 43, 84, 160,
    161–2
Comite Europeen de la Lutte
    Anti-Drogue (CELAD), 35–6,
    39, 41
Commissions of the European
    Parliament into illegal drugs
    Cooney commission, 31–2, 86
    Stewart-Clark commission, 31, 86
Comparative cross-national data
    EMCDDA standardizations, 83
    problems with, 47–8, 49, 58–9, 59,
    64, 67, 68, 70, 74, 82, 83–4
    use in drugs field, 48, 64, 67, 69, 75,
    82, 84
Cyprus, drug policy in, 87
Czech Republic, drug policy
    in the, 86

Decentralization, 16–17
Decriminalization, 31, 45, 86, 150
    in the Netherlands, 110, 112
    in Portugal, 74, 135–41, 147
de Gaulle, Charles, 9–10
Delors, Jacques, 10, 18–19, 24, 25
Denmark, alcohol policy in, 122

Denmark, drug policy in, 87, 121–9,
    146–7, 158–9
    Act on euphoriant drugs, 122–3,
    123–4, 124
    cannabis use, users and regulation,
    121, 122, 123–4, 127–8, 146–7
    Christiania, free city of, 121, 123,
    125, 127, 128, 146
    coercive treatment, 126
    debates on drug policy, 124, 126–7,
    146, 159
    harm reduction measures, 121,
    126–7
    hash clubs, 127–8
    heroin, use of, 125
    HIV/AIDS, 125
    methadone, provision of, 122, 124
    'Narkostrategi 90', 125
    repression, shift towards, 121, 127,
    128–9
    treatment facilities, 124, 125, 126
Denmark, politics in, 127
Dependent drug use and users, 33, 37,
    45–6, 59–64, 67, 93, 96–7, 109,
    112–15, 117, 122, 126, 157, 162
Drug control strategies
    demand reduction, 30, 36, 41, 43,
    87, 97
    supply reduction, 30, 37, 41, 43, 87,
    97, 102–3, 163
Drug policy, local level, 33, 41, 117,
    160, 161–2, 163
Drug policy, potential European
    styles of
    control, 157–8
    middle road, 44, 158–9
    tolerance, 155–7
Drug policy, universal lack of success
    of, 75, 84, 85, 160

Empty chair crisis, 9
Estonia, drug policy in, 86

European action plans on drugs/drugs
strategies, 35, 40, 41–4, 47, 154,
163
European city networks on drugs,
33–4, 100, 162–3
European Coalition for Just and
Effective Drug Policies (ENCOD),
42, 162
European Coal and Steel Community,
4, 8, 17, 18
European Commission, 8, 9–10, 39,
40, 43, 45
European Council, 10, 11, 13, 40–1,
43, 44
European criminal law, 153
European Economic
Community/European
Community, 4, 8–9, 18, 24
European economic policy, 1, 18–21
customs union, 9, 20
economic monetary union, 9, 11,
18–21, 25
European currency, 8, 11, 18–21
European monetary policy, 7, 8
European monetary system, 10
European single market, 18–21, 25,
27
harmonization of, 18–21, 24, 25, 26
European enlargement, 10, 11–12, 23,
25, 154
applicant countries, 40, 153
European Governance, 13, 14, 162
European harmonization, general
benefits of, 5
drawbacks to, 5–6
European Monitoring Centre for
Drugs and Drug Addiction
(EMCDDA), 36, 46, 47, 48–84,
133, 152, 163
European Monitoring Centre for
Drugs and Drug Addiction
statistics, 48–84, 85, 104, 117,
133, 147, 151, 163
correlation to types of drug policy,
83
dependent drug use, 59–64
drug markets and availability, 75–82
drug-related crime, 70–5
drug-related death, 68–9

drug-related infectious diseases,
64–7
prevalence of drug use, 49–59
European parliament, 30–2, 40, 86
European political policy, 1, 21–3, 26
common foreign and security
policy, 11, 21, 22–3
European political cooperation
(EPC), 11, 21–3
European regional policy, 5, 16–17, 26
European social policy, 1–2, 11, 17, 85
harmonization of, 17, 18, 24–7, 85,
159–60
European Union, 3, 11
Justice and Home Affairs (JHA), 11,
22–3, 28, 37, 38
Single European Act (SEA), 10–11,
24, 35
Treaty of Amsterdam, 11, 37–8
Treaty of Lisbon, 7, 12–13, 23, 25,
39–40
Treaty of Maastricht/Treaty on
European Union, 11, 14, 19,
22–3, 28, 36–7
Treaty of Nice, 11
Treaty of Paris, 4
Treaty of Rome, 4, 24
Europol, 37, 39

Fortuyn, Pim, 118
Free movement of people, 18, 25,
27, 35
Schengen agreement, 11, 35

Germany, drug policy in, 86, 115, 157
Greece, drug policy in, 87

Harmonization of illicit drug policy at
European level, 27, 41, 44, 85
desirability of, 2, 32, 43–4, 48, 85,
149–55, 158, 159, 160
divide in opinion about, 2, 46, 86,
143–4, 146, 158
likelihood of, 146, 148, 149, 155–9
prioritization of, 34–6, 152
viability of, 85, 155–9
Harm reduction, 43, 45–6, 67, 112,
113, 114, 116, 121, 126–7, 145,
157–8

Hepatitis B/C, 64, 66
HIV/AIDS, 64–7, 84, 98, 112–13, 125,
    145, 157–8
Horizontal Drugs Group (HDG),
    39, 40
Hungary, drug policy in, 87

International drug conventions,
    28–30, 156
    Convention against illicit traffic in
        narcotics and psychotropic
        substances, 30
    Convention on Psychotropic
        substances, 29–30
    Hague Opium Convention, 29, 106
    Shanghai Opium Convention, 28
    Single Convention on narcotic
        drugs, 29

Kissinger, Henry, 22

Latvia, drug policy in, 86
Legalization of drugs, 31, 32, 40, 45
Lithuania, drug policy in, 86
Luxembourg compromise, 9, 10
Luxembourg, drug policy in, 86

Monnet, Jean, 5, 8, 21
Multibeneficiary drugs programme,
    154
Multi level governance, 14–15, 26–7,
    33, 159–64

National sovereignty, 3, 5–6, 14–15,
    19, 21, 23, 28, 151, 153
Netherlands, alcohol policy in the,
    107, 110, 144
    temperance movements, 107
Netherlands, drug policy in the, 31,
    32, 33, 86, 105–20, 143–6
    Amsterdam users association, 112
    Baan commission, 109, 110
    cannabis use and users, 106–7, 108,
        109–10, 111, 144, 145
    cocaine, trade in, 105–6
    coffee shops, 111, 113–14, 116–17,
        118, 156
    expediency principle, 111
    hard drug use, 110

harm reduction, 112, 113, 114, 116,
    145
heroin on prescription/heroin trials,
    117, 119
heroin use and users, 109, 110,
    111–13, 114, 117
HIV/AIDS, 112–13
house dealers, 111
Hulsman commission, 108–9,
    109–10
International criticism of, 31, 115,
    156–7
low threshold services, 112, 114,
    116
medicinal cannabis, 119
methadone provision, 109, 112,
    113, 114, 117
normalization of users, 105, 112–13,
    114, 117, 143, 145
Opium Act, 106, 110, 111
opium producing colonies, 105
public nuisance, 115, 118–19,
    146
repression, growing tendency
    towards, 118, 119
separation of the markets, 105,
    110–11, 145
statistics on numbers of drug users,
    83
Straatjunks project, 115
synthetic drugs, 116, 118
Netherlands, politics in the, 118,
    119
Netherlands, societal pillars in the,
    107–8

Phare Programme, 154
Pompidou, Georges, 21,
    40–1
Pompidou group, 40–1
Portugal, drug policy in, 86, 130–41,
    147–8, 157
    Casal Ventoso open drug scene,
        133–4
    criticism of, 135–6, 139
    decriminalization of drugs for
        personal use, 135–7, 139–40,
        147–8
    dependent drug users/use, 133, 138

dissuasion committees, 136
drug policy reform, 130, 134, 135–7, 138
drugs in prisons, 139
evaluation of drug policy reform, 130, 137–8, 140
harm reduction, 130, 132–3, 134, 135, 138
heroin use and users, 131–2, 133, 138
interdisciplinary approach, 131
Projecto Vida, 132
scarcity of data, 130
drug trafficking, 131
Portugal, politics in, 131, 134, 135–6
Possession of drugs for personal use, European policy towards, 29, 30, 31, 32, 35, 45, 46, 86–7, 91, 119, 129, 150, 151, 156, 157
Prohibition/zero-tolerance approach, 29, 32, 43, 45, 150–1, 156, 157–8

Qualified Majority Voting (QMV), 9, 10, 11–13

Recession, effects of at European level, 10, 19–20, 25
Reseau Europeen d'Information sur les Drogues et les Toxicomanies (REITOX), 36

Schuman, Robert, 4–5
Schuman declaration, 4–5
Social dealing, 46
Spain, drug policy in, 31, 86, 157
Spillover, 6–7, 150, 153
Subsidiarity, 13–16, 26, 27, 33, 36, 41, 43, 149
Sweden, alcohol policy in, 90–1, 144
alcohol use, 91
System Bolaget/Bratt system, 91
temperance culture, 90–1
Sweden, drug policy in, 33, 86, 89–104, 143–6
action plans on drugs, 102–3, 155

amphetamines use and users, 89–90, 91, 96
Bejerot, Nils, 94–5, 96, 97
cannabis use and users, 90, 91, 92, 98, 144
coercive treatment, 98
criminalization of drug use, 99, 100
drug free society, desire for, 94, 97, 98, 103
harm reduction, 98–9, 103, 145, 146
Hassela treatment movement, 96–7
heroin use and users, 96
HIV/AIDS, 98–9
law enforcement approach, 92, 95, 97, 98, 99, 100, 102, 104
legal prescription project, 92–3, 94
liberal attitude to drug users, 90, 91–2, 93, 94, 95–6
LSD use and users, 91
moralistic policy, development of a, 94–5, 97, 98
Narcotic drugs Act, 95, 1968
Narcotic drugs Act, 95, 1972
Narcotics commissions, 98, 100, 101–2
National drugs coordinator, 102
National Organisation for a Drug Free Society (RNS), 94–5, 97, 98, 100
pursuit of users, 97
raveskomissionen, 100
statistics on numbers of drug users, 83, 92, 93, 95, 96, 97, 99, 101, 103, 104
Swedish model, export of the, 99
Swedish Organisation for Help and Assistance to Drug Users (RFHL), 94
treatment facilities, 92, 96, 97, 98–9, 100–1
UNODC report, 103
Sweden, economic crisis in, 100–1, 102
Sweden, politics in, 96, 100

Theories of European integration
confederalism, 7
federalism, 7–8, 10, 12–13, 14,
15–17, 26, 153
intergovernmentalism, 6, 7, 10, 21,
23
neo-functionalism, 6–7, 10, 14, 16,
159, 161
realism, 6–7
supranationalism, 6, 10, 21

Trafficking and traffickers, European
policy towards, 27, 28, 29, 30, 31,
35, 37, 38, 39, 40, 44–5, 85–6,
150, 153, 154, 155
European Minimum penalties, 45,
85–6, 163

United Kingdom, drug policy in the,
87

'War on drugs', 89, 127, 147, 156–8